Arms, Revenue, and Entitlements

Arms, Revenue, and Entitlements

U.S. Deficits in the Cold War, 1945–1991

William Mannen

LEXINGTON BOOKS
Lanham • Boulder • New York • London

Published by Lexington Books
An imprint of The Rowman & Littlefield Publishing Group, Inc.
4501 Forbes Boulevard, Suite 200, Lanham, Maryland 20706
www.rowman.com

6 Tinworth Street, London SE11 5AL, United Kingdom

British Library Cataloguing in Publication Information Available

Library of Congress Cataloging-in-Publication Data

Names: Mannen, William, 1986– author.
Title: Arms, revenue, and entitlements : U.S. deficits in the Cold War, 1945–1991 / William Mannen.
Description: Lanham : Lexington Books, 2020. | Includes bibliographical references and index. | Summary: "Arms, Revenue, and Entitlements: U.S. Deficits in the Cold War, 1945-1991 explores how defense, tax, and entitlement policies caused the U.S. government to become deficit normative during the Cold War era, arguing that only a comprehensive program can rein in deficits in the twenty-first century"— Provided by publisher.
Identifiers: LCCN 2019056198 (print) | LCCN 2019056199 (ebook) | ISBN 9781793607096 (cloth) | ISBN 9781793607102 (epub)
Subjects: LCSH: Budget deficits—United States—History—20th century. | Finance, Public—United States—History—1933- | Fiscal policy—United States—History—20th century. | United States—Armed Forces—Appropriations and expenditures. | World politics—1945-1989.
Classification: LCC HJ2051 .M366 2020 (print) | LCC HJ2051 (ebook) | DDC 336.3/4097309045—dc23
LC record available at https://lccn.loc.gov/2019056198
LC ebook record available at https://lccn.loc.gov/2019056199

Contents

Chapter One

From the Surplus to the Deficit Normative State

The long run trends in the ratio of debt to GDP through most of U.S. history show the pattern of rising debt during wartime and economic contractions followed by stabilization in debt levels during peacetime expansions. Yet today the federal debt assumes an unstoppable upward trajectory unprecedented in the annals of American public finance. In its extended baseline projections, the Congressional Budget Office (CBO) predicts that the ratio of debt to GDP will top 144% by 2049.[1] The federal budget now invariably produces deficits, which drives this debt. The last time the government generated a surplus occurred in FY 2001. The budget thereafter returned to deficit amid war and financial crisis. Yet even the four surpluses achieved in the late 1990s and very early 2000s only offered a reprieve from what had already become deficit normality.

Rising debt levels over the long run, triggered by near permanent deficits, must be recognized as harmful for both economic and institutional reasons, even if deficits should not be considered harmful per se such as during downturns. A standard justification for balancing the budget in the twentieth century centered on the threat that unrestrained deficits would produce inflation, and indeed the "Great Inflation" of the 1960s and 1970s arose at a time of rising government spending, in fact during a protracted war in Vietnam. This anti-inflationary justification may not be as germane today with the Federal Reserve struggling to hit its 2% inflation target. But the danger of rampant future inflation cannot be automatically discounted. What is more, the danger of rising government debt crowding out private investment and reducing output bears greater relevance in today's economy now that interest income accrued from Treasurys are increasingly diverted into foreign countries.

The institutional justifications for reining in deficits are equally powerful. Faced with constantly rising debt levels, the federal government will be forced into allocating more and more of its revenue into net interest payments (adjusted for interest income earned from government trust funds), hampering effective governance. In the past, net interest as a percentage of total outlays spiked whenever government spending grew, but it receded again with a subsequent decline in spending. This future stabilization in net interest will not occur in the event of continually rising debt levels. The CBO projects net interest payments to rise from 9% of total outlays in 2019 to 20% by 2049, by which point servicing net interest will cost more than total discretionary spending.[2]

The long run trends in the growth of debt should not obscure the role played by deficits in more immediate terms. Debt accumulates to the extent of deficits generated in a given fiscal year, and multiple factors, including events abroad and political dynamics at home, affect the generation of such deficits at specific points in time. Whatever the factors behind it, debt continues to rise as the government regularly sustains deficits year upon fiscal year, an invariability that is at the heart of the deficit normative state.

A situational perspective focuses on deficits as they are incurred in each fiscal year and the factors compelling these deficits. The budget and appropriations process inevitably occurs within a specific context shaped both by national security concerns and domestic political imperatives. Under a process first established with the Budget and Accounting Act of 1921, the president must submit a budget request by the first Monday in February for estimated spending levels in the following fiscal year. The fiscal year used to run from July 1 to June 30 until it was changed to an October 1–September 30 time frame starting in 1976. The legislation mandating this change also created the House and Senate Budget Committees, which designate spending levels for the two Appropriations Committees in each chamber. The Appropriations Committees then determine spending levels for the subcommittees. Congress ideally passes a series of twelve appropriations bills for the president to sign, though in recent years it has heavily relied on expedients like continuing resolutions, which keep the same level of spending intact from the previous fiscal year. This process does not occur in a void. Real world factors constantly impinge upon the budget. The transition to the deficit normative state occurred because for various reasons the president and Congress made tax and spending decisions that led to deficits, and these deficits became only more and more routine.

A surplus normative state existed in the 1800s because the budget registered more surpluses than deficits on an annual basis, and these surpluses tended to coincide with economic expansions. That is not to say the government never sustained a deficit or that national debt did not grow. Deficits were unavoidable in wartime or in periods of financial and economic distress. The Jackson Administration briefly succeeded in paying off the national debt in 1835, an accomplishment facilitated by sales of abundant publicly owned land. When the Administration inserted a specie clause into its contracts for the sale of land, it inadvertently triggered a financial panic and a downturn that sent the budget back into the red. The antebellum deficits paled in comparison to Civil War debt, which soared to 30% of GDP, its highest level since the 1790s, as the federal government organized a whole new scheme of taxation, currency, and banking to sustain the war effort. Many of these policy changes from the war remained in place after it ended, including higher tariff walls, which helped turn the budget quickly back to surplus.

Indeed from 1866 until 1894 the budget turned in an uninterrupted string of surpluses, even with bouts of depression and deflation. The size of government was much smaller back then, and economic growth was robust in most years, despite deficiencies in the country's monetary system. The government did not restore convertibility to gold until 1879 after having issued paper greenbacks during the war, while railroad booms turned to bust and caused panic in the major financial centers. Yet the railroad booms also fueled investment across the country. The transcontinental railroad, partly subsidized by the federal government, was completed in May 1869 with the last golden spike driven into the ground at Promontory, Utah. Capital and wealth became far more concentrated as businesses merged at an accelerating rate at the turn of the century. Over 1,000 firms vanished just in the year 1899.[3] As behemoths like U.S. Steel and Standard Oil wielded ever greater monopoly power in the business sphere, the political class responded with initiatives that marked the dawn of the regulatory state. Congress established the Interstate Commerce Commission in 1887, the first federal regulatory agency, and charged it with overseeing the railroads. It was followed three years later by the Sherman Anti-Trust Act, which outlawed combinations and conspiracies that unduly restrained competition. The corruption and other maladies of the Gilded Age aroused a full-scale progressive movement that led to additional reforms like the Pure Food and Drug Act of 1906 and the Fair Trade Commission in 1914 for more aggressively pursuing anti-trust violators. The regulatory state did not cause or lead to the deficit normative state per se, but it did increase discretionary spending to the extent of larger administrative expenses for running the new agencies.

The entitlement state as we know it today did not exist, but a forerunner of modern entitlements, pensions for Civil War veterans, did alter the trajectory in spending and affected budget balancing by the 1890s. The original pension program for veterans enacted in 1862 extended eligibility only to those Union soldiers who suffered a disability inflicted during the war, in addition to their widows and other dependents. The program remained fiscally limited through the 1870s until Republicans and Northern Democrats, pressured by lobbying groups like the Grand Army of the Republic veterans' association and lawyers handling disability cases, started dramatically expanding benefits. Congress first passed an Arrears Act in 1879, which retroactively paid out benefits to veterans whose determination of disability due to wartime service occurred well after the war itself had ended. By the late 1880s, with calls for increased benefits and even universal pensions growing louder, Congress tried to pass legislation extending eligibility to veterans with disabilities suffered after the war. President Grover Cleveland, a Northern Democrat who had incidentally avoided service in the Union Army, regularly resorted to his veto pen in stifling this legislation, but he was defeated in the next election by Benjamin Harrison, a former brevet Union general who fully pledged his support to expanding the program. In 1890 Congress passed the Dependent and Disability Pension Act, extending eligibility to veterans with postwar disabilities that impaired their ability to perform manual labor. The legislation vastly increased the government's annual spending, with pensions now constituting 40% of total outlays.[4]

The Civil War pension program has often been likened to modern day entitlements because it imposed uniform rules of eligibility to a vast swathe of the population. Like entitlements it led to increased spending that affected the government's ability to regularly generate surplus revenue. The budget turned in a deficit by 1894, only four years after passage of the Dependent Act but only one year after a financial panic that crippled the money market and led to economic depression. The budget had still managed to balance just after previous panics in 1873 and 1884, but now a devastating crisis, with the U.S. economy again integrated into the international gold standard, combined with the dolling out of some $140 million in pensions, produced a series of deficits for the rest of the 1890s, culminating in spending to fund the Spanish-American War. The budget at this could point could still not yet be described as deficit normative. The Civil War pension program was by definition transitory and subject to natural attrition. A stronger economy in the early 1900s, fueled by increased gold production and higher rates of inflation, also eased the budget back into surplus during expansions.

Going to war with Spain and intervening on behalf of Cuban independence signified another factor impacting the continuity of the surplus normative state. The U.S. emerged as a rising power in the late 1800s, and such a new role compelled more military spending inevitably affecting the budget. This effect on the budget was not at first dramatic. For a while in the early 1890s, pensions exceeded the combined expenditures for the Army and Navy. But the U.S.'s entry into the global military arena was bound to drive up costs. Benjamin Harrison proposed a shipbuilding program in 1889 that would rectify the Navy's dearth of battleships. In his annual report for 1889, Navy Secretary Benjamin Tracy laid the case for an Atlantic and a Pacific fleet each composed of battleships to secure the nation's coastlines. Instead of describing a modern navy as an instrument of empire, he recast seapower in largely defensive terms, seeing it as the only viable way for the U.S. to defend itself against belligerent European powers and a modernizing Japan. In armored warships the U.S. Navy severely lagged other nations and did not even rank as one of the world's top maritime forces. To remedy the dangerous imbalance in power, he called for a Navy of "20 battle-ships, 20 coast-defense ships, and 60 cruisers, or 100 vessels in all, which is believed to be a moderate estimate of the proper strength of the fleet."[5]

Tracy's recommendations reflected the thesis of Alfred Thayer Mahan in his seminal, soon to be published tome on seapower that large, blue water navies shape the course of world history. Some naval strategists would even go so far as to call the U.S. an "island nation" because of its long coastline on two different oceans. A modern navy with battleships was also bound to cost money. Yet Harrison's shipbuilding did not send the budget into deficit. It was much smaller than the pension program, and Harrison in fact presided over four straight years of surpluses. To put matters in perspective, by 1891 naval expenditures, including the costs of shipbuilding, totaled $26.1 million, compared to $48.7 million in Army-related spending, pensions costing $124.4 million, and a budget surplus of $37.3 million.[6] Naval expenditures, in other words, were that year smaller than the entire federal surplus. But revenue greatly fluctuated depending on the state of the economy, and the next year, just prior to a terrible financial crisis, naval spending marginally rose to $29.2 million while the surplus dropped to $9.9 million.[7]

Shipbuilding still put added pressure on the budget, regardless of the economy's gyrations. From a strategic vantage, shipbuilding ensured that the Navy had a modern fleet in being at the outset of the Spanish-American War. That war marked the high point of jingoism, an aggressive strand of patriotism contrary to the admonitions of defensive naval strategists, with the U.S. winning colonies and a new presence in the Pacific. These developments bore consequences stretching into the 1940s. The country was now obligated to defend the Philippines, Guam, and Wake, not to mention the recently annexed territory of Hawaii, and it more than ever needed the Navy to fulfill this function. Theodore Roosevelt launched the Great White Fleet in late 1907 to demonstrate American naval might just after the Japanese navy's decimation of the Russian fleet at Tsushima Straits only two years before. The U.S. was indeed hardly alone in the Pacific. The British, French, and German Empires all controlled islands throughout the region, with Japan seizing German Pacific territory during World War I. The Navy considered Japan its chief Pacific rival and formulated War Plan Orange as a desperate attempt to relieve the garrison holding Manila Bay after defeating Japanese naval forces in a decisive surface action somewhere in the western Pacific. The plan never came to fruition after Japan's surprise attack on the Pacific fleet battleships in Pearl Harbor while the previously underappreciated aircraft carriers remained fortuitously at sea.

The U.S.'s entry into the Pacific and the Caribbean at the end of the 1800s provides greater context for understanding isolationism. As a twentieth century phenomenon, isolationism was magnified by the bloodbath in Europe starting in 1914 and then the fear of another European war by the 1930s. This isolationism towards the horrendous slaughter going on in Europe or the prospects of another such slaughter was unsurprising, but it also did not necessarily signify rejection towards the rest of the world, especially other regions outside of Europe such as Latin America. Isolationism should be mainly thought of in relation to Europe and the World Wars. The U.S. emerged as a more engaged global power by the dawn of the twentieth century, and this new role did at times carry a budgetary impact, even if not always enormous. For instance, the federal budget ran deficits in 1904 and 1905 during and shortly after an economic slowdown, but Panama Canal spending also greatly contributed to these transitory deficits.[8] The budget then turned in a series of deficits starting in 1908 that resulted from the Panic of 1907 and its severe aftershocks. The surplus normative state survived for a while into the twentieth century, even with the beginnings of larger scale regulation over the economy and greater military power. The government in fact turned in another uninterrupted series of surpluses from 1920 through 1930 during the short-lived era of interwar prosperity at home. The Great Depression ended these surpluses in their tracks by 1931, and a surplus would not be reached again until 1947.

For taxation, the surplus normative state in the 1800s relied in large part on the tariff as a means for raising revenue. The tariff also served protectionist purposes, especially when Republican Congresses refrained from lowering the high Civil War–era duties in the late 1860s and 1870s. The federal government otherwise imposed excise taxes, with public land sales and other miscellaneous sources bringing in small amounts of additional revenue. To take the year 1890, for instance, when support for the tariff was still widespread, customs duties brought in $229.7 million in revenue as opposed to only $142.6 million from internal sources.[9]

Given their stewardship over industrial interests in the Midwest and Northeast, the Republicans, like their Whig forebearers, championed the tariff, while the Democrats had all along fought for free trade. A Democratic president, Grover Cleveland, and a Democratic Congress managed to enact the Wilson-Gorman Tariff during their one interregnum of joint power in the 1893–1895 session, but they failed to reduce overall tariff levels, and Cleveland refused to affix his signature to the law. They also revived the Civil War–era income tax in 1894, but the Supreme Court struck it down as unconstitutional the next year, concluding that it served as a direct tax that had to be levied proportionately with state populations. Even partial tariff reduction, meanwhile, did not stop Republicans from raising tariffs again in the late 1890s, or yet again in the early 1920s, which undid the Underwood Tariff signed into law by Woodrow Wilson. The Fordney-McCumber Tariff of 1922 became synonymous with Republican protectionism of that era, while the more reviled Smoot-Hawley Tariff of 1930 did much to dampen international trade without necessarily worsening the Great Depression. The push for Smoot-Hawley started as politics as usual for the Republicans after they again won the presidency and a huge majority in Congress in 1928. But by the time President Hoover signed the legislation the economy was entering a deep contraction, and the bill had already encountered stiff opposition from the academic and business communities.[10]

The Sixteenth Amendment to the Constitution authorizing an income tax, ratified in 1913, allowed the federal government to shift the tax burden onto personal and corporate incomes. But the personal exemption, written into the code at $3,000, or $78,000 in 2019 dollars, shut off the majority of taxpayers from liability. Taxes instead disproportionately hit the wealthy, and even under Republican administrations in the 1920s they brought in between 40% to 60% of revenue, with customs duties well under 20%.[11] The Revenue Acts of 1924 and 1926 reduced liability by expanding the personal exemption and cutting the normal and surtax rates. Treasury Secretary Andrew Mellon provided singular views on tax cutting, pointing to the need for lower rates and base broadening and even penning the famous tract *Taxation: The People's Business*. In his annual report for 1924 he assessed the Revenue Act of that year, along with President Coolidge deeming it inadequate and further opining that "if we attempt to levy taxes inherently too high, those whom we seek to tax will find some of the many ways of avoiding the realization of an income which can be reached by taxation, and the source of the revenue will decline."[12] Mellon wrote of tax cuts and base broadening in anticipation of the supply side movement some fifty years in the future. But in the next few decades economic depression and total war took tax rates in the opposite direction. Herbert Hoover by 1932 prioritized a balanced budget over lower taxes, and New Deal tax legislation led to even higher rates on the wealthy. World War II helped turn the tax code for the first time into a truly national system. In addition to hiking the top marginal rate to over 90%, Congress reduced the personal exemption, which had previously protected most middle income taxpayers from liability. Now they were brought into the system, causing income tax filings to rise by nearly 40 million during the war years.[13]

Meanwhile, multilateral trade agreements ratified after World War II only further detached the tariff from any lingering revenue raising purposes. Barriers were dramatically lowered again as a result of trade rounds in the 1960s and 1970s. By that point trade liberalization had gained greater support among both parties, especially the Republicans, though as domestic industries faced new competition overseas, resistance to more trade rounds grew.

But this populist resistance, which found its home in certain quarters of the Democratic Party in a reversal of its historical role, did not stop the long-term trend already underway, which was that the multilateral trade rounds helped unify the free world in an epic new struggle against communism, a struggle that was geopolitical, economic, military, and ideological. With tariff rates declining, the government relied ever more for its revenue on income taxes, mostly personal and to a lesser extent corporate. Perhaps unsurprisingly, the deficit normative state took hold once income taxes generated the overwhelming share of revenue. By 1970, personal income taxes brought in $90.4 billion in revenue, along with $32.8 billion from corporate income taxes, compared to $15.7 billion from excise taxes and only $2.4 billion from customs duties.[14]

The surplus normative state could not survive the duration of the Great Depression and World War II, but not until the period from 1945 to 1991, coinciding with the Cold War and momentous political changes at home, did the budget decisively turn deficit normative. This transition was not at first obvious, especially because the first two presidents during this period, Harry Truman and Dwight Eisenhower, both adamantly insisted upon balanced budgets. Their fiscal legacies improbably aligned because they both succeeded in balancing the budget part of the time in office, attributable to a shared commitment even though they belonged to opposing political parties and had become personally antagonistic to one another by 1952. Yet they only partly succeeded in balancing the budget, and their successors were even less successful. Truman secured surpluses in 1947, 1948, 1949, and 1951, while Eisenhower did so in 1956, 1957, and 1960. Post-Truman and Eisenhower, the budget turned in a surplus only once more during the Cold War, in FY 1969, remaining otherwise in deficit until the late 1990s when international tensions had considerably subsided.

No single factor caused the transition to deficit normality. The emergence of the entitlement state out of the economic wreckage of the 1930s did not single-handedly produce deficits, particularly since the most significant program enacted during the New Deal, Social Security, was funded through dedicated revenue sources. Postwar military commitments in Europe in the late 1940s, a dramatic break from interwar isolationism, offered the first potential challenge to surplus normality, even as the Truman Administration initially kept defense spending in check. This was the state of affairs until the shocking outbreak of war in Korea, which utterly overturned the Administration's fiscal and national security posture. The U.S. military emerged from the Korean War larger and more powerful, so much so that Eisenhower strived to use all his influence and credibility in these matters to keeping a lid on defense spending for the rest of the 1950s and preventing the country from descending into a militarized "garrison state."

The domestic political situation changed by the 1960s, with John Kennedy and Lyndon Johnson both calling for more activist steps in promoting economic growth and a higher standard of living, first with deep tax cuts and then increased social welfare spending. By the mid-1960s, entitlements had started contributing to deficits year in and year out as programs like Medicare and Medicaid relied at least partly on general revenue for funding instead of exclusively on payroll taxes. Spending for the Vietnam War also contributed to deficits, and the federal government could not achieve a surplus after FY 1969, even with the withdrawal from Vietnam. In the final epoch of this era, Ronald Reagan promoted another round of deep tax cuts and dramatically increased defense spending that sent debt to GDP soaring under conditions of peace and prosperity, which his successor, George H.W. Bush, handled as best he could while working with a Democratic Congress.

During the Cold War era defense could not alone take the blame for persistent deficits. Entitlements exerted an increasingly heavy pull on deficits after 1965. The tax code also shared responsibility for rising and continuous deficits through a series of exclusions, deductions, and credits: an exclusion the most advantageous of these breaks for the taxpayer, with some benefits such as employer-sponsored health insurance going entirely untaxed, deductions serving as expenses subtracted from income, whether from gross income ("above the line" on tax forms) or adjusted gross income ("below the line"), through which taxpayers reduce liability, and credits an even more aggressive way of reducing liability, functioning as percentages that are multiplied by taxes owed, not taxable income. The tax code is thus Janus-faced, looking forward in one direction to the collection of revenue and looking back in the other to taxpayer refunds to protect a multitude of diverse interests.

The oft-cited dilemma of guns and butter, pitting national security commitments against domestic priorities, should be more thoroughly modified as the paradox of arms, revenue, and entitlements. The competing demands of higher defense spending, lower taxes, and bigger entitlement programs increasingly offloaded onto general revenue cumulatively drove deficits over the span of decades, with the result today of deficit normality. Non-defense discretionary spending cannot be wholly excluded from a consideration of factors contributing to deficit normality in the budget sheet. This category of spending rose sharply as a result of the Great Society programs, with the federal government funneling dollars into housing, energy projects, education, and revenue sharing. As a percentage of GDP, it rose higher in recessions, first to 4.4% in 1975 and then 5.1% in 1980. Yet mandatory spending programs, which mainly take the form of entitlements and other benefits (net interest does not count as programmatic spending), rose to 10% of GDP in the same period, twice as high as non-defense discretionary spending.[15] Without ignoring non-defense discretionary spending, this narrative focuses on the major drivers of deficits in the second half of the twentieth century, first defense spending, also changes in the tax code, and then entitlements funded from general revenue.

If the government is to ever return to surplus normality, in which the budget generates surpluses at least in times of solid economic expansion, then the first step in this direction must be correspondingly comprehensive, to address equally defense spending at a sustainable level, a tax code that provides maximum revenue, and entitlements that do not unduly burden the general revenue base. Governance is a messy practice, and no single answer lends itself to the task of better controlling debt and perhaps returning to budget surpluses at some point down the road. But seeing exactly how we reached this point provides greater clarity when conceiving of and implementing future prescriptions.

A situational perspective serves as an effective way to depict the transition to deficit normality. The factors impacting how government spends money and raises revenue occur in real time, the effect of events at home and abroad. Policymakers respond in specific contexts, and often they cannot look beyond short-term horizons. This narrative relies mostly on nominal data not adjusted for inflation from the given period because that is what policymakers were working with at the time. From this approach we can observe how and under what circumstances deficits became normal as each presidential administration contended with new national and international challenges. The focus on presidential and not congressional leadership is unsurprising when considering the accretion of presidential power over the twentieth century. Members of Congress hold great sway during budgetary disputes. Congress must after all pass a budget for the fiscal year before the president signs it into law, and members of Congress may robustly oppose a president with a more relaxed attitude towards deficits. Yet by law the president submits a new budget request early in the new year, and the presidential administration sets the terms of debate over what spending items should be prioritized. In the time frame of 1945 to 1991 the possibilities of successful budget balancing corresponded, with some exceptions, to the inclinations of the administration in office, while members of Congress, even if at times willful and outspoken, tended to assume a more reactive role.

The main narrative ends in 1991 because by that point, at the Cold War's end, deficits had become normal, even with Congress and the president having worked feverishly to enact more aggressive deficit control legislation. The 1990s came to be regarded as a kind of hiatus from supreme national security threats and great power rivalry, and in the new century the same divergent demands of arms, revenue, and entitlements once again played out but now in a much more heated and vitriolic atmosphere.

A single momentous turning point in history can rarely be discerned, certainly at the time it is supposed to have happened and even decades later.

The same holds true for the shift from the surplus to the deficit normative state. But by looking to the factors impacting the budget in the second half of the twentieth century, new military commitments abroad and regional wars, changes in the tax code, and expansion in entitlements, we can gain a better understanding of how this shift came to occur and perhaps how fiscal balance might one day be restored.

NOTES

1. CBO, *The 2019 Long-Term Budget Outlook* (Washington, D.C.: Congressional Budget Office, June 2019), 1.
2. CBO, *2019 Outlook*, 21.
3. Ralph L. Nelson, *Merger Movements in American History, 1995–1956* (Princeton: Princeton University Press, 1959), 34.
4. Murray N. Rothbard, "Beginning the Welfare State: Civil War Veterans' Pensions," *The Quarterly Journal of Austrian Economics* 22, no. 1 (Spring 2019): 70–78.
5. Secretary of Navy, *Report of the Secretary of the Navy. 1889. In Two Parts. Part I* (Washington, D.C.: Government Printing Office, 1890), 11–12.
6. Secretary of Treasury, *Annual Report of the Secretary of the Treasury on the State of the Finances for the Year 1891* (Washington, D.C.: Government Printing Office, 1891), XXI.
7. Secretary of Treasury, *Annual Report of the Secretary of the Treasury on the State of the Finances for the Year 1892* (Washington, D.C.: Government Printing Office, 1892), XXI.
8. Secretary of Treasury, *Annual Report of the Secretary of the Treasury on the State of the Finances for the Fiscal Year Ended June 30, 1905* (Washington, D.C.: Government Printing Office, 1906), 7.
9. Secretary of Treasury, *Annual Report of the Secretary of the Treasury on the State of the Finances for the Year 1890* (Washington, D.C.: Government Printing Office, 1891), XXI.
10. Douglas A. Irwin, "From Smoot-Hawley to Reciprocal Trade Agreements: Changing the Course of U.S. Trade Policy in the 1930s," in *The Defining Moment: The Great Depression and the American Economy in the Twentieth Century*, ed. Michael D. Bordo, Claudia Goldin, and Eugene N. White (Chicago: University of Chicago Press, 1998), 333–35.
11. Secretary of Treasury, *Annual Report of the Secretary of the Treasury on the State of the Finances for the Fiscal Year Ended June 30, 1926* (Washington, D.C.: Government Printing Office, 1927), 19.
12. Secretary of Treasury, *Annual Report of the Secretary of the Treasury on the State of the Finances for the Fiscal Year Ended June 30, 1924* (Washington, D.C.: Government Printing Office, 1925), 4–5.
13. B.K. Atrostic and James R. Nunns, "Measuring Tax Burden: A Historical Perspective," in *Fifty Years of Economic Measurement: The Jubilee of the Conference on Research in Income and Wealth*, ed. Ernst R. Berndt and Jack E. Triplett (Chicago: University of Chicago Press, 1991), 349.
14. Secretary of Treasury, *Annual Report of the Secretary of the Treasury on the State of the Finances for the Fiscal Year Ended June 30, 1970* (Washington, D.C.: Government Printing Office, 1970), 4.
15. OMB, "Historical Tables" (PDF file), downloaded from Office of Management and Budget website, 9–10, accessed December 2018.

Chapter Two

Austerity Abandoned

Truman, 1945–1953

Harry Truman, a former haberdasher and senator from Missouri, assumed the presidency at a uniquely momentous point in history upon the death of Franklin Roosevelt. The Allies had already pushed deep into Germany by mid-April 1945, and Hitler would be dead by the very end of the month. In the Pacific, bloody days still lay ahead in the intense battle for Okinawa, and Truman himself would have to make undoubtedly the most important decision of his life of whether to drop a newly developed atomic bomb on Japan, which through nuclear fission had the explosive power to reduce whole cities to rubble. Rumblings of a new Cold War with the Soviet Union were not yet audible to most ears. Like the rest of the world, Americans had been horrified by the Bolshevik takeover in 1917 and the execution of the czar and his family. The U.S. had briefly landed troops in Archangel as part of a larger Allied expedition at the end of World War I, and only in 1933 did Roosevelt finally restore diplomatic relations with Moscow. Even then relations were at best cool, but the exigencies of war swept aside these attitudes as the Soviets mounted a defense against the German onslaught with the aid of "general winter," in time counterattacking over a 1,000 mile front in a campaign that culminated with the Red Flag flying over Berlin.

At the end of hostilities with the Axis and in the year afterwards, Truman could not have fully foreseen the dawn of the Cold War and the dilemmas that it would trigger between permanent military commitments abroad and political imperatives at home. He had supported the New Deal, and he wanted to carry on the Roosevelt legacy. While still believing in balanced budgets and frugality in administration, he primarily wanted to expand the reach of government in policy areas that had evaded Roosevelt. A large peacetime military, even in defense of freedom and democracy, did not necessarily square with his ingrained political beliefs, though his proud service on the Western Front in World War I might have foreshadowed a future belief in an interventionist role in the world. These attitudes were still a long way off in 1945. Truman's goal after victory over the Germans and Japanese was to ensure the peace through agreements with the Soviets and British and otherwise demobilize, to bring the boys home, and turn the government's attention back to domestic needs.

And indeed in the years following the war the Truman Administration succeeded in demobilizing the armed forces to assure reduced government expenditures and a stabilization of the national debt. By early 1946, some 50% of military personnel had been discharged. Another round of personnel cuts planned to slash the armed forces to a fraction, only 10%, of their strength from the war.[1] The Administration considered demobilization obviously necessary given the unprecedented national debt accumulated as a result of the war. Federal debt held by the public as a percentage of GDP topped 106% in 1946.[2] Demobilization helped account for Truman's success in converting the wartime deficits into surpluses by 1947, 1948, and 1949. The budget surplus for 1948 as a percentage of GDP was the highest ever in the postwar era at 4.3%.[3]

The budget surplus for the year before, 1947, turned out to be the first since 1930, not only seventeen years ago but of an entirely different era, when economic turmoil had just begun to tear apart the weak fabric of the interwar order. Now in the late 1940s the government's ability to turn in surpluses would be seriously complicated by decisions on national security and whether to rearm. Going into FY 1947 the Administration planned to spend just under $15 billion on the military, down from $49 billion the previous year. The next closest items in this planning framework were interest payments on the national debt at $5 billion and benefits and pensions for veterans at $4.2 billion.[4] The latter figure was driven by the G.I. Bill of 1944, a slew of educational grants, mortgage and business loans, job training assistance, and unemployment benefits for returning veterans. The budget could not be so simply described as one providing mainly for national defense. Spending on human resources was bound to rise in the postwar economy, especially with the G.I. Bill, but the Administration could only effectively secure a surplus by holding down defense expenditures, even if doing so did not necessarily imply rejection of a new role for the U.S. in international affairs.

Truman's budget request for the next fiscal year, 1948, submitted in early CY 1947, represented the high-water mark of demobilization and the lingering hope that tensions with the Soviets could be permanently avoided. The request also preceded the creation of the National Military Establishment (NME) by several months, which was intended to exert a unifying presence over the Departments of the Army and Navy through a new Office of the Secretary of Defense (OSD). For FY 1948, national defense was still commonly understood in terms of expenditures for the Army and Navy Departments. Congress would also create an independent Air Force under the National Security Act of 1947 but temporarily keep it budgeted with the Army. Truman put in a request for $11.2 billion in defense spending for 1948, lower than the estimated $14.7 billion in expenditures from FY 1947. This diminished spending could still sustain 1.6 million personnel, of whom 1 million served in the Army and just under 600,000 in the Navy.[5]

Yet within only the next few months world events began to weigh down on this program of austerity. The beginning of the Cold War cannot be easily pinpointed to a specific place and time. In 1946 tensions with the Soviets briefly lit up after they initially refused to withdraw their troops from northern Iran. The communist threat then appeared in much starker form early the next year in the eastern Mediterranean. Greece had fallen into civil war, and communist guerrilla forces threatened to take over. The British informed the Truman Administration that impending financial burdens prevented them from sending more aid to the non-communist Greek government, which they had supported since liberation from the Germans in 1944. While not plagued by civil war, Turkey was also exposed to Soviet aggression. The fall of both to communism, whether due to internal or external forces, potentially allowed the Soviets to descend upon the eastern Mediterranean. Convening with members of the Administration, including Under Secretary of State Dean Acheson, Truman grasped the importance of filling in this power vacuum and took his case to Congress. In an address before Congress that omitted any explicit reference to Soviet aggression, he explained that the fall of Greece and Turkey to totalitarian regimes could lead to rippling effects throughout the Middle East. For the most part Truman framed the request in larger terms of people struggling for their freedom, that the "[c]ollapse of free institutions and loss of independence would be disastrous not only for them but for the world. Discouragement and possibly failure would quickly be the lot of neighboring peoples striving to maintain their freedom and independence." Backing up these statements with deeds, Truman requested $400 million in emergency appropriations. He also needed authority to oversee the disbursement of these funds on the ground by transferring military and civilian officials to the eastern Mediterranean.[6] The expansive rhetoric of freedom and democracy, soon to be called the Truman Doctrine, reflected the emerging strategy to contain communist advances around the world. Congress agreeably went along in passing legislation for the funding.

Some $400 million in emergency appropriations represented a substantial but not enormous sum for the time, about $4.6 billion in 2019 dollars, and it did not override the Administration's urgent task of demobilization. Military aid to Greece and Turkey served as an isolated response to a perceived strategic threat. Whether or not isolated responses would suffice to check the tide of Soviet imperium over Eastern Europe was not yet clear.

UNIFICATION, AIRPOWER, REVOLT OF THE ADMIRALS

Demobilization served as the most obvious way to push down defense costs, with military spending plummeting from 77% of total outlays in 1946 to only 37% in 1947.[7] Yet the Administration also intended to keep costs to a minimum through unification of the defense establishment. Bureaucratic consolidation presented a number of ways to streamline funding and prevent the duplication of costly weapons system. How the newly created Military Establishment could contain costs and avoid duplication depended on an effective management over weapons development and procurement, with OSD providing a major supervisory role. To that end, the first defense secretary, James Forrestal, organized a Weapons Systems Evaluation Group (WSEG) to assess and decide between competing weapons systems and even differing strategic approaches.[8] WSEG's mandate was not strictly in the realm of cost-benefit analysis, a term not then in widespread use, but costs could certainly factor into its assessments of whether a given weapon system was worth pursuing. Procurement had also been greatly shaped by the new technological advances achieved during World War II. The services were gravitating to a "concurrency" concept for procurement. Concurrency meant that subparts and parts were developed, produced, and tested at the same time instead of the older and more rigid process of developing components time sequentially before production. Concurrency was not necessarily going to work, but it offered a way to more expeditiously test and produce increasingly complex weapons systems.[9]

The Air Force took the lead in experimenting with concurrency through its work on the B-36 Peacemaker, an intercontinental bomber that until being retrofitted with jet engines was entirely propeller driven, making it in fact the largest propeller driven aircraft ever produced. Manufactured by the Convair Corporation, the Air Force brought it into active service in 1948. The B-36 could fly 7,500 miles without landing to refuel, an incredible range, and physically it was over twice the size of the B-29 Superfortress, the existing strategic bomber in the Air Force's inventory. Military planners had begun designing the B-36 in 1941 before the attack on Pearl Harbor under the assumption that long-range bombers would need to strike Hitler's Europe directly from the U.S. instead of any available bases on Allied soil. World War II had ended, but now B-36s could fly roundtrip missions to outlying parts of Soviet Russia from bases in the U.S.

The military's relations with contractors also affected procurement. During World War II, the Army and Navy mainly negotiated contracts with defense companies in order to forgo an inefficient and time-consuming competitive bidding process. After the war, Congress passed the Armed Services Procurement Act that streamlined competitive bidding for the services. But the legislation permitted up to seventeen exceptions for negotiated contracts, which de facto paved the way for their widespread use by the military. As hardware became more advanced and concurrency took shape, the military could rely on only a few firms with the requisite know-how and avoid the rigidity of formalized competitive bidding.[10]

The key to avoiding duplication was stopping it at the core, and this could only come through greater oversight of the services' R&D activities. The National Security Act of 1947 instituted a new Board of R&D chaired by a civilian who answered to the defense secretary on the state of military R&D. Yet equipping the civilian leadership with new supervisory machinery was not going to overturn decades of service tradition. The Board only coordinated the R&D brewing from the ground up at each of the services. It consisted of committees devoted to discrete categories of technological capabilities and sought to prevent the services from developing duplicative systems.[11]

To varying degrees even the services themselves were decentralized in how they managed R&D. The Air Force set up a more centralized operation in 1950 with the Air Research and Development Command.[12] The Navy maintained a decentralized tradition, with R&D operations allocated among the separate Bureaus of Ships, Ordnance, and Aeronautics. These Bureaus conducted R&D internally through their own in-house facilities and externally through ties to the business sector and academia. New bodies in the services aimed to centralize R&D from the top down. The Navy's General Board and Board of Ship Characteristics oversaw shipbuilding. Congress mandated an Office of Naval Research (ONR) in 1946 to focus entirely on research to the exclusion of development. But these bodies did not fundamentally alter the decentralized makeup of Navy R&D, even after the creation of a new Research and Development Review Board to assign R&D priorities.[13] The Army's Logistics Division ran most of its in-house R&D activities, but like the other two services it also relied on contacts with outside laboratories.[14] As the civilian leadership worked to unify the military, more concerted steps were being taken to at least manage the flow of R&D without displacing the operations that already existed in each of the services. More importantly, the establishment of OSD and the R&D Board provided safeguards for stopping duplication before it became chronic.

Over a few short years the Military Establishment oversaw needed reforms until being further consolidated into the Department of Defense in 1949, bringing the hope that unification could keep defense costs to a minimum. Avoiding duplication was especially important with the emergence of costly new aircraft and guided missiles, both of which could conceivably have been developed by all four services (the Air Force impliedly replaced the Army as the primary agent for ground-based airpower, but not until 1966 did an interservice agreement expressly divest the Army of its remaining fixed wing transport aircraft).

Unification in the late 1940s also needed to be seen in terms of dilemmas over balanced forces. A balance of ground, aerial, and naval forces was deemed necessary after World War II since all three forces had contributed to winning the war, and indeed the budget figures for the services were initially comparable. But as the Truman Administration proceeded with austerity, policymakers began to engage in strategic thinking that implied disproportionately more funding for the Air Force than the Army and Navy. Only the Air Force had the technological ability at the time to deploy atomic weapons, and this advantage over the Soviets was central to U.S. strategy. Under the Atomic Energy Act of 1946, atomic weaponry remained in the hands of the civilian Atomic Energy Commission (AEC), which was authorized to turn over the weaponry to the military in an emergency. The U.S. did not initiate a rapid expansion in its stockpile of atomic bombs right after the war, and by mid-1947 the AEC held only a little over a dozen of these weapons. They were of the implosion variety used for the mission over Nagasaki and could only be delivered through improvised alterations to B-29s, which, before the deployment of B-36s, were alone large enough to carry this 10,000–pound payload.[15] With the Soviet Union still lacking the atomic bomb, military planners in a time of demobilization counted on the bomb as their ace, and that ace belonged to the Air Force.

The idea of expanding the Air Force quickly gained traction in policy circles. Truman appointed the lawyer and former State Department official Thomas Finletter to head a new commission in 1947 charged with studying the merits of strategic airpower. The commission conducted a wide-ranging investigation and heard the testimony of hundreds of witnesses from the Military Establishment. On January 1, 1948, the commission submitted its report resoundingly recommending a buildup for the Air Force. The report argued that the Navy no longer served as the first line of defense as new weapons under development in other countries would in time diminish the defensive utility of the Atlantic and Pacific. The Soviets possessed bombers that could travel on one-way missions of up to 4,000 miles, while guided missiles would soon have a range of 5,000 miles, warranting the need for enhanced air defense.[16]

The report described Phases I and II of rearmament and preparedness against aerial nuclear attack. Phase I was ongoing until January 1, 1953, or A-Day, when the Air Force achieved readiness. Phase II represented the period after A-Day.[17] At the time of the report, the Air Force consisted of only 55 air groups. The commission recommended a sufficient "force in being" by A-Day, amounting to "70 combat groups, and 22 special squadrons, supplemented by 27 National Guard groups and 34 groups of Air Reserve," all told 12,400 aircraft.[18] The report mentioned the need for expanded naval airpower, but it otherwise assigned major strategic responsibility to the Air Force, with the 70 groups, including 700 long-range bombers, operational as soon as January 1, 1950, and reserve aircraft ready just a few years later on A-Day.[19] The report also made clear that the increased Air Force expenditures would boost an ailing aviation industry, which was viewed as critical for national defense.[20]

As officials pondered whether to go forward with the proposals contained in the Finletter report, new guidelines were laid out for allocating service responsibility in the age of airpower. Of the four services, only the Army had lost most of its fixed wing aircraft with the creation of an independent Air Force. While the Marine Corps maintained a small force of combat aircraft to support amphibious operations, the Air Force and Navy were the two leading services involved in airpower. A few months after the release of the Finletter report, Forrestal met with the Joint Chiefs of Staff (JCS) at Truman's vacation home in Key West, Florida, to work out an agreement more coherently defining the "primary" and "collateral" functions of each of the services, but especially the Air Force and Navy with respect to airpower. Forrestal also intended the agreement to mitigate duplication and better clarify national strategic purposes. Pursuant to the so-called Key West Agreement, the Navy's primary functions included "local superiority (including air) in an area of naval operations" and "air operations as necessary for the accomplishment of objectives in a naval campaign."[21] For the Air Force, "general air superiority," "defeat[ing] enemy air forces," "control[ling] vital air areas," and "strategic air warfare" qualified as primary functions.[22]

But the Key West Agreement did not ease the festering tensions between the Air Force and Navy. These tensions, which finally erupted into the Revolt of the Admirals of 1949, centered on differences over the Air Force's B-36 and the Navy's proposed supercarrier. The Navy had already developed or modified aircraft suitable for carrying an atomic payload and taking off and landing on existing *Midway*-class carriers. More ambitiously the Navy now sought to build a new supercarrier that would greatly enhance its ability to carry out bombing campaigns against the U.S.S.R. The design for this carrier, the *United States*, included unusually large deck space maximized by eliminating the carrier's island superstructure, normally the command and control center for such a vessel. Members of the Air Force argued that the supercarrier was too vulnerable to enemy attacks to serve as a reliable launching pad for strategic bombers. The Navy, according to this argument, simply lacked a compelling reason, or at least not one justifying the cost, to build these carriers when the Air Force housed bombers on bases within reach of the Soviet Union. The *United States* had been under construction until the cost cutting Louis Johnson scrapped it in 1949 shortly after replacing Forrestal as Truman's second defense secretary. Johnson's decision set off charges of corruption and bribery that were subsequently found to be without basis. In fact, Johnson had simply not been persuaded by the arguments of Louis Denfeld, the Chief of Naval Operations (CNO), on the merits of the supercarrier. He was instead influenced by the Air Force Chief of Staff, Hoyt Vandenberg, who focused on the threats to such a massive naval target posed by aircraft, submarines, and other warships. Army Chief of Staff Omar Bradley also agreed with the Air Force that the supercarrier project was not necessary.[23]

After Congressional hearings clearing the Air Force and Johnson of corruption finished, new hearings were scheduled that turned attention to the merits of the B-36. During the ensuing Revolt of the Admirals, in which heated dissension towards the B-36 broke out among top naval brass, the Navy's representatives argued that the B-36 was vulnerable to fighter interceptors. Vandenberg's defense of the B-36 did not necessarily refute that point, even as he emphasized the aircraft's defensive and evasive capabilities. When the Navy brass disputed the very notion of strategic bombing, Vandenberg explained that it served overwhelmingly deterrent purposes. He also noted that the JCS closely oversaw the newly created Strategic Air Command (SAC), depriving the Air Force of the opportunity to use it for its own freewheeling purposes.[24]

The Navy brass became disgruntled because in their eyes the principal instruments of offensive power had been wrangled from them. Now they were left with support tasks like maintaining oceanic lines of communication or seizing new bases for offensive airstrikes. Yet only in the short-term did the Revolt of the Admirals represent a defeat for the Navy, with Denfeld and a few other top-ranking officers relieved of their command. The Pentagon ultimately renewed the supercarrier project after the Korean War, a conflict that revived interest in carriers.

For a two-year stretch from early CY 1946 to early CY 1948 the Administration succeeded in demobilization, all while tilting the emphasis in national defense to airpower. It otherwise relied on aid, military aid to the Greek and Turkish governments and a more ambitious plan for economic aid to European nations, to bolster the non-communist bloc and prevent an implosion into political turmoil and possibly communist takeover across the Atlantic.

BERLIN, CONTINGENCY PLANS, NSC 68

In January 1948, just at the time the Finletter committee returned its report, Truman submitted his budget request for FY 1949. The crafting of the budget request is the collective responsibility of the executive agencies, which in the late 1940s turned over their estimates to the Bureau of the Budget, later reorganized in 1970 as the Office of Management and Budget (OMB) lodged in the White House. The process of evaluating and compiling budget estimates begins a full year before the president submits the combined request to Congress. Yet the complex workings of the budget process do not imply a weak or powerless president. Truman, for example, could impose ceilings on spending to ensure an austerity budget, forcing the service chiefs to adhere to his budget preferences. After the president submits his budget request, including an enclosed budget message, by early February, House and Senate subcommittees work on appropriations before voting on them in committee and sending the bills to their respective chambers. Congress must first authorize executive agencies, programs, and activities in authorization bills and then appropriate funds through the appropriations subcommittees. The appropriations bills grant actual budget authority for the executive branch agencies to spend money from the Treasury, and so in that sense the terms appropriations and authority can be used interchangeably. Particularly in the context of defense spending, the budget process in Congress serves as a live political issue with requests being debated and Congressional committees hearing testimony from members of the OSD, the JCS, and other organs of the military. This process becomes all the hotter from a political perspective when world events force a drastic revaluation of defense needs as the budget bills course their way through Congress, which is exactly what happened in early CY 1948. These factors may often delay passage into law of appropriations bills while also forcing a greater reliance on supplemental requests, whether for the current or upcoming fiscal year, an example of this being the aid to Greece and Turkey asked for by Truman in March 1947.

When Truman submitted his budget request for FY 1949, the Greek government continued to battle communist guerrillas, Soviet dictator Joseph Stalin had tightened his grip over most of Eastern Europe, and in June of the past year Secretary of State George Marshall announced the European Recovery Program (ERP). Yet these circumstances had not caused a turnaround in the Administration's ingrained austerity. With demobilization over, the Administration now focused on stabilizing combat forces at current levels. Truman put in a request for $11 billion in defense spending compared to $10.7 billion from the year before. Even within this tight budget, Truman identified the importance of aircraft procurement and the replacement of obsolescent aircraft for both the Air Force and Navy, seeking to increase funds by $150 million for this purpose. While the Administration did not totally abandon notions of balanced forces, it had shifted its focus to airpower at least for the time being. Truman noted that of the spending authority for FY 1949 and beyond, "nearly 50 percent will be devoted to defense aviation" to help maintain fifty-five Air Force groups. The Air Force received about 50% of Army appropriations since the Army and Air Force were not yet separately budgeted.[25]

Shortly after Truman submitted his budget request, the service chiefs and Forrestal alike began scrambling for additional FY 1949 spending to fund increased personnel strength. U.S. forces were stretched around the world, along the Pacific Rim and in Europe, not to mention contingency planning in the eastern Mediterranean that might, depending on adverse events, turn into a heavier presence. Forrestal emphasized the importance of ground forces to back up the Air Force, an argument that conformed to the conventional wisdom of a balanced defense. By mid-March, Truman decided to impose a $1.5 billion cap on supplemental requests for the year. Though the cap could be subject to upward revision, Truman remained committed to austerity.[26]

Truman's cap on supplemental appropriations served as a blunt, straightforward way to restrain military spending. He did not want to interfere with the workings of the newly created Military Establishment, but he ultimately had to decide on a figure in order to keep a lid on spending, even at the risk of coming up with a seemingly arbitrary number. The president's decision to allow a supplemental request to go forward only raised the thorny question of where the money should go. The Finletter report's recommendation of a 70–group Air Force buttressed the case among air advocates that this arm of defense deserved prioritization. The Air Force itself now saw the buildup to 70 groups as a central goal. Under the assumption of balanced forces, a buildup to 70 air groups in turn necessitated an expanded Army and Navy. Yet Truman generally held firm in his conviction that an unrestrained rise in defense spending would ruin the economy. By the time Truman acquiesced in forwarding to Congress an amended supplemental of $3.159 billion, an appropriations bill had already ended up giving the Administration $822 million more for air procurement than he had requested, with authority under the bill expiring at the end of June 1950. Truman signed the bill in May 1948, just as the Berlin crisis was starting to escalate, but stated that he would not spend the additional $822 million for the foreseeable future, which stunted efforts to accelerate the Air Force's expansion.[27] Congress ultimately enacted a combined $13.169 billion in defense appropriations for FY 1949.[28]

Truman's decision to allow a supplemental coincided with his willingness to contemplate an increase in force levels as tensions with the Soviets began to seriously rise. The day before he assigned the cap on supplemental requests, and shortly after the Soviets backed a communist coup in Czechoslovakia, Truman delivered a joint address before Congress on March 17, 1948, pleading for its support on the ERP, a re-imposition of selective service, and the implementation of universal military training (UMT). Truman had long supported UMT as a cost-efficient way to keep large swathes of the civilian population combat ready in the event of war, but it had not gained much support in Congress. The coup in Czechoslovakia added meaning to Truman's bellicose rhetoric that "the Soviet Union and its agents have destroyed the independence and democratic character of a whole series of nations in

Eastern and Central Europe."[29] Unlike a year ago when seeking aid for Greece and Turkey, Truman now mentioned the Soviets directly by name. Congress never acted on UMT, but it eventually passed legislation for selective service and the ERP. Truman did not propose selective service to build up a massive conscript military, and nor did Congress interpret the proposal in this way. Selective service was instead intended to help keep force levels stable and to enable an at most moderate increase in personnel strength in the event of an emergency.

Then another crisis in the heart of Europe threatened more than previous flareups to upset Truman's stable budget outlook. The crisis over Berlin showed all too clearly the necessity of keeping combat forces in Europe, most of all air units. Airpower would indeed help resolve the crisis but in the most unlikely of ways. The Allies had agreed at the Potsdam conference in the summer of 1945 to cooperate in forming a unified Germany that was nonetheless demilitarized and perhaps even economically weakened. Yet differences over reparations and ideology motivated the Western Allies to create a new West German government out of their occupation zones. Western officials were more inclined to support a regeneration of German industry as the path to an independent national economy, and a key step in this direction involved the issuance of a new currency. The Council of Foreign Ministers (CFM) talks in London over postwar Germany, which included the Soviets, broke down by early 1948. Stalin thereafter indicated his intention to turn East Germany into another communist satellite in the region, and the Western Allies prepared to merge their occupation zones. Stalin retaliated by moving against the single most vulnerable point in the Western occupation area, West Berlin, which was in fact located a hundred miles inside East Germany. The four wartime Allies administered Berlin separately from their other occupation zones in Germany as part of a city-specific Kommandatura.

Watchful for signs that Stalin might betray the trust of the Kommandatura, members of the military and intelligence communities kept the Truman Administration apprised of Soviet belligerence towards West Berlin. The Berlin crisis started in earnest when the Soviets instituted new permit and inspections requirements for ground transit into West Berlin. The Soviets had up until this time implicitly allowed the Western Allies to use the autobahn and a railway for shipping in supplies, with only an additional quadripartite agreement formally guaranteeing Western access to Berlin through designated air corridors. The Soviet interference with ground access therefore did not violate any official agreement among the Allies, but it still heightened tensions and threatened the inadvertent outbreak of war. The U.S. Military Governor in Germany, General Lucius Clay, did not want to put U.S. personnel escorting passenger trains in the position of having to accede to Soviet demands for inspection. As a result, he organized an airlift using on-hand C-47 transports for supplying the U.S.'s garrison in the city. The aircraft were not large enough to furnish the Western sector indefinitely with food and coal, but the small airlift proved the Air Force's ability to carry out such a logistical feat under current budgetary circumstances.

The Soviets upped the ante by withdrawing from the Kommandatura and then using Western proposals for currency reform in their occupation sectors of the city as a pretext to order a blockade on all rail, road, and sea access to West Berlin. Because the airlift did not at first appear to be a workable way for supplying the city, military officials contemplated sending a motorized column up the autobahn as part of a relief effort, but by this time the U.S., U.K., and France had only occupation troops left in Germany. West Berlin could still be supplied through an expansion in the current airlift. Truman authorized Clay to continue the airlift with all available C-47s and larger C-54 transports. A few days later on June 28 Truman approved Pentagon requests to form a new B-29 group in Germany and to send two additional B-29 groups to England, all of which were conventionally armed.[30] Given the logistical strains caused by the airlift, the Administration sought to break the impasse with the Soviets through dialogue, but negotiations temporarily stalled as the Soviets tied the situation in Berlin to larger questions over German reunification. The airlift was going to have to work on a long-term basis until these larger issues could be somehow resolved diplomatically.

At a meeting of the National Security Council (NSC) in the White House in late July, Clay, who had briefly returned from his post in Europe, thought the airlift remained viable into the autumn, but he needed at least another 75 C-54s with which to fly in coal for the upcoming winter. Representing the Air Force view, Chief of Staff Vandenberg cautioned that, in addition to posing logistical challenges, sending in more transports to Berlin rendered a larger share of valuable U.S. transport aircraft vulnerable to decimation if hostilities suddenly erupted. He also indicated that the U.S. did not have adequate infrastructure to accommodate the additional aircraft, but Clay answered that he was already planning for local Germans to build another airfield in West Berlin. The NSC decided to send in the additional aircraft.[31] The Air Force's concerns were still valid. A crucial lesson from World War II had been the importance of defending airbases and aircraft with abundant ground forces, but now the Red Army outnumbered the Western Allies in the center of Europe. A few days later, Forrestal sent to the NSC a memorandum enclosed with JCS views on the Berlin situation. After first affirming that the airlift was achievable, the JCS nonetheless conceded that such air transport operations would, in addition to a depletion in available fuel, "further and seriously reduce our air capabilities for implementing emergency war plans including the essential support by the Military Air Transport Service of those plans."[32]

Using up much of the Air Force's transport capacity for the relief of West Berlin was a gamble since Stalin might have only threatened the city as a diversion before engaging in even more hostile action elsewhere. However improbable this scenario, transport aircraft were still extremely exposed as a result of the airlift, and it tied up the Air Force's logistics while hindering its ability to respond to a Soviet attack. Even the beefed-up B-29 presence in Western Europe included only conventionally armed aircraft. The single B-29 group equipped with atomic bombs remained stateside for the duration of the crisis. The Air Force nonetheless successfully orchestrated the airlift. The stream of C-54 and C-47 flights carrying cargo for the West Berlin population continued without interruption through the winter of 1948–49 until September, several months after the Soviets lifted the blockade. Lifting the blockade was an agreement between the Western Allies and the Soviets to resuscitate the CFM talks over Germany. This new round of talks predictably made no progress on the outstanding disputes, as the Americans, British, and French prepared to form a new West German government. But the Soviets did not reimpose the blockade, and the Administration deemed it safe enough to end the airlift.

The Berlin airlift turned out to be a remarkable success, but it further reinforced the view that the Administration was attempting to defend the free world on a shoestring defense budget, especially since Truman had refrained from using additional spending authority for aircraft procurement. Tumultuous world events shaped budget considerations in 1948. Truman seemed most amenable to supplemental spending early in CY 1948 when the communist threat appeared gravest after the coup in Czechoslovakia and the early warning signs that the Soviets might cut off all access to West Berlin. The situation in Europe paradoxically looked to have stabilized once the Air Force demonstrated the success of the airlift, to the point where it could be continued indefinitely, even if it wore down equipment and personnel. Congress had also passed legislation implementing selective service and the ERP, the latter obligating the U.S. to spend $13 billion on economic aid to Europe over a long-term timeframe, which as a gross figure was comparable to the annual defense budget. In looking ahead to FY 1950, Truman wanted to stay the course with an austerity defense budget, signaling that the supplemental request for FY 1949 had been an aberration. He assigned a cap of $15 billion for defense spending in 1950.[33]

Truman's cap may have held down spending, but it uneasily coexisted with the military's global responsibilities in the postwar era. The JCS directed interservice contingency planning that was only viable to the extent of adequate funding. In 1948, the JCS adopted a new contingency plan codenamed Halfmoon (later called Fleetwood) that laid out strategic goals in the event of a third world war caused by Soviet aggression. The Soviets would hypothetically gain preponderant control over the Eurasian landmass, while the U.S. and its closest allies sought to maintain key points along the periphery. Two key points already reflected a U.S. military presence, the U.K. and

Okinawa, outlying islands from which bombers could strike the U.S.S.R. while the U.S. would gear up its war economy in order to stage a ground campaign.[34] The planners behind Halfmoon/Fleetwood also understood the importance of maintaining a defensive position in the Middle East and the Mediterranean. The Suez-Cairo region served as an additional base for strategic air operations against the Soviet Union, but the supply lines for this region extended along the Mediterranean. As the Soviets pushed into Southern Europe, they would be positioned to cut off these lines, forcing the U.S. Navy to deploy the bulk of its heavy warships, including carriers, to defend the area. At the same time, B-36s would strike the Soviet Union from the relative security of North America. The blueprint only planned operations a year out from the start date, so objectives for an Allied ground offensive were not detailed. But under the direst of assumptions the Soviets would gain control over a vast stretch of territory, including critically important oilfields.[35]

While still constituted as the Army Air Corps, the Air Force had a few years earlier worked out a plan called Makefast that similarly envisioned Britain and Egypt as launching pads for an atomic air offensive against the U.S.S.R. with the intention of crippling Soviet petroleum and industrial infrastructure. Now operating under a planned austerity budget for FY 1950, the new SAC commander General Curtis LeMay thought that forty-eight air groups would still be adequate for such an offensive, but that lower number necessitated organizational consolidation and a focus on the attack instead of defense.[36] Military planners understood that airpower could not alone win a war against the Soviet Union, but it could severely degrade the communist bloc's ability to wage armed conflict over the long-term while the U.S. and other non-communist allies mobilized for a ground offensive. Planners also knew that Western conventional ground forces would not be robust enough to decisively defeat the Soviets at the outset of war. A strengthening of U.S. ground forces only increased the odds of slowing the Soviet advance or at least holding some territory on the European continent.

Even after Truman's cap had been revised downward to $14.4 billion, Forrestal worked with the JCS to concoct alternatives of $16.9 billion and $23 billion under the rationale that they better served the Halfmoon/Fleetwood blueprint. Forrestal personally recommended to Truman the $16.9 billion figure, but Truman afterwards wondered why Forrestal had come up with the alternative in the first place and decided to stay with $14.4 billion.[37] In his request to Congress, Truman unambiguously presented the defense budget for FY 1950 in a context of austerity, especially with the economy having undergone an unexpected boom since the end of the war. He stated that "[i]n a period of high prosperity it is not sound public policy for the Government to operate at a deficit. A Government surplus at this time is vitally important to provide a margin for contingencies, to permit reduction of the public debt, to provide an adequate base for the future financing of our present commitments, and to reduce inflationary pressures." This assertion prefaced a request for $4 billion in new taxes.[38] Among the services, the Air Force received $4.6 billion in requested funding, with comparable requests for the Army and Navy. Yet combat strength took a toll due to Truman's renewed commitment to austerity, with the Air Force reorganized into 48 groups, while the Army stayed at 10 active divisions and the Navy maintained 288 active combat ships.[39] Congress ended up legislating $14.3 billion in defense appropriations for the year, which conformed with Truman's wishes.[40]

A defense budget of just over $14 billion had also forced the JCS to amend their contingency planes. Truman appointed Dwight Eisenhower, at the time president of Columbia University, to head the JCS as its acting chairman in early 1949 until a permanent successor could be named. Eisenhower wondered whether Truman's cap could satisfy the military's increasing commitments around the world when factoring in inflation. The JCS would have to make cuts not only in planned capabilities but also in contingency objectives, which required revisions to the updated version of Halfmoon/Fleetwood that included a more detailed catalogue of atomic bombing targets in the Soviet Union. This revised war plan, now called Offtackle, was designed to fit within the Administration's narrowing budget parameters. It did so on a global scale by abandoning Suez-Cairo as a forward base of operations, which had in turn necessitated vulnerable supply lines through the Mediterranean, and instead planned for a U.S. position in the more defensible Northwest Africa area, then under French control. Like earlier plans, Offtackle assumed the quick loss of Western Europe to a Soviet ground assault, even while Eisenhower had initially asserted in a memorandum shortly after his appointment the importance of holding a defensive line along the Rhine. Such a defense was probably not viable, but U.S. forces could attempt to maintain a line near the Pyrenees. They would also be required to defend the western approaches to the Mediterranean in order to keep open lines of communication with Gibraltar and the position in Northwest Africa. The drafters of Offtackle intensified the planned bombing campaign against the U.S.S.R., seeing it as a way to possibly stall the Soviet ground assault if it brought Soviet war production to a virtual halt. The bombing groups responsible for carrying out this campaign would fly from bases in the U.K. and Northwest Africa. Another bombing group would still be assigned to Okinawa, but Offtackle like earlier iterations assumed a defensive posture along the Pacific Rim.[41]

Truman's cost cutting wrought consequences for military planning, including an abandonment in the defense over the short-term of most of the Mediterranean and Suez. In that sense, Truman's confidence in maintaining peace and security might have looked misplaced as Stalin communized Eastern and Central Europe, therefore warranting higher military spending consistent with contingency objectives. But however brutal a dictator Stalin might have been in his own country, and however much he employed secret police tactics for setting up satellite dictatorships in most places where Soviet troops marched, one must also consider that the wartime Allies had just ended the deadliest and most destructive war in history, in which Soviet military and civilian losses reached as high as 27 million compared to just over 400,000 U.S. military deaths. When Stalin insisted to Western leaders that the Soviet people simply could not endure more war no matter what their leaders told them, he may very well have conveyed an underlying truth that put into proper perspective the assumption of a Russian bear clawing its way deeper into Europe. The Soviets also had understandable concerns for preventing another invasion of their homeland from Central Europe. While this did not justify imposing one party communist rule in the areas they occupied, let alone cutting off surface access to West Berlin, they had an obvious interest in the political composition of states along their immediate border. And as with the Western Allies they had just as much right to station occupation troops in Germany for the foreseeable future. Finally, the U.S.'s monopoly over the atomic bomb was fleeting, but Soviet development did not overturn new conventions in nuclear deterrence, especially as the U.S. continued to modernize its arsenal. The JCS had to formulate contingency plans to clarify core objectives, a function of any standing military, but all the same most assessments of the Soviets at the time concluded that they did not want to start another war.

Thus if Truman had been confident reining in defense spending at the beginning of CY 1949, then he was probably even more so at the start of 1950. The situation in Europe had now fully stabilized from the crisis conditions of early 1948. ERP aid was boosting reconstruction, the Soviets had lifted the Berlin blockade, and the North Atlantic Treaty Organization (NATO) had been established. The creation of a West German government had not led to the total dissipation of tensions with the Soviets over Germany, who could still pressure Western officials to begin another round of CFM talks on reunification. But at least NATO promised a new military and logistical machinery for Western defense. In Greece, the non-communist government had at last defeated the guerillas, a victory facilitated by the break in relations between the Soviets and the Yugoslav dictator Josip Broz Tito. Tito disavowed the Greek guerrillas after they refused to transfer their allegiance from the Soviets to his own personal leadership. The Greek communists were thereafter denied a base of operations just within the Yugoslav border, greatly hampering their ability to carry on the insurrection. With continued military aid to Greece and Turkey, the eastern Mediterranean had been secured in all but contingency planning. These developments in Europe had been offset by major reverses in Asia, notably the fall of mainland China to Maoist forces, which added fire to the Red Scare at home. Yet despite this setback, the Truman Administration wanted a defense budget that restrained spending over the long-term. This long-term posture was also advisable from a technological perspective. Outmoded weapons systems could be more efficiently weeded out and replaced on a tighter budget than if a crash buildup were confined to a single year.

When Truman submitted his budget request for FY 1951 at the beginning of 1950 the economy had gone through a recession, which was contributing to a projected $5.1 billion deficit over the near term.[42] The Air Force for the first time decisively won the largest share of requested funding among the services at $4.4 billion, compared to $4 billion for the Army and $3.9 billion for the Navy, for a combined defense budget of $13.7 billion.[43] Yet the continued tilt towards airpower did not keep Truman from opining in his budget message that "national defense must be sufficient to provide us with the balanced military strength we must maintain in the present world situation, at a level which can be sustained over a period of years."[44] The diversion of funding into the Air Force had arguably been done to offset past weaknesses without overturning underlying assumptions towards national defense. The Air Force still consisted of only 48 groups and 8,800 active aircraft before the Korean War, its objective of 70 groups a distant goal, but these figures compared to the equally modest 238 combat ships and 5,900 active aircraft for the Navy and 10 active divisions for the Army.[45] Truman further emphasized the need for stability in defense planning, noting that "[f]or the past 2 years we have been adjusting our military programs to achieve a balanced structure which can be maintained over a period of years without an undue use of national resources."[46] He submitted this budget request five months before the outbreak of the Korean War. Congress would not seriously act on it until after the commencement of hostilities, which irreversibly cast aside such cautious assumptions. Yet the budget message is still noteworthy for its insistence on stable spending patterns.

At the time that Truman submitted this budget request, he made two important decisions. First, he authorized testing for a hydrogen bomb to keep the U.S. one step ahead of the Soviets, who had now successfully exploded an atomic device. The venture into thermonuclear weapons threatened a more dangerous arms race, but the Administration, according to many officials at the time, had little choice until negotiations could resume with the Soviets hopefully at some point after Stalin's death. Truman also commissioned a study to provide a framework for long-term defense planning. Paul Nitze, who had recently replaced George Kennan as head of the State Department's Policy Planning Staff, took the helm of an informal interdepartmental working group responsible for drafting the document. Nitze personally expended much labor on the document that came to be known as NSC 68. In April 1950, Truman referred it to the NSC for final approval.

While Truman might have been responsible for commissioning the paper, the final product did not wholly reflect his outlook when he first received it over two months before the start of the Korean War. NSC 68 described in grave terms the Soviets as a totalitarian menace to world peace. It emphasized the demands placed upon the U.S. and its allies to build up their conventional and nuclear forces in order to contain communist advances. Budget austerity could not impede such a necessary buildup. The free world risked falling behind the Soviets now that they had successfully tested an atomic bomb. The document flatly stated that "[b]udgetary considerations will need to be subordinated to the stark fact that our very independence as a nation may be at stake." NSC 68 instead focused on the inherent strengths of the U.S. economy to sustain such a buildup. U.S. GNP was estimated as four times larger than that of the Soviet Union, but the U.S. spent only 6.5% of its GNP on defense compared to 13.8% for the Soviets. Nitze and the other authors of NSC 68 avoided viewing higher defense spending as a drain on the economy. On the contrary, NSC 68 predicted that "[w]ith a high level of economic activity, the United States could soon attain a gross national product of $300 billion per year. . . . Progress in this direction would permit, and might itself be aided by, a build-up of the economic and military strength of the United States and the free world[.]"[47]

NSC 68 did not provide any cost figure for this planned buildup, probably because its drafters knew that an actual figure included in the written document itself could impede its positive reception in Congress and the White House. Yet NSC 68 recommendations were widely believed to entail another $50 billion in defense spending. Truman refrained from explicitly approving NSC 68 upon reviewing it in April 1950, and in his memo forwarding the document to the NSC he urged the director of the Bureau of the Budget, his chief economic adviser, and the treasury secretary to convene and discuss the budgetary ramifications of the report, a sign of the close relation between his national security and fiscal agendas.[48] In just a few months, the Administration would be overwhelmed by the invasion of South Korea. It would no longer be operating under normal peacetime conditions, and its perspective on defense would change drastically. The Korean War affected not only U.S. responses in Asia but in Europe as well, as allies suddenly feared that the Kremlin was masterminding communist movements around the world and might target their countries next in a surprise war of aggression. The influence of NSC 68 on the Truman White House cannot be separated from the disturbing global context in which it was eventually approved.

At the same time, the establishment of NATO represented a more durable embodiment after the isolated responses of Truman Doctrine aid and the Berlin airlift. The idea of establishing NATO came relatively quickly amid the tumult of 1948. Britain, France, and the Low Countries had already concluded a collective security organization, which then morphed into

NATO after U.S. military officials joined in the talks. But the genesis of NATO and its subsequent Senate ratification in July 1949 did not automatically signal the deployment of large numbers of U.S. ground forces to Europe. Truman's budget request for FY 1951, after NATO had been ratified, made no provision for such a deployment. He only referred to NATO commitments in the FY 1951 request in relation to military aid.[49]

For another two-year stretch from early CY 1948 to early CY 1950 the Administration faced heightening world tension, which it met with the logistical triumph of the Berlin airlift and the creation of NATO while not losing sight of its underlying fiscal goals. But the very integrity of the Administration in balancing the budget also invited criticism that it failed to back up its increasingly ambitious foreign policy pronouncements with requisite military might. Well into CY 1950 the Administration had not proceeded with rearmament, and Truman at first responded ambivalently to the recommendations in NSC 68. In whatever case, the Administration had succeeded in balancing the budget during the tense peace of the late 1940s, which had conversely turned into a Cold War.

RECONVERSION, NATIONAL HEALTH INSURANCE, TAXES, FAIR DEAL

While the Administration faced threats to peace abroad, it embarked upon the transition from a totalistic wartime regime to a peacetime economy at home. Reconversion to such an economy signaled a return to normal market forces, including the albeit delayed termination of wage and price controls and the ending of war-related government contracts. But unlike the domestic economy, the international economy operated abnormally until the late 1950s. Among belligerents, only the U.S. economy emerged from the war not only undamaged but operating at full capacity. At war's end it produced well over half the world's manufactured goods and housed two-thirds of its gold stock. The U.S. maintained large trade surpluses with Europe, and this situation would not significantly change until European countries rebuilt their battered economies with U.S. aid. Current accounts in goods and services remained officially inconvertible in the late 1940s and through most of the 1950s, and governments had little recourse except to impose controls on capital and trade. By the mid-1950s the international situation became steadily more normal with the help of ERP aid, which fomented much-needed investment and productivity in Europe. Both real and monetary factors remained in a state of transition. Even the international monetary system planned out at Bretton Woods, New Hampshire, in 1944 would not be fully activated until 1958 with the convertibility of current accounts. The planners at the Bretton Woods conference wanted to do everything possible to avoid the "beggar thy neighbor" devaluations of the 1930s and opted instead for a modified gold standard, with only the U.S. dollar directly pegged to gold but other currencies pegged to the dollar subject to adjustment within narrow bands. Now that gold bullion had been nationalized in government vaults, a legacy of the Depression, world leaders hoped that they could turn the classical gold standard into a more modern and workable system that helped keep balance of payments even among trade partners.

For the Truman Administration in September 1945, with the Pacific war reaching a surprisingly quick conclusion, casting a huge relief over a country and a world exhausted with war, these considerations still waited well into the future. Truman inherited a highly abnormal international economic setting and fears at home of a return to depression once military contracts dried up for industry. The termination of these contracts and demobilization of combat forces were bound to produce budget surpluses, even with tax cuts. Yet from very early in the postwar era Truman did not intend simply to preside over reconversion. He was after all an acolyte of the New Deal. In Franklin Roosevelt's state of the union address in January 1944, well before the Democratic Party put Truman on the ticket, the president had propounded a "second Bill of Rights" that included among other things the right to employment, medical care, and education. Inhabiting an unusual and transitory moment of economic primacy, Truman worked to expand the entitlement state and complete the New Deal.

The beginning of the modern entitlement state in the U.S. during the Great Depression did not necessarily portend deficit normality, even as the government repeatedly turned in deficits due to economic conditions after 1930. Roosevelt's New Deal coalition enacted sweeping changes to government, but it implemented elaborate funding schemes for most entitlement programs that were intended to avoid triggering deficits. Legislation establishing Social Security, Railroad Retirement, and Unemployment Insurance (UI) directed that payroll taxes on employers and employees fund these programs. These dedicated sources served as an alternative means to general revenue collected through income and excise taxes. Social Security relied on a 1% payroll tax on both employers and employees up to a wage base of $3,000, which cut off liability above that ceiling. The Railroad Retirement program, which funded retirement benefits for railroad workers, similarly imposed a 2.75% tax on employers and employees capped at $300 in income. The Department of Labor partnered with the states in overseeing the UI program. Federal and state unemployment taxes on employers funded UI, with the tax in effect passed on to employees. States were expected to build up reserves that could be drawn down during recessions. These complicated funding schemes on the surface demonstrated that social insurance could potentially cohere with balanced budgets under improved economic conditions.

Yet these policies did not entirely isolate the funding mechanism for Social Security, the largest of these programs, from general revenue. The Social Security Administration was tied to a trust fund model, with revenue generated from payroll taxes invested in Treasury bonds. Interest earned from the bonds in turn funded the payment of benefits. Payroll taxes funded general spending to the extent the Treasury used the principal from the bonds sold to Social Security for meeting government expenditures. These funding arrangements continued to facilitate the expansion of Social Security to survivors of beneficiaries, including wives over sixtfy-five years of age, widows with dependent children, and dependent children themselves. Uncovered groups included farm and domestic workers, the self-employed, federal workers, and employees of non-profit organizations.

Truman decided to mobilize public support in the wake of the Allied victories by pushing for legislation in one important area that had escaped Roosevelt's agenda, health care. Truman remained consistently committed to balanced budgets and mindful of the dangers of rampant debt, but from very early in his presidency he wanted to fulfill a big part of Roosevelt's Second Bill of Rights with the creation of a national health insurance program. Truman's proposal to Congress for such a program in November 1945 was not necessarily novel. Only a few years before at the height of the war a group of senators wrote a bill for a similar system funded from payroll taxes, but it never emerged from committee. As described in an address to Congress, Truman's means for funding relied on a combination of mandatory premiums paid by all covered persons and general revenue, which he left at Congress's discretion to work out in detail. Truman urgently noted that many physicians were returning from the war. Now was the time, he claimed, to fund medical care in rural and poor areas through government assistance. He repeatedly insisted in his address that, for various reasons, this proposal did not amount to "socialized medicine," among them being localized administration over hospitals and physicians, the discretion of physicians and patients to opt in or out of the system (though premiums were still mandatory), and the preservation of existing physician-patient relationships.[50]

Truman left the door open for a major expansion in the entitlement state to be funded from general revenue as opposed to new payroll taxes. Premium payments triggered at a threshold of $3,000 in income would also contribute to the centralized fund that Truman proposed, but except for basic insurance principles he offered no other safeguard for containing rising medical costs in part funded from general revenue. Truman of course only sketched out an idea in an address before Congress, and Democratic backers soon worked to translate these ideas into a viable bill. But no legislation ever reached the floor of the House or Senate, let alone Truman's desk. Entrenched interests such as the American Medical Association had long opposed governmental intrusion into health care. A national health insurance program, so the argument went, threatened to wipe out private health insurance, even if Truman appeared to be avoiding a highly centralized, top down model. Opponents of the plan went so far as to link it to communism, and acts of Soviet aggression in Europe did little to assuage public opinion in that respect. After Truman won reelection, he could not muster enough support to push a bill out of committee. The exigency of the Korean War finally extinguished any hope of passing some version of Truman's initial proposal.

The initial proposal of November 1945 coincided with the less political but still highly urgent task of reconverting the economy to civilian production, which had to be managed carefully to avoid economic disturbances and the feared return of depression. Though the population craved consumer goods after years of rationing, the postwar transition did not play out in the smoothest possible way for the Administration, which contended with labor strife and inflation well through 1946. The sharp drop-off in government spending officially caused a contraction in GDP in 1946 and 1947 (in addition to 1945) before it reached 4% growth in 1948, but the economy was not in any meaningful sense in a recession. Resurgent consumer demand and reenergized private investment propelled the economy forward, and through this transition Truman continued to focus on a tight fiscal policy. He proposed tax cuts and phase-outs of wartime taxes as the conscript military demobilized. But he only wanted tax cuts moderate enough not to interfere with paying down the national debt in addition to funding his health care proposal if it ever passed in Congress, which from the vantage of late 1945 was unclear.

Truman's treasury secretary, Fred Vinson, echoed these same sentiments when testifying before Congress in October 1945. Vinson advised only modest tax cuts because the Administration still anticipated onerous spending commitments a year out from the war, and anyhow Congress did not have time to push through comprehensive tax legislation if it wanted the cuts to be ready for CY 1946. He thought that tax cuts should be kept no deeper than $5 billion.[51] Congress subsequently passed the Revenue Act of 1945, signed into law by Truman, which cut corporate and personal taxes and repealed the excess profits tax. At the time, corporate and personal taxes were still bifurcated between normal rates and surtaxes. The law did not alter normal corporate rates, but it cut the corporate surtaxes from 10% to 6% for brackets $25,000 or under, maintained a 22% surtax for incomes up to $50,000, and lowered the surtax from 16% to 14% in the top bracket over $50,000. As a result, among corporations the combined normal rate and surtax for the highest bracket dropped from 40% to 38%. The legislation notably maintained a "notch" or bubble rate for corporate incomes between $25,000–$50,000, which were hit with a combined 53% statutory rate, higher than the next income bracket over $50,000. The law further applied an across the board 3% cut to personal surtax rates while expanding the personal exemption to

$500. The combined normal and surtax rate on the top bracket still sat at 86.45%. Wartime excise taxes, meanwhile, were already slated to expire shortly after the cessation of hostilities.[52]

For Truman the 1945 Revenue Act had been more than adequate in boosting business investment and consumption without setting off an inflationary storm. In the budget message from early CY 1946, he doubted the prospects for more aggressive tax cutting in the future and noted that "[t]he level of anticipated expenditures for the fiscal year 1947 and the volume of outstanding public debt require the maintenance of large revenues." The Administration's concerns over revenue loss and inflation were closely tied to its central goal of debt stabilization, which in turn hinged upon low nominal interest rates then at only 2%. The federal government had recently finished off war-related borrowing with the Victory Loan. On-hand cash at the Treasury Department allowed the government to now pay down the debt from $278 billion to an estimated $271 billion during the course of FY 1947. The government was not in any danger of running up against the $300 billion statutory debt limit.[53]

The Administration intended to pay down the national debt in near programmatic terms. Larger tax cuts threatened to trigger peacetime deficits and cause a breach in the debt limit while fueling inflation and raising nominal borrowing costs. For a few important reasons, then, the Administration sought only a moderate tax cut in order to preserve a base of revenue that could also fund any future expansion in the entitlement state. A booming economy and full employment would hopefully generate larger tax revenue and make this agenda all the more feasible. Yet even though the Administration had limited ambitions for the 1945 Revenue Act, the legislation turned out to be highly significant from an economic standpoint, leading to nearly $6 billion in revenue loss in current dollars and helping to spark a postwar boom that ended any remaining fears of a return to the Great Depression. The revenue loss would not be exceeded by any later tax laws in current dollars until the 1964 Revenue Act. As a percentage of GDP, it was larger at 2.67% than any other piece of tax legislation in the period from 1940 to 1968.[54]

The year 1946 still turned bad politically for Truman, culminating in a Republican takeover of both the House and Senate. Truman's objectives otherwise remained the same, especially as the economy heated up. His budget for FY 1948 planned for a small surplus that would grow larger in the next few years. Truman held that "[a]s long as business, employment, and national income continue high, we should maintain tax revenues at levels that will not only meet current expenditures but also leave a surplus for retirement of the public debt. There is no justification now for tax reduction."[55] The Administration had already paid down the debt by $20 billion to a total of now $259 billion. To further stabilize the debt, the Treasury sold non-negotiable savings bonds to the public and used the proceeds to retire normal negotiable bonds traded among banks. These operations shifted debt holdings from banks to general members of the public while reducing excess liquidity in the Treasury markets.[56]

Republican control of Congress prevented Truman from seriously pursuing national health insurance for the time being, but he wanted to preserve the Administration's policy structure for the budget and the economy. With the Cold War not yet fully evident and major expansion in the entitlement state on hold, early CY 1947 offered a moment when the permanent return to peacetime budget surpluses still seemed possible. Yet Republicans prepared to utilize their large majorities in Congress for another round of tax cuts. John Snyder, who had replaced Vinson as treasury secretary, testified in March 1947 before the House Ways and Means Committee, arguing against tax reductions for reasons mirroring those in Truman's own statements. Snyder emphasized not only the sheer strength of the economy but also the high degree of confidence characterizing the current business climate. New production techniques perfected during the war could now be geared to civilian ends. From his standpoint, a tax cut was at present plainly unnecessary.[57]

Congress nonetheless proceeded with legislation for up to $4 billion in tax cuts, and Truman ended up vetoing two bills in the summer of 1947. The Republicans in Congress failed to override the vetoes both times, coming just a few votes short of a two-thirds majority in the Senate. They finally succeeded a year later in overcoming Truman's third veto. Congress passed the Revenue Act of 1948 in April of that year, just at the outset of the Berlin airlift and subsequent to Truman's request for ERP funding, selective service, and UMT. Congress also passed the tax law in a presidential election year in which most political pundits considered Truman a lame duck. Among other provisions, the Revenue Act of 1948 lowered the top personal income tax rate from 86.45% to 82.1% while extending cuts to all other income brackets, the lowest bracket coming down from 19% to 16.6%. The law also increased the personal exemption by $100 to $200 depending upon filing status and number of dependents, in addition to an over $500 exemption for those with disabilities.[58] The Act led to a $5 billion revenue loss in current dollars and equaled 1.87% of GDP.[59]

The Administration had reached its budgetary apex in FY 1948, which ended just after passage of the tax cuts. The budget for that fiscal year registered a surplus of $8.4 billion, a feat to be repeated only twice more, and to a lesser degree, during Truman's presidency.[60] In the second term the Administration encountered recession, war, and new overseas commitments in Europe, all seriously complicating budget balancing. The fact that Truman's presidency even lasted to 1953 was due to his dramatic upset victory in the 1948 election. In his whistle-stop campaign across the country he derided the "do nothing" Congress and called for various prescriptions to speed up the transition back to the civilian economy. With his own reelection and Democratic recapture of Congress, Truman enjoyed a fresh mandate to again focus on domestic initiatives as the Berlin crisis wound down. Truman laid out the Fair Deal package in his state of the union address in January 1949, which entailed a $4 billion hike on corporate, gift, and estate taxes to fund among other things federal assistance for low income housing and slum clearance, national health insurance, expansion of Social Security coverage, and construction of the St. Lawrence Seaway.[61]

Truman at the outset of his second term wanted to raise taxes to exclusively fund Fair Deal programs under the assumption that a shooting war with the Soviets could be avoided through deterrence. The 1950 tax legislation emanated from the White House with this intention, and Truman secured a few of his Fair Deal objectives before being totally engulfed by the Korean War. The first of these was the Housing Act of 1949, which funded slum clearance, construction of public housing, and rent support for low income households. Six months later in January 1950 Truman signed into law a near doubling of the minimum wage from 40 to 75 cents per hour for workers covered under the Fair Labor Standards Act. Raising the minimum wage served as a particular form of government intervention in the economy that did not explicitly require additional revenue and possibly passed costs on to employers. The Housing Act, however, did necessitate additional revenue to replace slums with over 800,000 new housing units.[62] Housing initiatives did not lead to enormous expenditures. By FY 1951 funding for low rent housing was expected to climb to $136 million, while slum clearance cost about $156 million.[63]

But Truman's most important domestic legacy was to continue the process of enlarging the entitlement state even in an age of global military commitments. By the time he took office, Social Security had already been substantially revised and expanded. The 1939 Amendments, in addition to extending coverage to survivors of beneficiaries, altered benefit calculators to maximize monthly payments to retirees. The budget surpluses of the late 1940s had delayed planned increases in payroll taxes, but by 1950 Congress and the Administration cooperated in increasing payroll taxes on employers and employees to 1.5% each for a combined 3% rate. These payroll tax hikes were implemented in tandem with a series of benefit increases adjusted ad hoc for inflation. The most significant component of the 1950 Amendments extended coverage to an additional 10 million workers, including farmers, domestic laborers, self-employed persons not within professions requiring official certification such as law and medicine, and some federal employees not eligible for civil service pensions. Truman thus expanded Social Security while keeping its funding edifice intact, reinforcing a pattern that turned it into a universal program.

KOREA, FISCAL REPERCUSSIONS, REARMAMENT IN EUROPE

The Administration had never intended to fight a war in Korea. In the wake of the rapid North Korean offensive down the peninsula in the summer of 1950, the military commander in the Far East, Douglas MacArthur, was at first forced to throw underequipped, undermanned occupation units stationed in Japan into the maelstrom of combat, which made all too clear the U.S.'s lack of preparedness. The sudden onset of hostilities cast a negative light on the preceding years of military austerity, which had decisively contributed to the fiscal stability that Truman deemed a central objective of the Administration. The responses to the communist threat in the late 1940s focused on Europe, first with military aid, then economic aid, then the airlift, and finally NATO, which in 1950 still had a long way to go before being built up into a viable military force. JCS contingency plans assumed that the U.S. and its allies would struggle to secure a perimeter in Europe at the onset of hostilities with the Soviets, whether at the Rhine or possibly in Iberia.

For various reasons, any equivalent security perimeter in or bordering the Asian landmass was not as clear-cut. With a few exceptions in Burma, U.S. ground forces had not penetrated in depth into Asia during the war. The U.S. presence in China was largely limited to airpower. MacArthur, as Allied commander of the Southwest Pacific theater, directed two landings on the island of Borneo in the Dutch East Indies in the last months of the war using mainly Australian troops. The major thrust of U.S. forces had been up the Solomons ladder, along the northern coast of New Guinea, across the central Pacific, and into the Philippines. By the end of the war in the Pacific in September 1945, U.S. forces had liberated, invaded, or were in the process of occupying outlying islands along the East Asian Pacific Rim, specifically the Philippines, the Ryukyus, and the Japanese Home Islands. And at the northernmost extent of the Pacific, the U.S. held Alaska and the Aleutians as American-owned territory. The axis of this advance skirted the edge of the Asian landmass. Marines had also landed along the mainland coast of northeastern China to back the shipping in of supplies and reinforcements of Nationalist troops, but the Administration later pulled out these units as the Chinese civil war intensified.

U.S. forces had also landed in Korea. Having been officially relegated a Japanese colony since 1910, U.S. and Soviet troops both went into the country in the closing days of World War II. During the war Allied representatives formally agreed to a reunified Korea, but the Potsdam conference authorized the U.S. and U.S.S.R. to carve out occupation zones demarcated by the 38th Parallel. The U.S. thereafter introduced a resolution before the U.N. General Assembly calling for U.N.-supervised national elections in a reunified Korea. The resolution passed in the General Assembly but without the support of the Soviets, who were turning North Korea into a heavily armed satellite state that could outmatch the South Korean constabulary in any ground fighting. Because the Soviets did not accept a request for multi-party elections in a unified Korea, the U.S. proceeded with elections in the South in 1948.

Many high-level officials during this period called for a U.S. pullout from South Korea. Shortly after becoming defense secretary, Forrestal asked the JCS for their opinion on Korea options. The JCS doubted the wisdom of keeping troops in the South, further explaining that "[i]n the event of hostilities in the Far East, our present forces in Korea would be a military liability and could not be maintained there without substantial reinforcements prior to the initiation of hostilities. Moreover, any offensive operation the United States might wish to conduct on the Asiatic continent most probably would by-pass the Korean peninsula." Even if Soviet-backed forces occupied the southern half of Korea, the U.S. could respond with "neutralization by air action" from nearby bases. The JCS concluded that national security was better served by redeploying the 45,000 troops in Korea to an area of greater importance.[64] As the JCS formulated contingencies such as Halfmoon/Fleetwood and Offtackle, they planned for strategic defense in East Asia. Such a defense could be sustained through aerial and naval operations staged from offshore fortresses like Okinawa without the need for a landing on the Asiatic mainland.

An NSC directive from April 2, 1948, presented a similarly dubious picture of the commitment to Korea. The directive outlined three options for the Administration: total disengagement, economic and military support without a formal guarantee, or extending a formal security guarantee to the South with or without continued troop presence in the country. The NSC decided in favor of the second option in order to achieve "a settlement of the Korean problem which would enable the U.S. to withdraw from Korea as soon as possible with the minimum of bad effects."[65] Yet absent such a settlement with the North U.S. forces would not be withdrawn under favorable conditions. A CIA report from February 1949 put the matter more bluntly, predicting that "[w]ithdrawal of U.S. forces from Korea in the spring of 1949 would probably in time be followed by an invasion," which "would probably result in a collapse of the U.S.-supported Republic of Korea." South Korean forces would not be strong enough to fend off the invasion before January 1950. On the other hand, the retention of U.S. forces in Korea "would not only discourage the threatened invasion but would assist in sustaining the will and ability of the Koreans themselves to resist any future invasion once they had the military force to do so[.]"[66]

The Administration temporarily delayed the withdrawal of troops until after the formation of the South Korean government in 1949. Military assistance to South Korea was also not extensive. Truman signed into law the Mutual Defense Assistance Act in October 1949, which provided military aid to both NATO and non-NATO allies. Under the Act South Korea had to share $27.6 million in aid with Iran and the Philippines for FY 1950. During 1949, with NATO still nothing but parchment, the JCS doubted the U.S. could defend Western Europe and the Middle East from communist invasion, let alone South Korea. Secretary of State Dean Acheson famously failed to include South Korea within any formal security perimeter in a speech before the National Press Club in January 1950. Acheson was discussing the commitment to Japan and its security, whose "defense must and shall be maintained," before referring to a "defensive perimeter" from the Aleutians to Japan and then extending south to include the Ryukyus and the Philippines. He did not otherwise elaborate on what he meant by "defensive perimeter" but did mention that the U.N. would respond to any act of aggression against other areas in East Asia, an implied reference to Korea.[67] Acheson's statements reflected conventional views at the time. This "defensive perimeter" extended to areas where the U.S. already maintained military forces and basing rights. Acheson for that reason did not include Taiwan in the perimeter, now home to the Nationalist government of Chiang Kai-Shek.

The Administration ended up waging a hot war in a Northeast Asian country supposedly outside its security perimeter while it brought into being a permanent military alliance on the other side of the world. Various reasons may account for the Truman Administration's decision to intervene in Korea. The Administration above all wanted to prove its mettle in stopping communist aggression. Even with monumental accomplishments like the Marshall Plan and NATO under his belt, Truman's domestic standing had been weakened due to the loss of China to communism and the Red Scare. The North Korean invasion should not have surprised members of the Administration, but the imminent communist takeover of the South served as a shock and may have led to a vague sense that Japan might now be threatened. Japan certainly served as a base of operations during the war. Whatever the reason for Truman's decision to order intervention and seek U.N. authorization, the Korean War ended for good Truman's defense austerity. Funding military operations in Korea was now bound to drive up spending. Perhaps had the U.N. forces achieved a decisive victory shortly after the Inchon amphibious landing in September 1950 the Administration could have returned to its normal level of spending. But the Chinese wintertime counteroffensive along the Yalu River in the far north of Korea and the threat of conflict in Europe negated any such possibility. The Korean War also affected defense spending over the long-term, beyond Truman's tenure in office. The military emerged permanently larger as a result of the war, especially the Air Force, while the threat of invasion to Europe no longer seemed quite so hypothetical, in turn elevating the importance of NATO.

Truman's budget request for FY 1952 reflected the tense situation. He framed the budget as one "for our national security in a period of grave danger," with no end in sight for the war.[68] Congress had already legislated emergency appropriations to the amount of $28.7 billion since the war started, on top of $10 billion in planned authority requested by Truman for FY 1952. Truman could not even provide detailed numbers for the FY 1952 request because of the innumerable military imponderables, but he estimated that defense spending would come to roughly $61 billion.[69] These figures were a dramatic rise from the original $13 billion in defense spending requested a year earlier. Instead of a quick "police action," as Truman initially referred to the conflict, the Pentagon found itself having to fund a protracted slugfest. Congress ended up appropriating $55.5 billion for defense in FY 1952.[70] To control the ongoing buildup, which had led to the creation of 95 Air Force wings (a renaming of groups) by CY 1952, Truman imposed a "stretch out" spending protocol for the foreseeable future that limited defense spending to $60 billion for FY 1953.[71] Congress eventually appropriated $44.3 billion by the time Truman signed the budget act into law.[72]

The war also added new urgency for a bill to increase tax revenue. Congress passed the Revenue Act of 1950 that September, which raised personal income taxes across the board. The Act increased the top personal rate from 82.1% to 91% and the lowest rate from 16.6% to 20%. It also revised corporate tax rates by eliminating the "notch" or bubble rate on incomes between $25,000 and $50,000 and instead imposing a two-tiered rate structure. Companies earning income below $25,000 paid the normal 25% statutory rate. Higher corporate incomes were subject to a 20% surtax, which when combined with the normal rate came to 45% on the higher income.[73] China's entry into the war late in 1950 only necessitated extra revenue raising legislation. Congress passed an excess profits tax by the end of 1950 requiring companies to pay a 30% tax on income in excess of an average of earnings during a designated base period from prior years. The drafters of the bill inserted a clause scheduling the tax to expire at the end of FY 1953. However, the law added to this tax a permanent rate hike of 2% on the corporate surtax.[74] With U.N. forces retreating below the 38th Parallel, Truman called for more revenue, even with the Revenue Act of 1950 and the excess profits tax already expected to contribute to an over $10.5 billion rise in taxes for FY 1952.[75] The resulting legislation, the Revenue Act of 1951, included regressive components. Congress still hiked rates by 9% for incomes over $26,000, but it imposed an 11% tax increase on incomes $2,000 or lower and 11 ¾% on incomes $26,000 or lower. The top personal rate now reached 92%. Congress also slapped on a number of excise tax hikes while increasing the normal corporate rate by 5% and the long-term capital gains rate on individuals and corporations by 1%, to now 26%.[76] The three tax laws brought in a combined revenue of $13.2 billion.[77]

The Korean War taxes serve as a prime example of government raising revenue in a highly concerted manner in order to fund the waging of a limited, regional conflict. Truman insisted throughout this period on pay as you go tax rules for the war effort, stating outright in his budget request for 1952 that "[h]igh taxes are indispensable to our successful mobilization" both to furnish the government with revenue and to put a damper on inflation.[78] Personal income tax rates were extremely high by 1953 and arguably prohibitive. However, the fiscal effects of the war perhaps further motivated Truman and Eisenhower into ending it, in addition to the human losses, even if only through an armistice instead of a peace agreement. For all of Truman's pay-go rhetoric, he left office presiding over rising deficits. The war taxes had managed to turn in a $3.5 billion surplus for FY 1951, but subsequent years brought in deficits, with FY 1954 estimated at up to $10 billion in the red.[79]

Truman failed to secure an armistice during his remaining time in office. Differences between the two sides over the repatriation of POWs caused the armistice talks to drag on interminably as the bloodshed continued. Yet while Truman failed to end a shooting war in Asia, he bolstered the chances for security in Europe by working with allies to strengthen the military forces there and gain greater deterrent advantage. Turning NATO from a paper treaty into a cohesive military force required a new level of spending on the part of all the treaty members, including and especially the U.S. Spending needed to be dramatically raised over a roughly four-year period so that NATO forces would achieve readiness by 1954, the year thought to be of maximum danger by the Administration. The outbreak of the Korean War only added to this sense of urgency, and the Administration faced these new commitments in Europe just as it was requesting huge new supplementals for war spending in Korea. As a symbol of American commitment to Europe, Truman designated Eisenhower as Supreme Allied Commander–Europe to oversee NATO forces in late 1950, a reprisal of his role during World War II. By April 1951, Eisenhower was setting up the Supreme Headquarters for the Allied Powers in Europe (SHAPE) in northeastern France.

Over a year before the activation of SHAPE, NATO officials had begun planning the new organization's force structure and core strategy. NATO's Standing Group, an executive body that directed the day to day work of the Military Committee, forged ahead through its subordinate working teams on hashing out interim targets for readiness prior to 1954. These intermediate planning targets did not gauge contingencies over the long run, focusing instead on the immediate ability to stop a Soviet assault. In its report to the Military Committee, the Standing Group recommended "[f]irst priority to be given to the achievement, and effectiveness of those forces programmed for 1 July, 1951, which are destined to meet the first enemy onslaught in Europe," including upkeep for tactical air combat groups, air defense, and ground forces. In meeting this priority, the Standing Group estimated the availability of fifteen infantry divisions and three armored divisions by the initial target date of July 1, 1951, which would fulfill the first phase of preparations for the Medium Term Plan (MTP).[80]

The Standing Group proposed specialization on the part of national militaries to help fulfill the goals laid out in this MTP by 1954. NATO members were authorized to specialize in different capabilities, both for the time being and to a lesser extent as rearmament began in earnest. Specialization complemented the planned integration of European and North American forces under SHAPE. The Standing Group indicated in a May 26, 1950, directive "the NATO aim to establish collectively balanced forces throughout the whole NATO area, rather than within each nation individually[.]" In applying this principle over the short-term, the Standing Group assigned the European countries with responsibility for "ground forces and tactical air forces," the U.S. and U.K. for "organization and control of ocean lines of communication," and the U.S. for "strategic bombing assisted as practicable by other nations."[81]

These assignments served as expedients until rearmament could lead to more general sharing of ground, air, and naval burdens. When Eisenhower activated SHAPE in April 1951, the U.S.'s ground contribution was limited to occupation troops in Germany, totaling a single infantry division, three armored cavalry regiments, and a regimental combat team stationed in West Berlin, though by that year the U.S. also planned to deploy three more infantry divisions and a full armored division to SHAPE.[82] The 1951 reinforcements helped close the gap between the American ground contribution and the British and French contingents attached to NATO. The U.S. would be expanding its ground responsibilities well before the MTP interim target date, in addition to increasing the number of fighter-bomber wings deployed to Europe. The infusion of American manpower offset the diversion of French troops to Indochina and then Algeria, where they were engaged in bitter counterinsurgencies, a preoccupation shared with the British to a lesser extent in Malaya. Truman's stretch out helped fund the deployments to Europe, but the U.S.'s NATO commitments were expected to be costly. In 1951, NATO's Pricing Committee estimated that the U.S. would incur $106 billion over a four-year buildup and then up to $24 billion per year thereafter.[83]

Even with the Administration's deployment of four divisions, the Europeans over the long run were going to have to field most of the ground forces to defend the non-communist side of the continent, or the cork of the wine bottle as Eisenhower characterized it. NATO rearmament has in retrospect invited accusations that it inevitably reinforced historic Russian paranoia over encirclement, induced a Soviet counter buildup, and even implicated culpability for the very origins of the Cold War and all its resulting financial costs. While Stalin retained large numbers of troops in Eastern Europe in the late 1940s, Soviet forces may very well have lacked the logistical means to even mount a general offensive against the West. But these considerations fall into irrelevance when bearing in mind justifiable Western distrust of Stalin by 1950, even if he tended to behave more as a traditional Eurasian despot intent on maintaining his power base than as a zealous Bolshevik. Building up military forces derives from a situation of fear and distrust, and fear of another North Korean–type invasion of the West, combined with distrust over Stalin as a partner in peace, drove the effort to rearm. Now the challenge, first facing Truman and then his successors, was to organize a new alliance, unprecedented in American history and a violation of George Washington's farewell address, in a way that did not lead to exorbitant and uncontrollable costs.

Truman met this challenge. He succeeded more than any other president during the Cold War era in balancing the budget, doing so a total four times. He had an inherent aversion to deficits and was willing to pay for most domestic programs and higher military spending through tax hikes, his funding proposal for national health insurance serving as one apparent exception. Demobilization naturally catered to these fiscal instincts, and in that respect Truman was dealt a good hand. The dismantling of the wartime political economic regime helped turn in a surplus within two years of the end of the war, a hand further bolstered by revived domestic consumption and European demand for exports. Truman's cards started to change as the threat of communist advances became more dire. Even so, he did not submit to panic and kept a tight lid on defense spending while still effectively responding to challenges in Europe. The outbreak of war in Korea shows what can happen when an external event, in this case armed conflict, unexpectedly transforms the trajectory of spending and taxes. The Korean War started because the regime of Kim Il-Sung decided to invade, but in the countdown to invasion the Administration exhibited a lack of interest in adequately supporting the South that sharply contrasted with the subsequent intervention on the ground. By early 1950 the Administration had committed most of its attention to the security situation in Europe, and hindsight is always perfect, but the asymmetry should still be noted. One wonders that if the Administration had supplied the South with more military aid and delayed the pullout of U.S. troops until the country achieved full readiness the invasion could have been prevented. Truman nonetheless consistently adhered to the conviction that future generations should not have to bear the burdens of debt incurred in the present. He strived to apply this principle in the face of adversity and as the U.S. assumed a new role of leadership in the world.

NOTES

1. President of U.S., *The Budget of the United States Government for the Fiscal Year Ending June 30, 1947* (Washington, D.C.: Government Printing Office, 1946), XIX–XX.

2. Federal Reserve Bank of St. Louis Economic Data, "Gross Federal Debt Held by the Public as Percent of Gross Domestic Product," https://fred.stlouisfed.org/series/FYPUGDA188S, accessed August 2018.

3. Federal Reserve Bank of St. Louis Economic Data, "Federal Surplus or Deficit as Percent of Gross Domestic Product," https://fred.stlouisfed.org/series/FYFSGDA188S, accessed February 2019.

4. President, *1947 Budget*, LXXVIII.

5. President of U.S., *The Budget of the United States Government for the Fiscal Year Ending June 30, 1948* (Washington, D.C.: Government Printing Office, 1947), M16–M17.

6. "Recommendation for Assistance to Greece and Turkey." President Harry Truman. Address before Congress. March 12, 1947.

7. OMB, "Historical Tables," 50.

8. Elliott V. Converse, III, *History of Acquisition in the Department of Defense, Vol I., Rearming for the Cold War: 1945–1960* (Washington, D.C.: Historical Office, Office of the Secretary of Defense, 2012), 30.

9. Converse, *Rearming for the Cold War*, 171.

10. Ibid., 43–45.

11. Steven L. Rearden, *History of the Secretary of Defense, Vol. I, The Formative Years: 1947–1950* (Washington, D.C.: Historical Office, Office of the Secretary of Defense, 1984), 97–99.

12. Converse, *Rearming for the Cold War*, 222–23.

13. Ibid., 332 - 39.

14. Ibid., 150–51.

15. Rearden, *Formative Years*, 439.

16. *Survival in the Air Age: A Report by the President's Air Policy Commission* (Washington, D.C.: Government Printing Office, 1948), 16–18.

17. Ibid., 19.

18. Ibid., 24–25.

19. Ibid., 31.

20. Ibid., 46.

21. James Forrestal, "Functions of the Armed Forces and the Joint Chiefs of Staff," in *The United States Air Force: Basic Documents on Roles and Missions*, ed. Richard I. Wolfe (Washington, D.C.: Office of Air Force History, U.S. Air Force, 1987), 161.

22. Ibid., 163.

23. Phillip S. Meilinger, *The Admirals' Revolt of 1949: Lessons for Today* (Carlisle, PA: Army War College, 1989), 86–88.

24. Meilinger, *Admirals' Revolt*, 90 – 93.

25. President of U.S., *The Budget of the United States Government for the Fiscal Year Ending June 30, 1949* (Washington, D.C.: Government Printing Office, 1948), M14–M17.

26. Rearden, *Formative Years*, 317–18.

27. Ibid., 326–28.

28. Ibid., 334.

29. The American Presidency Project, "Harry S. Truman: Special Message to the Congress on the Threat to Freedom in Europe, March 17, 1948," http://www.presidency.ucsb.edu/ws/index.php?pid=13130, accessed August 2018.

30. Kenneth W. Condit, *History of the Joint Chiefs of Staff, The Joint Chiefs of Staff and National Policy, Vol. II: 1947–1949* (Washington, D.C.: Office of Joint History, Office of the Chairman of the Joint Chiefs of Staff, 1996), 69 – 70.

31. Ibid., 72.

32. Folder: "Report to the National Security Council: U.S. Military Courses of Action with Respect to the Situation in Berlin, July 28 1948." Collection: The Berlin Airlift. Series: President's Secretary's Files. Harry S. Truman Presidential Library & Museum.

33. Rearden, *Formative Years*, 335.

34. Ibid., 336–37.

35. Condit, *Joint Chiefs 1947–1949*, 156–57.

36. Robert F. Futrell, "The Influence of the Air Power Concept on Air Force Planning, 1945–1962," in *Military Planning in the Twentieth Century: Proceedings of the Eleventh Military History Symposium*, 10–12 October 1984, ed. Lt. Col. Harry R. Borowski (Washington, D.C.: Office of Air Force History, U.S. Air Force, 1986), 258–59.
37. Rearden, *Formative Years*, 350–51.
38. President of U.S., *The Budget of the United States Government for the Fiscal Year Ending June 30, 1950* (Washington, D.C.: Government Printing Office, 1949), M5.
39. President, *1950 Budget*, M21–M23.
40. Rearden, *Formative Years*, 360.
41. Condit, *Joint Chiefs 1947–1949*, 159 - 63.
42. President of U.S., *The Budget of the United States Government for the Fiscal Year Ending June 30, 1951* (Washington, D.C.: Government Printing Office, 1950), M5.
43. Ibid., M27.
44. Ibid., M10.
45. Ibid., M29.
46. Ibid., M26.
47. Folder: "A Report to the National Security Council—NSC 68, April 12, 1950." Collection: Ideological Foundations of the Cold War. Series: President's Secretary's Files. Harry S. Truman Presidential Library & Museum.
48. "NSC 68."
49. President, *1951 Budget*, M25.
50. "Special Message to the Congress Recommending a Comprehensive Health Care Program." President Harry Truman. Address Before Congress. November 19, 1945. Harry S. Truman Presidential Library & Museum.
51. Secretary of Treasury, *Annual Report of the Secretary of the Treasury on the State of the Finances for the Fiscal Year Ended June 30, 1946* (Washington, D.C.: Government Printing Office, 1947), 90.
52. Ibid., 92–93.
53. President, *1947 Budget*, LIV - LV.
54. Jerry Tempalski, "Revenue Effects of Major Tax Bills," Office of Tax Analysis, U.S. Treasury Department, Working Paper No. 81 (September 2006), 15.
55. President, *1948 Budget*, M5.
56. Ibid., M13.
57. Secretary of Treasury, *Annual Report of the Secretary of the Treasury on the State of the Finances for the Fiscal Year Ended June 30, 1947* (Washington, D.C.: Government Printing Office, 1948), 218.
58. Secretary of Treasury, *Annual Report of the Secretary of the Treasury on the State of the Finances for the Fiscal Year Ended June 30, 1948* (Washington, D.C.: Government Printing Office, 1949), 51.
59. Tempalski, "Revenue Effects," 15.
60. President, *1950 Budget*, M6.
61. The American Presidency Project, "Harry S. Truman: Annual Message to the Congress on the State of the Union, January 5, 1949," http://www.presidency.ucsb.edu/ws/?pid=13293, accessed September 2018.
62. "Provisions of the Housing Act of 1949," *Monthly Labor Review* 69, no. 2 (August 1949): 156, JSTOR, https://www.jstor.org/stable/41831843?readnow=1&refreqid=excelsior%3A5c079267e5246e1a9de85ede3906fbec&seq=1#page_scan_tab_contents, accessed August 2018.
63. President, *1951 Budget*, M49.
64. James F. Schnabel and Robert J. Watson, *History of the Joint Chiefs of Staff, The Joint Chiefs of Staff and National Policy, Vol. III: 1950–1951* (Washington, D.C.: Office of Joint History, Office of the Chairman of the Joint Chiefs of Staff, 1998), 6–7.
65. Folder: "The Position of the United States with Respect to Korea; National Security Council Report 8, April 2, 1948." Collection: The Korean War and Its Origins. Series: President's Secretary's Files. Harry S. Truman Presidential Library & Museum.

66. Folder: "Consequences of U.S. Troop Withdrawal from Korea in Spring, 1949, February 28, 1949." Collection: The Korean War and Its Origins. Series: President's Secretary's Files. Harry S. Truman Presidential Library & Museum.
67. "Speech on the Far East." Secretary of State Dean Acheson. National Press Club. Washington, D.C. January 12, 1950.
68. President of U.S., *The Budget of the United States Government for the Fiscal Year Ending June 30, 1952* (Washington, D.C.: Government Printing Office, 1951), M5.
69. President, *1952 Budget*, M14.
70. Doris M. Condit, *History of the Office of the Secretary of Defense, Vol. II, The Test of War: 1950–1953* (Washington, D.C.: Historical Office, Office of the Secretary of Defense, 1998), 258.
71. Ibid., 276.
72. Ibid., 282.
73. Secretary of Treasury, *Annual Report of the Secretary of the Treasury on the State of the Finances for the Fiscal Year Ended June 30, 1950* (Washington, D.C.: Government Printing Office, 1951), 36–37.
74. Secretary of Treasury, *Annual Report of the Secretary of the Treasury on the State of the Finances for the Fiscal Year Ended June 30, 1951* (Washington, D.C.: Government Printing Office, 1952), 47–48.
75. President, *1952 Budget*, M12.
76. Secretary of Treasury, *1951 Treasury Annual Report*, 50–51.
77. Tempalski, "Revenue Effects," 15.
78. President, *1952 Budget*, M11.
79. President of U.S., *The Budget of the United States Government for the Fiscal Year Ending June 30, 1954* (Washington, D.C.: Government Printing Office, 1953), M6.
80. Standing Group. "Report by the Standing Group to the Military Committee on Data Pertaining to NATO Medium Term Plan." MC 0015/1, Military Committee Series. NATO Archives, Brussels, Belgium.
81. Standing Group. "A Directive by the Standing Group to Regional Planning Groups on the Revision of the NATO Medium Term Defence Plan." SG 020/15, Standing Group Series. NATO Archives, Brussels, Belgium.
82. Standing Group. "Note by the Secretaries to the Standing Group on Allocation of Forces to SACEUR." SG 108/1, Standing Group Series. NATO Archives, Brussels, Belgium.
83. Standing Group. "Report by the Standing Group to the North Atlantic Council Deputies on Costing of the Medium Term Defense Plan." SG 083/4, Standing Group Series. NATO Archives, Brussels, Belgium.

Chapter Three

Austerity Retried

Eisenhower, 1953–1961

Dwight Eisenhower brought a uniquely internationalist background to the White House, mainly by virtue of having commanded Allied forces in the North African and European theaters during World War II and later returning to his old post after the establishment of NATO. His nomination for the ticket over Senator Robert Taft turned the Republican Party away from isolationist impulses and ensured that the very principle of waging Cold War would not become a partisan issue, even if all related foreign policy concerns were bound to be subjected to partisan rancor. Eisenhower himself was not really a partisan figure. With the entitlement state already an accomplished fact, he vowed not to roll back Social Security. He stood to the right of Truman, though like Truman his views on the budget were essentially rigid. He wanted the math to add up, only he wanted to reach this goal through spending cuts instead of tax hikes whenever possible. In office his budgetary compass did not totally differ from Truman's. He saw that forestalling deficits required curtailed defense spending. He was less amenable to activist packages like the Fair Deal, but as with Truman his views on the budget and defense policy were bound by a consistent logic. The Korean War temporarily cast aside this logic, both for Truman and Eisenhower, and Eisenhower assumed not only the presidency but also command over a two years' stalemate along the 38th Parallel.

NEW LOOK, CONTINENTAL DEFENSE

Whether the austerity label should even be ascribed to Eisenhower in the first place is a matter of interpretation. After all, he in no way demobilized military forces after the Korean War as Truman had done after World War II. The adage that the military came out of the Korean War in superior shape than when going into it carries an indisputable degree of truth. Indeed, defense spending as a percentage of GDP in the postwar era reached its highest point during the Eisenhower Administration, staying consistently over 9% through 1961. Yet austerity should be understood in a broader context, implying not only the effort to outright reduce government expenditures but also to actively restrain their otherwise self-propelled rise. By circumstance if Eisenhower wanted to balance the budget, then he had to mainly tighten defense spending because it made up over two-thirds of total federal outlays when he came into office. Truman had successfully reduced defense spending to 30.6% of total outlays by 1948, but the Korean War and rearmament pushed it back up to 69.4% in 1953.[1] Eisenhower's defense policy early in his tenure became known as the New Look, and it reflected an innate fiscal cautiousness. No member of the Administration explicitly articulated the New Look right at the outset of Eisenhower's presidency. As a concept it evolved to mean reduced defense costs at a sustainable level while containing the communists over the long run through reliance on strategic weapons. With the military consuming most of the discretionary budget and the entitlement state still confined mainly to Social Security, Eisenhower had little alternative but to integrate his budgetary objectives with his defense policy. He promised to hold the line on spending rather than reduce the size of government, and this largely meant holding the line on defense spending.

Yet the New Look was never intended to inhibit innovation in military technology, least of all in missiles. It served more as a shorthand for the fear of excessive defense spending crowding out private economic investment. The Administration eventually codified the New Look with NSC 162, which addressed related questions of economic growth, defense preparedness, and a focus on nuclear weapons as a means of deterrence. The document asserted that "[a] sound, strong, and growing U.S. economy is necessary to support over the long pull a satisfactory posture of defense in the free world and a U.S. capability rapidly and effectively to change to full mobilization."[2] During Eisenhower's time in office, the NSC staff issued Basic National Security Policy (BNSP) statements distilling strategic approaches that adhered to the gist of the New Look.

The notion of "massive retaliation" complemented the New Look, which Secretary of State John Foster Dulles propounded in a major address in early 1954. He called for a "maximum deterrent at a bearable cost" and argued that the Soviets wanted to induce an unsustainable military buildup in the West eventually resulting in economic implosion, the ultimate communist aim. The U.S. would thus only be playing into communist hands by gearing up its military expenditures and recklessly ignoring the risks to its economy. On the downside, the New Look seemed to shackle the military into relying on a single response to any form of Soviet aggression, strategic bombing, or as Dulles termed it "massive retaliatory power," instead of smaller scale regional responses.[3]

Eisenhower's first budget request in January 1954 actualized the New Look. He implicitly rebuked Truman's stretch out when mentioning that "[o]ur military planning in previous years had been based on several successive assumed fixed dates of maximum danger" that sought "to achieve maximum readiness by each such date." The stretch out preceding the year of perceived maximum danger, 1954, contrasted with Eisenhower's own approach for the budget, which operated indefinitely "over the extended period of uneasy peace." The key to national defense remained airpower. Prioritizing airpower helped produce savings for the overall budget.[4] Eisenhower sought to reduce spending for the Army to $8.2 billion while slightly increasing spending for the Navy up to $9.9 billion. The Air Force fared better than the Army with only a $200 million reduction in spending, leaving it with $11.2 billion.[5] With these allocations in place, the military could expand total aircraft from the current 33,000 to a planned 40,000 while simultaneously increasing the jet-powered portion of this total from 33% to over 50%. Such a projected expansion ensured a 137–wing Air Force, in addition to Navy and Marine airpower.[6]

Eisenhower and his first defense secretary, corporate mogul Charles Wilson, took other steps towards reducing defense costs. The Administration, for instance, sought to cut non-combat personnel as much as possible without directly affecting combat units, which allowed Army divisions to stay in Europe. Bureaucratic reorganization was seen as another way to reduce costs. The Administration issued an executive order in 1953 bringing the R&D Board into OSD instead of allowing it to serve as a free-standing body within the Department. The 1958 Defense Reorganization Act also consolidated R&D functions by creating an office of director of defense research and engineering and strengthened civilian control over the Pentagon by mandating the chain of combat command from the president, to OSD, to individual military commands, bypassing the JCS and turning it more into an advisory board.[7]

Civilian supervision over R&D functioned primarily to coordinate the operations of the services. The Army and Navy still maintained the most intensive in-house laboratories. Yet now the two services took steps towards centralizing their own R&D activities. The Navy ended up combining the Bureaus of Aeronautics and Ordnance into a single Bureau of Naval Weapons, which took over most of the Navy's R&D, while further creating a new assistant secretary of the navy for research and development. This consolidation followed in the wake of the Defense Reorganization Act, and it also resolved long running questions over how Aeronautics and Ordnance were supposed to share responsibility for missile development.[8] The Army similarly took steps towards centralization now that the deputy chief of staff for plans and research would be vested with the R&D activities managed by the Logistics Division.[9]

Bureaucratic reorganization may have helped streamline costs over the long run, but ending the Korean War through a negotiated truce in July 1953 permitted an immediate reduction in spending. The whole premise of the New Look, first articulated in NSC 162 and then put into action with Eisenhower's budget request for FY 1955, in fact relied on ending the war in Korea. In bringing the war to an end, the Administration could further calibrate a military doctrine predicated upon nuclear weapons and "massive retaliation," in the process generating cost savings. Nuclear weapons were not cheap, especially after factoring in advances in missile development, but a mixed arsenal of bombers and missiles still offered a way to offset cutbacks in conventional forces while credibly defending defined security perimeters in other parts of the world.

The Administration succeeded in reducing defense appropriations to $28.8 billion for FY 1955.[10] The budget for FY 1955 represented an all-time low in the post-Korea era of "uneasy peace," and for the rest of his presidency Eisenhower remained adamant in keeping total defense expenditures in the $40 billion range (which included funds appropriated in previous years), even contemplating the imposition of fixed ceilings if necessary. The New Look still allowed increased spending for critical new weapons systems, in particular guided missiles. Expenditures in this area rose from $631 million in 1955 to an estimated $918 million in 1956 and $1.3 billion in 1957. Eisenhower requested up to $1.8 billion in spending authority for guided missiles for FY 1957.[11] By the time he submitted his next to last budget request in January 1960, he planned for $45.6 billion in defense expenditures, just less than the $46 billion from 1952 and in part pushed up by inflation. His budget message argued for continuing a restrained defense policy into the 1960s, especially as missile technology replaced older modes of warfare. The Administration had cut the Army down to 14 divisions, while the Air Force now hovered at 91 combat wings. Yet advances in missile technology complicated previous assumptions of balanced forces, with Eisenhower cautioning that "[t]he change of emphasis from conventional-type to missile-type warfare must be made with care" in "one of the greatest transitions in history."[12]

The New Look deemphasized conventional forces in large part because the Warsaw Pact enjoyed a numerical upper-hand, both in terms of front-line troops in East Germany and Poland and reserves in the western Soviet Union, and for various reasons the Western alliance simply did not have the wherewithal to totally overcome this disparity through sheer number of conscripts. At the Lisbon conference in February 1952, NATO chiefs had laid out ambitious force goals of up to 96 combined divisions, but European economies were still in a state of recovery and could not furnish the means to immediately reach these targets. By 1953 NATO had 36 divisions actively ready on M-Day, the day NATO mobilized its forces in response to a hypothetical Soviet onslaught. A year later this figure rose to 41 divisions, with the U.S. contributing six. In M-Day + 30 contingencies, 30 days after the assault, NATO planned to muster just over 86 divisions. Assuming Soviet subs had not totally cut the sea lanes, the U.S. could deploy over nine divisions.[13] While these figures may have seemed formidable, they compared to an estimated four million Soviet combat forces, along with a growing contribution of personnel from the Eastern European satellites. As a report from the NATO Military Committee from this period noted, in the aftermath of the war "Soviet armed forces were not demobilized to the same extent as were those of the Western Powers. Instead, a considerable program of reorganization and training was initiated. As a result, the Soviet Union now has in being a powerful military machine."[14]

While these intelligence assessments may have overestimated Soviet capabilities, reasonable concerns persisted over NATO conventional capabilities. Many Western European divisions were simply not at full strength. Proponents of the New Look emphasized the use of tactical nuclear weapons, which had the potential of negating the Warsaw Pact's numerical edge with tremendous explosive power on the battlefield. The pertinent question became one of time, that is how long NATO ground forces could hold out while the alliance's air forces engaged in a bombing campaign against Russia that might eventually hinder lengthening Soviet supply lines. In an early example of tactical nukes, the Army began loading atomic artillery shells into 280mm M65 cannons, one of which was test fired at White Sands Proving Ground, Nevada, in May 1953. The Army later deployed a handful of these "Atomic Annies" to Europe, where they were added to the NATO force structure. Equipping Army cannons with atomic shells gave NATO forces a greater chance of stunting or slowing a Soviet armored assault anticipated through the Fulda Gap in central Germany. The Standing Group to the NATO Military Committee recognized the importance of tactical nuclear weapons, recommending in its guidance for the 1955 Annual Review that general forces ready on M-Day encompass an "integrated atomic capability."[15]

Development of the M65 "Atomic Annie" underscored the growing importance of technology to augment NATO firepower. R&D allowed the military to increasingly miniaturize nuclear warheads and reduce their yields for ever smaller weapons systems, such as the Davy Crockett recoilless rifle introduced in the early 1960s. Conceived and developed during the New Look era, the Davy Crockett was handled by a three-man crew and included a lighter and heavier version. Nuclear war had come a long way, to the point where three soldiers could operate a heavy rifle discharging an atomic projectile. An undated study from this period discussed a handful of other unusual defense technologies, including kinetic energy-directed anti-tank weapons, long-range mine laying and remote control over the mines, and the release of biological and chemical toxins on advancing enemy armies.[16]

From the standpoint of the twenty-first century, the effort to normalize nuclear war through miniaturized platforms may seem dismaying. Putting aside strategic bombing between the U.S. and U.S.S.R., even just the limited use of tactical nuclear weapons in a conflict centered in Europe would have been devastating to the military and civilian populations alike, both in terms of direct impacts and radioactive fallout. But perhaps the wisdom of the New Look was to acknowledge that the nuclear age had changed all assumptions underlying armed conflict. While in Third World conflicts a hegemon such as the U.S. might refrain from using atomic or thermonuclear weapons against a weaker rival, war between great powers like the U.S. and U.S.S.R. was bound to turn nuclear sooner or later. By developing nuclear weapons not only on a strategic but on a tactical level as well, the U.S. military increased its capacity for credible defense and demonstrated the potential destructiveness of even a regional conflagration.

The nuclear age had certainly forced the Army to reevaluate its own assumptions of warfare. Military planners briefly reconfigured battle formations away from the accustomed divisional grouping of battalions and regiments to a more flexible and atomized "pentomic" combat division composed of five subsidiary units. In a nuclear attack, pentomic divisions would be extremely exposed and could not be concentrated. They would instead need to hunker down in defensive positions and then only mass together at the right time, probably at night, to mount an operation. The Army brass eventually found the "pentomic" division ineffective and discarded it after only a few years.[17] The idea turned out to be unworkable, but getting rid of it did not resolve long-running concerns that the Army had become irrelevant. The Army was of course not irrelevant, and it still needed to develop its armored capabilities in the event of a dreaded tank battle in Europe. It worked on a line of tanks until readying the M60 Patton for deployment in 1960, which would serve as the Army's main battle tank over a twenty-year period.

The Navy also grappled with its role in the nuclear age. While the Soviet Union lacked a significant surface threat, the Navy still needed to face off against an expanding Soviet sub force. The Soviets were rapidly building and deploying attack subs that could menace the U.S.'s supply lines to Europe and Asia in the event of a crisis. These supply lines were as vulnerable as they had been during the World Wars, when German U-boats had at times threatened to cut off Allied shipping. Defense against the attack subs required more advanced anti-submarine warfare capabilities, whether from surface ships or attack subs. But the Navy still wanted an offensive role after it lost the debate over the *United States*, and the Korean War revived its hopes. The war again demonstrated the importance of carrier-based airpower, with Navy fighters encountering Soviet MiG-15s in tough dogfights. During the war Congress authorized construction of a new *Forrestal* class supercarrier that could transport heavy bombers equipped with atomic weapons. Constructed with an angled flight deck and four catapults, the Navy commissioned the *Forrestal* in 1955, securing the service's involvement in strategic bombing contingencies.

Under CNO Arleigh Burke, the Navy also underwent advances in nuclear propulsion and electronic data systems. The *Nautilus*, the world's first nuclear powered sub, was launched in 1955 and could stay underwater indefinitely. The launching of the *Nautilus* did not imply a future all-nuclear surface fleet, in which the advantages of nuclear power were not as clear, but the new sub was followed six years later by the *Enterprise* nuclear powered carrier. Burke also focused on improving the Navy's use of advanced electronics. A major innovation was implementing an integrated electronic system for fleet operations in which information on enemy movements could be updated automatically.[18]

The Air Force remained most directly responsible for deterring Soviet aggression through the development of a series of new heavy and medium bombers. The B-36 had first been deployed in 1948 and would go on to have a ten-year service life. Initially powered by piston engines, it was retrofitted with jet engines to give it a better chance of evading MiG-15s. The Air Force soon added to its inventory the B-47 Stratojet, a medium bomber with a range of 5,000 miles. The B-47 was equipped with cannon but had been specifically designed for delivering a nuclear payload. It remained in service until 1965. In assessing future heavy bomber options, the Air Force decided to forego the YB-60 all turbo-jet version of the B-36 in favor of the B-52 Stratofortress, which unlike the B-36 had been originally designed with jet engines and swept wings. Though Boeing had wanted to manufacture the B-52 at its own plant in Washington State, it ended up building the aircraft at a facility in Wichita, Kansas, where production was deemed less vulnerable to enemy airstrikes. The Air Force also pursued another medium bomber, the B-58 Hustler, to eventually replace the B-47 and reach supersonic speed at high altitudes. The delta winged B-58 was plagued by a high accident rate, and it played no role in regional conflicts. The Air Force purchased a little over a 100 of the aircraft and phased it out starting in 1969, while the B-52's service life would extend well into the twenty-first century.

Air Force strategy conformed to massive retaliation in the clearest of terms. SAC intended to destroy Soviet airpower in the initial moments of a nuclear war. After eliminating this aerial threat in the skies over Eurasia,

SAC could then focus on staging a bombing campaign against the Soviet Union. The Tactical Air Command (TAC) formulated similar contingencies and focused its fighter-bombers like the F-105 Thunderchief on destroying enemy targets with nuclear weapons at the outset of war with communist nations.[19]

The mirror opposite of massive retaliation was air defense over North America. Allocating funding to defense against enemy aerial attack might have seemed an unending drain of resources. But a confluence of factors compelled the Eisenhower Administration into building a system of North American, or continental, air defense and early warning. The Soviets had successfully tested a thermonuclear weapon in 1953 while simultaneously developing long-range aircraft potentially capable of carrying out roundtrip missions to the U.S., the Tu-95 "Bear" and M-4 "Bison" bombers. Even before these developments the Truman Administration had foreseen the Soviet aerial threat to the U.S. The first step towards continental defense was building radar stations in strategic locations such as industrial areas, including production sites for the U.S.'s own heavy bombers. The Pentagon approved a plan to build 24 improvised Lashup radar sites concentrated in the Northeast and around bases in New Mexico and the Pacific Northwest before undergoing work on a more permanent and comprehensive network of radar stations.[20]

NSC 159/4, issued in September 1953, formalized the Eisenhower Administration's approval of continental defense. The drafters of the document infused it with a shrill tone that reflected the Administration's alarm following the Soviet thermonuclear detonation. It recommended all possible extensions in the early warning system across North America while indicating that "a minimum of at least two hours is an immediate necessity" for early warning of attack. NSC 159/4 also emphasized the need for building up new fighter interceptor groups and missile defenses to increase the "kill ratio" of incoming bombers, seeing this as the primary means for enhancing security against nuclear attack. It conceded that "[t]his process will be costly but essential if the objectives of the Continental Defense Program are to succeed." The document even predicted that defenses would need to be automatically expanded "consistent with any significant increase in Soviet capabilities."[21]

Except in the territories of Alaska and Hawaii, radar stations located in the U.S. did not greatly improve the military's alert capabilities. Seaward extensions, on the other hand, in the form of radar picket vessels and advance early warning (AEW) aircraft flying along the Atlantic and Pacific coasts could increase the margin of forewarning. The Air Force also explored the idea of building a few Texas Tower stations in shoal waters right off the Northeast coast. They were presumably nicknamed this due to their similar appearance to offshore oil rigs. Because their radar beams stretched up to 500 miles into the ocean, the Texas Towers provided an extra half-hour's warning for the heavily populated areas to the rear. The Air Force ended up building three such towers, but they lasted only into the early 1960s. A hurricane seriously damaged one of the towers and forced it to be reconstructed. It was then hit by an unexpected storm while being repaired and collapsed into the ocean, killing all the on-site personnel. The Air Force thereafter dismantled the other two remaining towers.[22]

If the Pentagon wanted to build an effective outlying radar network, then it needed to cover a predominant swathe of the North American landmass. Such coverage could incorporate existing radar stations in Alaska, Hawaii, the domestic U.S., and Canada. The Canadian military had already begun preparations for a Mid-Canada line along the 55th Parallel, which consisted not of actual radar stations but a sensory fence capable of detecting aircraft.[23] A study group headed by James Killian of the Massachusetts Institute of Technology recommended such an expansive early warning system. In addition to the Mid-Canada line and the Pinetree network (the latter a north-south line of radar stations straddling the U.S.–Canada border), a Distant Early Warning (DEW) line would stretch across North America near the Arctic Circle and potentially include parts of Greenland. The DEW and Mid-Canada line also entailed seaward extensions to the Azores and Hawaii. The Air Force eventually backed the DEW once it determined that radar stations could be maintained in the Arctic climate. But early warning was only one element of continental defense. The Air Force also planned to deploy 75 new fighter groups to intercept incoming Soviet aircraft. Existing fighter aircraft were currently available for this purpose, but the Air Force was in the process of developing a new breed of fighters specialized in the interception of bombers at high altitude that would be ready in 1955. Interceptors could in a few years be armed with a new nuclear tipped Falcon surface to surface missile, while as an interim measure on-hand aircraft would be equipped with atomic rockets. The Air Force also continued to pursue development of the Bomarc surface to air missile (SAM) with Boeing, keeping pace with the Army's work on the Nike SAM.[24]

The civilian leadership and the JCS had to grapple not only with Soviet capabilities but air strategies as well, which were in turn affected by the range of their aircraft. The Soviets might rely on different routes for their missions, whether directly over the Arctic or along the more indirect Atlantic and Pacific flanks. For instance, if the Soviets wanted to attack New York and other cities in the Northeast, they could launch their bombers from the northwestern tip of Russia near Murmansk. The bombers would then have to make a broad loop around Norway to minimize their contact with NATO airspace, though they would inevitably fly within the vicinity of Iceland and Greenland. A DEW line from Alaska to Baffin Island, Canada, provided warning against an Arctic approach, while Atlantic seaward extensions, especially those linking up with parts of Northwest Europe, guarded against a loop through the Norwegian Sea.

With enough funding, the JCS could approve plans for warning systems against all possible routes, and this is largely what it did. The JCS approved the DEW line in January 1955, but it still had to resolve an interservice dispute over which seaward extensions to choose. If the Pentagon only funded the DEW and not the seaward extensions, then with adequate range Soviet aircraft could outflank the DEW by flying a half-circle into the Atlantic and Pacific and approach the East and West Coasts head-on. The Navy supported a Greenland-Iceland-Faroes-Britain extension, while the Air Force preferred a line from Cape Farewell in southern Greenland to the Azores, which would also replace the Newfoundland-Azores extension of the Mid-Canada line. The Air Force finally conceded to the Navy's proposal after it conclusively determined that radar stations could be set up in Greenland, with the understanding that the Cape Farewell-Azores line would serve as a backup.[25] The JCS also approved advancing the Pacific extension westward from a Kodiak, Alaska-Hawaii line to Adak, Alaska-Midway.[26]

The defense establishment, in working with the corporate and academic communities, had the technological means to perfect a system of continental defense, which was formed into a joint Continental Air Defense Command (CONAD). The more uncertain issue now centered on rising costs associated with CONAD, including an increased number of fighter interceptor groups, battalions of Bomarc missiles directed by a computerized Semi-Automatic Ground Environment (SAGE), and networks of radar stations, AEW aircraft, and radar picket ships located across thousands of miles. In this respect, continental defense seriously complicated the Administration's New Look approach. Massive retaliation had been closely tied to budget cutting because the military could focus on offensive strength, which conformed with the Air Force's primary function. Continental defense threatened to undo this whole approach because, pursuant to the very language of NSC 159/4, it would cost a great deal of money. Some Air Force brass even worried that exaggerated claims by scientists on the value of continental defense would undermine the impetus behind strategic bombing.[27]

For Eisenhower, the dilemmas of allocating money between offensive and defensive capabilities pointed to no easy or clear answer. He continued to seek an austerity budget, which would on some level restrain spending for CONAD, even if stretched out over several years. Eisenhower had not embraced continental defense, but he was also in no position to outright reject it. Momentum had been growing for air defense and early warning at the political, military, and scientific levels before he assumed office. In September 1953, Eisenhower and his national security staff discussed proceeding with NSC 159/4 at the White House. While Eisenhower grumbled about the threatened militarization of the economy, he did not stop the NSC from issuing the document as a directive. According to the meeting minutes, he raised the concern that "if we went beyond a certain point, we would have to face the likelihood that our stockpile of war materials would suffer obsolescence, not to mention terrific costs of maintenance." Eisenhower preferred "a minimum military establishment and mobilization base that could be expanded promptly in case of need."[28]

Eisenhower's remark touched on the central challenges of the era. With technology improving so rapidly, the military had to avoid incurring the excessive costs of weapons systems and other hardware that might end up being outdated in only a few years. This danger existed for both a crash and a stretch out budget. The corollary to this assumption, however, that spending could be contained and only increased in the event of a crisis included some built-in problems. Once the military found itself in the middle of a crisis, it had in the nuclear age an exceedingly brief period of time in which to improve its defenses. With CONAD there was really no margin for error. If air defenses were even somewhat inadequate, whole cities and industrial areas could be obliterated within the first hours of war. The continental defense view presupposed that capabilities needed to be made as airtight as possible. Everything short of that could lead to disaster, which necessitated high costs. But on the other hand continental defense suffered from criticism that trying to achieve a kill-rate of 90% to 100% of incoming Soviet aircraft was futile. And even if only a few Soviet bombers penetrated the defensive air screen and dropped their nuclear bombs, they would inflict untold devastation for miles and death upon hundreds of thousands, perhaps millions, of people. A system of infallible continental defense looked impossible.

Under the Eisenhower budgets, the early warning system was not perfect but expanding. In a memo to Eisenhower in August 1958, Killian, a strong proponent of continental defense, noted that the picket ships and AEW aircraft part of the seaward extensions were not integrated into a computerized data system. Alerts could only be sent out manually, which would lead to a delayed reaction to enemy aircraft. Ground radar, however, was part of the SAGE computerized system that also directed Bomarc anti-aircraft responses.[29] Were the Soviets to strike, then if feasible they might send their bombers on a far more southerly route through the Atlantic or Pacific. After becoming chief scientific adviser to Eisenhower, Killian remained apprised of holes in continental defense, including inadequate AEW aircraft coverage and reports that the seaward lines "at present do not extend far enough to prevent an 'end run' by long-range bombers."[30]

Eisenhower's budgets did not buy airtight continental defense, though according to most intelligence assessments the Soviets were not able to launch a general air attack before 1957 in any event. While frequently mentioned in the budget message for FY 1955, the Administration did not present continental defense as a discrete item of the budget. Eisenhower publicly announced that he sought a $1 billion increase for continental defense going into FY 1955, but in reality the figure stood closer to $800 million.[31] Whatever the request, CONAD would take years before achieving full readiness, whether in terms of high altitude fighter interceptor groups, Bomarc and Nike battalions, and early warning networks. These expanding capabilities translated into nearly $5 billion in CONAD spending by FY 1957.[32]

Despite forewarnings from outside consultants like Killian or the electronics manufacturer Robert Sprague, Eisenhower prevented CONAD spending from spiraling out of control in a time of acute anxiety over Soviet intentions. Accelerated missile development in the U.S. and Soviet Union eventually vindicated Eisenhower's decision to refrain from going all-out for CONAD in budgetary terms. The Soviets would end up focusing their buildup on land-based offensive missiles instead of bombers, to the point where CONAD and the Bomarc were finally dismantled in the 1970s, outlived by the joint U.S.-Canadian North American Aerospace Defense Command (NORAD) overseeing early warning in the missile age.

MISSILES, SPUTNIK, SUMMIT SETBACKS

Missile development above all demonstrated the importance of avoiding a crash buildup before technologies could be fully exploited or even understood. The Army first began work on missiles at its Redstone Arsenal in Huntsville, Alabama, after originally establishing the facility in 1941 to test chemical weapons. Only towards the end of the war did the Army start experimenting with unguided rockets. By that point the Germans had launched the V-1 "flying bomb" in response to the Normandy invasion, which served as an early version of a cruise missile capable of a trajectory entirely within the atmosphere. The Germans then started firing off the V-2 rocket, a precursor to the modern ballistic missile in its ability to penetrate the atmosphere and then arc back down to earth. After the war, German rocket scientists were attached to the Army as part of Operation Paperclip, benefiting the Army's developmental work. The Army thereafter produced the Corporal guided missile fitted with an atomic warhead. The Air Force also began developing a ballistic missile in the late 1940s but scrapped the project due to cost cutting. However, as the Army turned Redstone into a missile facility in 1949 and accelerated its testing of Corporal, the Air Force renewed its own missile program. Missile development lagged during the Truman Administration as the services contended with cutbacks in funds and then the Korean War. But with the arms race in full swing during the Eisenhower era, the focus shifted back to missiles and miniaturization of thermonuclear warheads.

Arguments soon arose over which service or services should run missile development. The rationale for a unified defense establishment had been to avoid duplication and keep costs contained, and nowhere was this more important than an entirely new mode of warfare in the form of guided missiles. Army brass viewed missiles as an extension of artillery befitting its core responsibilities of fielding ground forces. Indeed, if the Army's surface to surface missile (SSM) program proceeded far enough, it could at some point conceivably rely on missiles directly within its control for close-in support instead of tactical aircraft flown by the Air Force. Yet at the same time, a missile with a long enough range was eventually bound to count as a strategic weapon, to the point where intercontinental ballistic missiles (ICBMs) clearly fell within the Air Force's exclusive domain. Sea-launched missiles, meanwhile, by definition implicated the Navy.

In the debate regarding which service controlled which kinds of missiles, Air Force Chief of Staff Vandenberg argued that SAMs entirely came within the Air Force's responsibility because they were guided weapons theoretically comparable to manned aircraft. Vandenberg also would have permitted the Army to develop and deploy SSMs with an offensive range of up to about 70 miles, though he lengthened this range to 150 miles to allow the firing of missiles from behind the front lines. These restrictions were meant to suit the Army's tactical requirement for enhanced firepower in a battlefield setting. Anything more belonged to the Air Force. Yet the dispute remained unresolved, becoming even further complicated after the Army acquired Navy-built Regulus SSMs to convert into a land-based platform. Regulus achieved a maximum range of 500 nautical miles, which according to Air Force officers was well in excess of the Army's tactical needs.[33] The JCS sidestepped the matter for the time being without issuing a comprehensive ruling on SSMs and SAMs. Such a ruling waited until September 1954, when the JCS determined that the Army could deploy SSMs for tactical battlefield purposes but without providing a range restriction on these types of missiles. The Air Force by default was responsible for developing missiles with longer ranges, the most important being ICBMs. Army SAMs would be deployed to defend specific sites and limited to a horizontal range of 50 miles. OSD approved this decision a few months later.[34]

In approving the JCS decision, the Administration granted its imprimatur for regulating missile development in a way that kept service responsibilities roughly divided. Among SAMs, the Air Force's Bomarc sustained a range of over 400 miles, compared to about 25 miles for the Army's Nike-Ajax, the first of its deployable SAMs. A subsequent expansion in the Army's authorized range to 100 miles accommodated the next missile in the Nike program, Hercules, with a range of up to 75 miles. However, after revived discussion the Army lost the debate on eliminating range restrictions altogether. It also lost authorization to work on a land version of the Navy's Talos, which was turned over to the Air Force.[35] But custody issues pertaining to SSMs and Intermediate Range Ballistic Missiles (IRBMs) had yet to be fully determined. OSD permitted the Army to continue developing its own IRBM, the Jupiter, with the understanding that an ultimate decision over its deployment be deferred until later. The Air Force was exclusively invested with responsibility for ICBMs, which conformed to its mandate for strategic command of the skies, but it was also tasked with developing the Thor IRBM. The Navy was likewise authorized to begin development of a sea-based version of the Army's IRBM. Secretary Wilson finally issued a ruling in November 1956 that resolved the interlinked questions surrounding SSMs and IRBMs. He imposed a new range limitation of 200 miles on the Army for all types of missiles. The Army could not deploy any missiles with ranges over this limit. This limitation assumed that the Army would want to place its missiles 100 miles behind the front lines, so in effect Army SSMs would be limited to a range of 100 miles into enemy territory. As a result of this decision, the Army could not deploy the Jupiter IRBM, which had a range of over 1,000 miles.[36]

While imposing a range limitation on Army SSMs may have seemed arbitrary and unfair to the senior service, it fulfilled the Administration's pledge of cost efficiency. If the Army had been allowed to develop supposedly tactical missiles with ever longer ranges, then it could have duplicated similar Air Force projects and generated higher than necessary costs. Regarding SAMs, the Bomarc was intended to intercept fleets of Soviet bombers well before they reached their intended targets. Nike-Ajax and Hercules missiles, by contrast, defended specific sites such as military bases and cities from incoming enemy aircraft that had made it through the initial screen of Bomarc missiles and fighter interceptor squadrons. Yet controversy continued over duplication and if resources should have been directed into only one of these missile systems.

The recommendations of scientific experts had created momentum for the Administration to pursue ICBM and IRBM programs. In February 1955, the Technological Capabilities Panel of the Scientific Advisory Committee headed by Killian returned a confidential report decisively recommending such steps. The Killian report foresaw the nuclear arms race between the U.S. and U.S.S.R. occurring over the course of four overlapping but discrete periods. In the current Period I, the U.S. enjoyed overwhelming atomic advantage, but this advantage would steadily diminish with Soviet advancements in multimegaton weapons. By Period IV, "[a]n attack by either side would result in mutual destruction" given that "each country will possess enough multimegaton weapons and adequate means of delivering them[.]" The panel seemed to imply that Period IV was inevitable, but it still urged the Administration into doing what it could to delay reaching that point and maintain its advantage. The panel even alluded to an "escape" from Period IV if the U.S.

developed paradigm-shifting technology, a veiled reference to anti-ballistic missile (ABM) defense. In its recommendations, the report did not neglect continental defense. It encouraged the completion of the still unfinished seaward extensions in the early warning network and the more effective dispersal of SAC aircraft. But the report concluded that offensive missile technology needed to be fully utilized, however this might affect the potency of defensive systems in general over the long-term. In that regard, the report accorded "highest priority" to ICBM development while also making clear the importance of IRBMs with shorter ranges.[37]

A month later Eisenhower discussed implementing the report at the White House with the NSC and a few members of the advisory committee, including Killian. Drawing from the report, Eisenhower asked whether the U.S. should take advantage of its current lead in multimegaton weapons by pursuing a bilateral moratorium on nuclear testing with the Soviets. One scientific adviser cautioned against such an approach because while the yields of U.S. nuclear weapons had reached maximum potential, scientists had not yet perfected the miniaturization of these weapons onto missiles. Testing should therefore not be foreclosed until missiles were successfully fit with nuclear warheads. Even a partial moratorium among the two powers would be unwise because it would not necessarily restrain the Soviets from testing in contravention of such an agreement and gaining an edge in weapons development.[38]

A voluntary moratorium on testing would wait a few more years, and in the interim Eisenhower gave the go-ahead for full-scale missile development. The Air Force ran its Atlas/Titan ICBM and Thor IRBM programs as a Special Project Office (SPO), using the "concurrency" model to accelerate development. The Navy eventually decided to withdraw from the Jupiter program to pursue a smaller missile compatible with deployment aboard a submarine. Called Polaris and also managed as an SPO, the Navy worked on a submarine launched ballistic missile (SLBM) that could be fueled more safely and easily through a semi-solid substance instead of with liquid fuel. All the other ICBMs and IRBMs from this period—Atlas, Titan, Thor, and Jupiter – were liquid fueled.

Yet the Administration still exerted restraint over the funding costs for ballistic missiles, even if it had designated their development a national priority. Eisenhower personally monitored which missiles Wilson was funding and which he was eliminating. In July 1957, Wilson informed Eisenhower that the Army's Nike-Ajax SAM and its Corporal SSM were both being phased out, along with the Navy's Regulus I. This news elicited a positive response from Eisenhower and a follow-up inquiry regarding potential missile duplication. Eisenhower cut right into the core ICBM/IRBM programs, wondering whether Atlas and Titan were duplicative or Thor and Jupiter and also mentioning the SAMs Nike and Talos. Soon after Eisenhower's prodding, Wilson retired the Air Force's Navaho, which had never advanced beyond prototype but served as a model for later deployed ICBMs.[39]

World events were bound to rock this posture of stability, with a huge one occurring in October 1957 when the Soviets successfully launched the satellite Sputnik into space. Fear of technological eclipse by the Soviets suddenly overtook those in the halls of officialdom in Washington, D.C. Just a month after the launch, the Special Resources Panel of the Scientific Advisory Committee released a report on the status of nuclear capabilities, commonly known as the Gaither report after the panel's director, Robert Gaither. The release of the Gaither report could not have been better timed to reinforce fears within the government that the Soviets were outpacing the U.S. in satellites and ballistic missiles. The report noted that in the immediate aftermath of World War II the U.S. had successfully deterred the Soviets from aggressive moves in Western Europe through a combination of aerial and naval supremacy topped by an unmatched atomic capability. But the Soviets had allocated a massive portion of their industrial output to a sustained military buildup and modernization of their air, naval, and nuclear forces, to the point where they now had an estimated "1,500 B-29 type bombers," many of which had been retrofitted with jet propulsion, another "3,000 jet bombers" of shorter range, "250 to 300 new long-range submarines," and "at least 1,500 nuclear weapons." The report went on to note that the Soviets had "probably surpassed us in ICBM development," complemented by their increasingly sophisticated air defenses consisting of thousands of fighter interceptors and nests of SAM launchers concentrated at critical sites.[40]

Sputnik embodied this feared buildup from behind the Iron Curtain in a stunning way, in that an artificial object under the auspices of the Soviet government now orbited the Earth, but in reality it was not as much of a shock as it appeared to be. The Administration had viewed space satellites as peripheral to core ICBM development, which explained the apparent lack of progress in launching one in the first place. With satellites now dominating public attention, this prudence looked in hindsight like negligence. At an NSC meeting at the White House attended by Eisenhower a few days after the Sputnik launch, Air Force Secretary Donald Quarles reiterated that, unlike the Soviets, the U.S. had separated a peaceful satellite program dedicated to scientific research from the militarized development of ICBMs. The Soviets were pouring money into weapons technology, and their ability to launch Sputnik was a natural product of these efforts. The Soviets had quite simply been determined to be the first ones in space.[41]

Eisenhower's intention to separate space satellites from the ICBM program ensured that the venture into outer space would not consume ever larger amounts of money. But in the wake of the Sputnik launch the Administration could not ignore public pressure. The Administration first had to blast U.S. satellites into space, which it shortly succeeded in doing, first with the Jupiter rocket-powered Explorer 1 in January 1958 and then two months later with Vanguard, unlike Explorer a solar-powered satellite that remains in orbit to this day. From a national security standpoint the Sputnik launch only further motivated the Administration into getting its ICBM program off the ground, literally and figuratively. The Gaither report offered recommendations exactly along these lines, urging huge increases in planned ICBM and IRBM arsenals, acceleration of Polaris, and readying IRBMs for deployment before the end of 1958 and ICBMs a year later. In broader terms, the report seemed to cast doubt on continental defense, at least if the Soviets successfully developed radar-jamming technologies, noting that "[i]f the attack were at low altitude, or at high altitude with electronic countermeasures (jamming), little protection would be afforded[.]" The crux of the report hinged on the assumption that "[t]he protection of the United States and its population rests, therefore, primarily upon the deterrence provided by SAC," which further necessitated the installation of SAMs near SAC airbases. The report concluded that "[t]he measures of highest value, to strengthen our deterrent and offensive capabilities, are estimated to cost over the next five years (1959–1963) a total of $19 billions."[42]

Eisenhower could not reflexively countenance such high costs, even if stretched out over five years. At an NSC meeting to discuss the Gaither report, he remarked to the effect that "it was essential that we neither become panicked nor allow ourselves to be complacent. It was necessary urgently to make an economic, psychological, and political survey of what could and should be done."[43] Inflation had already contributed to upward pressure on defense costs, with defense appropriations for FY 1958 coming to $33.8 billion, on top of another $1.5 billion for military construction. Of the total from the regular bill, the Air Force received $15.9 billion, just over twice as much money budgeted for the Army at $7.3 billion, while the Navy got $9.9 billion. Spending authority for FY 1959 would probably need to be about $3 billion higher because authority from previous years had been exhausted.[44] Eisenhower opposed any further increases in spending beyond this additional amount, but he had to accept supplementals that enabled accelerated timetables for ICBM and IRBM deployment. To that end, the new defense secretary, Neil McElroy, transferred funds designated for FY 1959 to a FY 1958 supplemental that expedited the deployment schedule for Thor and Jupiter until a combined eight squadrons would be deployed by 1960. The supplemental totaled $1.26 billion, including $253.5 million for Thor and Jupiter, $108.5 million for Atlas, $350 million for three new Polaris subs, $219 million on SAC defenses, and $329 million on early warning against incoming enemy missiles, which had now become vital.[45]

Eisenhower also allowed expanded ICBM production. The FY 1959 budget authorized nine Atlas squads and four Titan squads, with Atlas scheduled for deployment in 1959 and Titan in 1961. Members of the Administration wanted to forego larger-scale Titan production because another ICBM was already in development, the solid fueled Minuteman. A year after the Sputnik launch the Air Force pressed the case for an additional seven Titan squads in the FY 1960 budget, and the Administration relented by revising its budget request.[46]

Yet the planned Titan expansion did not assuage worries on Capitol Hill that the U.S. lagged the Soviets in missile production. Having already weathered fear of a "bomber gap"—sightings of Bear and Bison aircraft during a Moscow military parade led to pressure in Congress to accelerate B-52 production—the Administration now faced paranoia over a "missile gap." Eisenhower consistently believed that the military's goal should be to stay ahead in overall terms, especially after factoring in the current lead in bombers. His restraint was again tested when the Soviet leader Nikita Khrushchev issued the Berlin ultimatum of November 1958, giving NATO six months to withdraw its forces from West Berlin. In a radio and television broadcast on March 16, 1959, Eisenhower continued to insist on lean defense budgets as a safeguard against the U.S. becoming a "garrison state." He mentioned recent missile R&D programs and heralded "a constant parade of improvement, with newer and better weapons constantly crowding out the older and less efficient ones." Eisenhower could accurately point to a combined 41 separate missile systems run by the military, whether still in the R&D stage or ready for deployment.[47] Fears over the "missile gap" and the Berlin ultimatum, the latter of which evaporated after the deadline passed without incident, did not trigger a new arms buildup. Congress ultimately approved defense appropriations of $39.2 billion for FY 1960.[48]

Amid Eisenhower's "constant parade of improvement," the Air Force successfully tested Atlas in late November 1958 for a range of over 6,000 miles across the Pacific Ocean. The Atlas D version achieved Initial Operational Capability (IOC) the next year after another series of tests, but only the F version could be siloed underground and raised to the surface through an elevator. The Air Force next planned for the lighter, solid fueled Minuteman. Deployed in deep, underground siloes, the Minuteman's launch process could be completed within one minute, hence its name. Even with budget constraints, Eisenhower saw missiles as cutting-edge technology and requested an increase of $581 million for the procurement of missiles in FY 1961, putting the total figure at $3.8 billion.[49]

The Air Force began deploying IRBMs during this period, with Thor squads stationed in England and Jupiters in Italy and Turkey. The Polaris program also turned out to be an important contribution to the nuclear arsenal. The Navy moved the program along briskly, even though it was the last of the three services to become seriously involved with IRBMs. When the first Polaris sub, the *George Washington*, took to sea with its complement of sixteen ballistic missiles in 1960, Eisenhower thought a preemptive Soviet first strike would now be nothing short of suicidal. The Polaris subs, dubbed "ships" instead of "boats" unlike other submarines because of the gravity of their mission, were invulnerable to such a strike and guaranteed a reprisal attack from any point along the Russian coast. The only restriction on expanding their deterrent value was the cost of producing the subs and missiles themselves. For FY 1961, Eisenhower wanted funding for another three Polaris subs, even as part of a longer-term program.[50]

The Administration oversaw the emergence of revolutionary military technologies without letting costs get out of control. Eisenhower also successfully prevented a destabilizing buildup in the face of an array of eruptions abroad that might have rattled a different administration. He encountered crises in the East China Sea, Indochina, the Middle East, Hungary, and Berlin. His ability to restrain the rise in spending even in these dangerous times resembled Truman's insistence on keeping down defense costs following the first Berlin crisis and the threat of Soviet pressure on Western Europe. The Korean War interrupted the austerity from the early and middle phases of Truman's presidency into the Eisenhower era, but Eisenhower avoided becoming entangled in another regional war. He refused nuclear or conventional assistance to the French after their redoubt at Dien Bien Phu came under siege by the Viet Minh in 1954. Two years later he condemned the joint British, French, and Israeli operation to seize the Suez Canal and the Sinai Peninsula as a hairbrained scheme that only further alienated the nationalist Egyptian regime of Gamal Abdel Nasser from the Western bloc.

Yet Eisenhower was also not averse to deploying forces abroad. Only two years after the Suez crisis, he ordered the landing of Marines in Lebanon after the fall of the Hashemite monarchy in Iraq threatened the non-communist Lebanese government. He supported the Chinese Nationalists during their low-intensity conflict with the communists for control of the Quemoy and Matsu islands hugging the coastline, to the point of sending in warships for supply missions in 1958. He never used military force in the region, but the threat was real. He even hinted at using tactical nuclear weapons to end the standoff on the Korean peninsula. Eisenhower also had no qualms with engaging in covert operations in places as diverse as Iran, Guatemala, and possibly the Congo. The Bay of Pigs operation to overthrow Fidel Castro in Cuba had been planned and prepared for in the final months of his presidency.

And even though Eisenhower refrained from unilaterally trying to rescue the French at Dien Bien Phu, he still viewed Southeast Asia as a strategically pivotal region, off-handedly coining the term domino theory during a press conference. Eisenhower's fortune was that during his presidency South Vietnam, the non-communist regime formed out of the Geneva Accords, did not face the prospect of immediate implosion as it would in 1964–65. By that point Eisenhower did urge President Johnson on a visit to the White House to escalate the Vietnam War. Nor during his own presidency did he rule out the possibility of outright military intervention in Vietnam. In April 1958 Eisenhower approved NSC 5809 regarding options in Southeast Asia, including the possible application of military force in response to communist insurgencies fomented within allied states in the region.[51]

Finally, Eisenhower took strides towards arms control as part of a larger attempt to mitigate the arms race, which would in turn hopefully compress defense spending over the long-term. He did not succeed in these endeavors. The Soviets rejected his first proposal for Open Skies at the Geneva conference in 1955, in which the U.S. and U.S.S.R. would have mutually granted access to one another's air space for surveillance purposes. Eisenhower apparently did not see any problem with the idea of unrestricted aerial surveillance, but he knew that covert overflights threatened to wreck negotiations with the Soviets, which ended up happening in May 1960. Until a Soviet SAM shot down the U-2 spy plane flown by Gary Francis Powers, the Administration depended on the CIA's U-2 flights for gauging Soviet missile developments. The lack of any concrete information about the Soviet arsenal fed worries of a missile gap more than anything else. In December 1953 at the U.N., Eisenhower advanced another idea that he thought would reduce tensions, Atoms for Peace, a sharing of nuclear energy technology for peaceful, civilian purposes, but the Soviets also rejected this proposal. The death of Stalin in 1953 had potentially set the stage for a new era of East-West thaw, but such hopes were dashed during the next ten years. In a foreboding of Khrushchev's brinksmanship over Berlin, the U-2 incident, and missiles in Cuba, a CIA report from April 1953 assessing the situation in Russia upon Stalin's death warned that "the new regime will probably find it more difficult to abandon positions than did Stalin and might feel itself compelled to react more strongly if moves of the West confronted it with the need for major decisions."[52] Eisenhower failed to achieve a foreign policy breakthrough, but in the anxious, uncertain post-Stalin era he used all his goodwill and credibility to maintain a fragile peace.

TAX OVERHAUL, SOCIAL SECURITY

Eisenhower's insistence on lean defense budgets conformed with his broader outlook of limited government in domestic affairs. But a mandate for limited government did not imply an undoing of the New Deal. He supported Social Security and even added a new cabinet level Department of Health, Education, and Welfare, which consolidated a variety of disparate offices. As the first Republican president since Herbert Hoover, Eisenhower was foremost intent on balancing the budget. While Truman emphasized paying down the national debt in a programmatic manner, Eisenhower wanted any resulting budget surplus transferred directly back to the private economy through tax breaks. The goal of this fiscal policy, as stated in his budget message for FY 1955, would be "to return to the people, to spend for themselves and in their own way, the largest possible share of the money that the Government has been spending for them."[53] While Eisenhower's proposals were not tantamount to supply side tax cuts, he still thought tax reform could expedite economic growth, asserting in an address before Congress in February 1953 that "[w]e must develop a system of taxation which will impose the least possible obstacle to the dynamic growth of the country."[54]

The government faced a deficit for FY 1954 and could not afford to slash taxes across the board. Spending would also have to be steadily cut, but even so the budget was not going to immediately balance. For this reason, the Administration planned to extend the excess profits tax for an additional six months until the end of CY 1953, delay a rewriting of the excise tax laws until next year, and forgo cutting corporate rates. As Eisenhower saw it, the $9 billion generated from current corporate rates, with the top rate at 52%, offset the phase-out of the excess profits tax, which he viewed as unfavorable to business. At the same time, he wanted personal income tax rates to return to levels prior to the Revenue Act of 1951 while delaying a hike in the Social Security payroll tax from 1.5% to 2% until the start of 1955.[55]

Eisenhower instinctively sought to cut taxes, but he was also mindful that any changes in the tax laws would invariably affect the government's intake of revenue. As he had earlier proposed, income tax levels returned to their pre-Korean War levels by early 1954, the top rate brought down to 91% and the bottom rate to 20%. The effect of these cuts was progressive, also consistent with Eisenhower's wishes, with lower earners receiving breaks of about 10% compared to top earners who saw their liability fall by only 1%. Yet the Republican Congress did deviate from Eisenhower's tax agenda by delaying until March 1955 rather than rescinding the 5% cut in corporate taxes. Congress also took aim at taxes on consumption with the Excise Tax Reduction Act. The legislation cut taxes on consumer merchandise such as kitchen and heating appliances and on some manufacturing goods like light bulbs and cameras. Yet in keeping with the cautious fiscal prescriptions of this era, Congress carried forward for another year taxes laid on a handful of goods that were slated for expiration like cars, distilled spirits, cigarettes, and malt liquor.[56]

The more ambitious overhaul of the Internal Revenue Code in 1954 incentivized business activity through a number of reforms. The new code, for instance, introduced accelerated depreciation for capital investment. Before the code rewrite, companies could deduct ordinary business expenses per year from their taxable income, but larger investments that generated income needed to be capitalized under the straight-line method of depreciation, with allowances for cost and wear and tear allocated evenly over the useful life of the asset. The code now authorized a declining balance method for increased write offs closer in time to when the asset was first acquired. Such a provision intended to bring the tax laws closer in unison with actual depreciation of capital equipment. Among other revisions, the code eased the maligned "double taxation" on companies by introducing an exclusion from income for stock dividends $50 or under and a 4% tax credit for dividends over $50. This provision made easier the formation of capital stock among businesses instead of reliance on debt financing. The new code also clarified the tax rules governing R&D activities by explicitly allowing small businesses, along with larger corporations, to deduct R&D-related spending per year as ordinary expenses or to capitalize it for a period of at least five years (the R& D tax credit would not be written into the code for another twenty-seven years). Another measure included an expansion of carrybacks for losses from 1 to 2 years, with carryforwards maintained at 5 years. Finally, the code relaxed rules against excessive retained earnings by allowing companies to present in their tax returns any retained earnings as a response to foreseeable commercial needs and not as an illegitimate way to escape liability. This provision de facto exempted taxes on retained earnings of $60,000 or less, with only amounts in excess taxable.[57] Tax laws in the early Eisenhower Administration would lead to about a $1.2 billion loss in revenue, significantly smaller than the $11 billion during the early and middle phase of the Truman presidency, which was partly attributable to the Republican Congress.[58]

The Administration did not pursue any other major changes in the tax laws after 1954. It avoided taking steps that would seriously disturb the inflow of revenue, which was in keeping with its goal of both balancing the budget and fulfilling its defense commitments. Eisenhower also inherited from Truman a Social Security Administration that was growing and which had strong public support. Like Truman he expanded benefits and strengthened funding for the program without causing it to begin triggering deficits. The program remained funded through payroll taxes instead of general revenue. Eisenhower continued the payroll tax hikes and benefit increases adjusted ad hoc for inflation, albeit after an initial delay early in his administration. In the 1954 Amendments Eisenhower signed into law a new expansion in coverage to self-employed workers in the agricultural sector, members of certified professions such as law and medicine, and other groups on a voluntary basis, such as people already enrolled in state and local retirement programs and clergy. The Amendment brought in another 6 million people into Social Security, comparable to the 1950 expansion, while an additional 4 million people were now eligible to join voluntarily.

Congress also created disability insurance under the program. It first implemented a "freeze" for physical disability that Eisenhower signed in 1954. If a worker now did not earn income in a given year due to disability, the absence of income could not factor into the computation of benefits. Months or years with little or no income for these disabled workers would otherwise have reduced the benefits available to them, but the freeze simply excluded those periods of no-pay from computation altogether. The freeze opened the way for disability benefits starting in 1956, first for disabled workers between the ages of fifty and sixty-four, then expanding to include the dependents of disabled workers, and eventually in 1960 disabled workers of all ages. Social Security thus turned into a program for Old Age, Survivors, and Disability Insurance (OASDI).

Eisenhower's signature domestic achievement, a new system of interstate highways crisscrossing the nation, relied for its funding on a trust that collected revenue through gasoline taxes. This revenue was projected to rise as more motorists made use of the interstates. A few of his ideas did not fit so neatly into this framework, like a limited government health reinsurance program to guarantee private plans, but this backstop would have come to no more than $25 million, and in any event Congress did not act on it. Eisenhower was concerned with deficits for the same reasons as Truman, that accumulating debt would eventually burden future generations. Yet other factors compelled Eisenhower to push back against unrestrained spending. He was especially worried that excessive defense spending would turn the private economy into a kind of "garrison state" churning out military hardware instead of consumer goods. This higher level of spending would also exacerbate inflation and destabilize the very way of life to which Americans had grown accustomed. Other urgencies therefore existed for Eisenhower besides the sheer drain caused by deficits, and these urgencies lay at the heart of the warning in his farewell address of a "military-industrial complex."

For all his efforts at keeping spending under control, Eisenhower earned only a modestly successful record at turning in balanced budgets occasionally, if not regularly. The budget ran surpluses of $1.6 billion in both 1956 and 1957 before registering deficits of $2.8 billion in 1958 and then an unusually high $12.4 billion in 1959, worsened by fluctuations in the business cycle. Tight spending brought the budget back to a small surplus of $1.2 billion in 1960.[59] Eisenhower's success in budget balancing was hardly total. Over half of his presidency was marked by deficits, though admittedly the deficits in the early years were affected by Truman budgets and the Korean War.[60]

This checkered record demonstrated the inherent challenge of balancing the budget in the postwar era, even with a fiscally resolute president, an entitlement state still isolated from general revenue, and the exertion of restraint over defense spending. Yet to consistently focus on curbing spending, especially during a dangerous time such as the 1950s, required a certain military prestige that Eisenhower, by virtue of his wartime exploits, provided. He had been one of only a handful of military officers to rise to the five star rank of General of the Army during World War II, and while these five stars did not entirely save him from public criticism of a supposedly lax defense policy, he still projected an image of benign calm under the surface of which the arms race continued in lock step. This stability engendered a strategic posture more tightly bound to the dictates of the budget than in any other period of the Cold War.

NOTES

1. OMB, "Historical Tables," 50–52.
2. *Foreign Relations of the United States, 1952–1954, National Security Affairs, Volume II, Part I*, ed. Lisle A. Rose and Neal H. Petersen (Washington, D.C.: Government Printing Office, 1984), Document 101, https://history.state.gov/historicaldocuments/frus1952–54v02p1/d101, accessed June 2019.
3. "The Evolution of Foreign Policy." Secretary of State John Foster Dulles. Council on Foreign Relations. New York. January 12, 1954.
4. President of U.S., *The Budget of the United States Government for the Fiscal Year Ending June 30, 1955* (Washington, D.C.: Government Printing Office, 1954), M38 – M39.
5. President, *1955 Budget*, M42.
6. Ibid., M44.
7. John Norton Moore and Robert F. Turner, "The Legal Structure of Defense Organization," memorandum prepared for the President's Blue Ribbon Commission on Defense Management, January 1986, 24–26.
8. Converse, *Rearming for the Cold War*, 552.
9. Ibid., 606.
10. Richard M. Leighton, *History of the Office of the Secretary of Defense, Vol. III, Strategy, Money, and the New Look: 1953–1956* (Washington, D.C.: Historical Office, Office of the Secretary of Defense, 2001), 254.
11. President of U.S., *The Budget of the United States Government for the Fiscal Year Ending June 30, 1957* (Washington, D.C.: Government Printing Office, 1956), M24.
12. President of U.S., *The Budget of the United States Government for the Fiscal Year Ending June 30, 1961* (Washington, D.C.: Government Printing Office, 1960), M15–M16.
13. Standing Group. "Memorandum for the Military Representatives: Force Goals for 1952, 1953, and 1954." SGM-0648–52, Standing Group Memoranda. NATO Archives, Brussels, Belgium.
14. Military Committee. "Report from the Military Committee to the North Atlantic Defense Committee on North Atlantic Treaty Organization Medium Term Plan." DC 013, DC—Subject Files Defence Committee. NATO Archives, Brussels, Belgium.
15. Standing Group. "Report by the Standing Group to the North Atlantic Military Committee on Guidance for 1955 Annual Review." SG 190/17, Standing Group Series. NATO Archives, Brussels, Belgium.
16. "Report on Army's R&D programs including nuclear and non-nuclear firepower, mines, chemical warfare, SSMs, air defense, space and satellites, air and surface mobility, combat surveillance and nuclear research, undated." Office of the Staff Secretary Records. Subject Series. Alphabetical Subseries. Box 2, Army [Vol. I] (10). Dwight Eisenhower Presidential Library and Museum.
17. Converse, *Rearming for the Cold War*, 601.
18. Ibid., 530–32.
19. Futrell, "Air Power Concept," 266.
20. Kenneth Schaffel, *The Emerging Shield: The Air Force and the Evolution of Continental Air Defense: 1945 – 1960* (Washington, D.C.: Office of Air Force History, U.S. Air Force, 1991), 93–95.
21. *Foreign Relations of the United States, 1952–1954, National Security Affairs, Volume II, Part I*, eds. Lisle H. Rose and Neal H. Petersen (Washington, D.C.: Government Printing

Office, 1984), Document 92, https://history.state.gov/historicaldocuments/frus1952–54v02p1/d92, accessed June 2019.

22. Schaffel, *Emerging Shield*, 217 – 20.

23. Ibid., 210.

24. Ibid., 188.

25. Kenneth W. Condit, *History of the Joint Chiefs of Staff, Vol. VI, The Joint Chiefs of Staff and National Policy: 1955–1956* (Washington, D.C.: Office of Joint History, Office of the Chairman of the Joint Chiefs of Staff, 1998), 275–77.

26. Condit, *Joint Chiefs 1955–1956*, 281.

27. Schaffel, *Emerging Shield*, 176–77.

28. *Foreign Relations of the United States, 1952–1954, National Security Affairs, Volume II, Part I*, eds. Lisle H. Rose and Neal H. Petersen (Washington, D.C.: Government Printing Office, 1984), Document 91, https://history.state.gov/historicaldocuments/frus1952–54v02p1/d91, accessed June 2019.

29. "Memo regarding current and proposed air defense radar coverage, August 22, 1958." White House Office of the Special Assistant for Science and Technology. Box 4, Air Defense (1). Dwight Eisenhower Presidential Library and Museum.

30. "Memo to Dr. Killian re Present Problems Relating to Radar Early Warning of Manned Bomber Attack, October 10, 1958." White House Office of the Special Assistant for Science and Technology. Box 1, Air Defense. Dwight Eisenhower Presidential Library and Museum.

31. Leighton, *Strategy, Money, and the New Look*, 135.

32. Ibid., 293.

33. Robert J. Watson, *History of the Joint Chiefs of Staff, Vol. V, The Joint Chiefs of Staff and National Policy, 1953–1954* (Washington, D.C.: Office of Joint History, Office of the Chairman of the Joint Chiefs of Staff, 1998), 180–81.

34. Watson, *Joint Chiefs 1953–1954*, 184–85.

35. Condit, *Joint Chiefs 1955–1956*, 61–65.

36. Ibid., 71–72.

37. *Foreign Relations of the United States, Panel, 1955–1957, National Security Policy, Volume XIX*, eds. William Klingaman, David S. Patterson, and Ilana Stern (Washington, D.C.: Government Printing Office, 1990), Document 9, https://history.state.gov/historicaldocuments/frus1955–57v19/d9, accessed June 2019.

38. *Foreign Relations of the United States, Panel, 1955–1957, National Security Policy, Volume XIX*, eds. William Klingaman, David S. Patterson, and Ilana Stern (Washington, D.C.: Government Printing Office, 1990), Document 17, https://history.state.gov/historicaldocuments/frus1955–57v19/d17, accessed June 2019.

39. Robert J. Watson, *History of the Office of the Secretary of Defense, Vol. IV, Into the Missile Age: 1956–1960* (Washington, D.C.: Historical Office, Office of the Secretary of Defense, 1997), 175–76.

40. *Foreign Relations of the United States, Panel, 1955–1957, National Security Policy, Volume XIX*, eds. William Klingaman, David S. Patterson, and Ilana Stern (Washington, D.C.: Government Printing Office, 1990), Document 158, https://history.state.gov/historicaldocuments/frus1955–57v19/d158, accessed June 2019.

41. *Foreign Relations of the United States, Panel, 1955–1957, National Security Policy, Volume XIX*, eds. William Klingaman, David S. Patterson, and Ilana Stern (Washington, D.C.: Government Printing Office, 1990), Document 146, https://history.state.gov/historicaldocuments/frus1955–57v19/d146, accessed June 2019.

42. Document 158.

43. *Foreign Relations of the United States, Panel, 1955–1957, National Security Policy, Volume XIX*, eds. William Klingaman, David S. Patterson, and Ilana Stern (Washington, D.C.: Government Printing Office, 1990), Document 156, https://history.state.gov/historicaldocuments/frus1955–57v19/d156, accessed June 2019.

44. Watson, *Into the Missile Age*, 100–101.

45. Ibid., 147.

46. Ibid., 363–64.

47. The American Presidency Project, "Dwight D. Eisenhower: Radio and Television Report to the American People: Security in the Free World, March 16, 1959," http://www.presidency.ucsb.edu/ws/index.php?pid=11682, accessed September 2018.
48. Watson, *Into the Missile Age*, 320.
49. President, *1961 Budget*, M19.
50. Ibid., M21.
51. *Foreign Relations of the United States, 1958–1960, East Asia-Pacific Region; Cambodia; Laos; Volume XVI*, eds. Edward C. Keefer and David W. Mabon (Washington, D.C.: Government Printing Office, 1992), Document 12, https://history.state.gov/historicaldocuments/frus1958–60v16, accessed June 2019.
52. "Memo re CIA estimate of probable consequences of the death of Stalin, April 10, 1953." NSC Staff Papers. Special Staff File. Box 7, Special Staff Memos (2). Dwight Eisenhower Presidential Library and Museum.
53. President, *1955 Budget*, M12.
54. The American Presidency Project, "Dwight D. Eisenhower: Annual Message to the Congress on the State of the Union, February 2, 1953," http://www.presidency.ucsb.edu/ws/?pid=9829, accessed September 2018.
55. The American Presidency Project, "Dwight D. Eisenhower: Special Message to the Congress Recommending Tax Legislation, May 20, 1953," http://www.presidency.ucsb.edu/ws/?pid=9856, accessed September 2018.
56. Secretary of Treasury, *Annual Report of the Secretary of the Treasury on the State of the Finances for the Fiscal Year Ended June 30, 1954* (Washington, D.C.: Government Printing Office, 1955), 44–45.
57. Secretary of Treasury, *1954 Treasury Annual Report*, 49–51.
58. Tempalski, "Revenue Effects," 15.
59. President of U.S., *The Budget of the United States Government for the Fiscal Year Ending June 30, 1962* (Washington, D.C.: Government Printing Office, 1961), M4.
60. President of U.S., *The Budget of the United States Government for the Fiscal Year Ending June 30, 1959* (Washington, D.C.: Government Printing Office, 1958), M4.

Chapter Four

Idealism and Overreach

Kennedy and Johnson, 1961–1969

John Kennedy ran for president in 1960 opposed to the Eisenhower record in rhetoric if not entirely in reason, all the more so because he was running against Eisenhower's vice president, Richard Nixon. Through this political positioning Kennedy, elected senator of Massachusetts in 1952 and a product of familial wealth and privilege, opposed eight years of relative stability and prosperity that to a casual observer might nonetheless have appeared lackluster. Kennedy invoked more spirited and forward-looking rhetoric for both domestic and foreign issues. He wanted to "get America moving again" in economic terms while also vowing to "bear any burden" against communist encroachments around the world. He most likely did not want for the government to incur larger and continuous deficits, but he brought a certain degree of finesse to defense policy that served as a departure from the stubborn insistence on square budgetary logic defining the Eisenhower era. In domestic affairs Kennedy was instinctively more activist than Eisenhower, even if his truncated presidency led to no crowning legislative achievements. While Eisenhower had worked to gradually enlarge Social Security through existing structures, Kennedy supported an expansion of the entitlement state into public health insurance, even if limited to senior citizens and the needy. He also became far more willing to incur deficits in order to sustain stronger economic growth. The Administration had to adapt to a more normal international trade setting, with the U.S. on track to again becoming a net importer of manufactured goods. In overall terms U.S. economic might was declining, and this trend affected policymaking.

FLEXIBLE RESPONSE, BERLIN, CUBA

Given that the Eisenhower Administration had promulgated massive retaliation and then offensive missile strength as a central component of strategy, Kennedy explored alternative ways of responding to Soviet pressure. He further wanted to replace Eisenhower's occasional indulgence for covert operations in peripheral regions with a sustained and earnest check on communist advances in the Third World through counterguerrilla activities. Some of these differences with Eisenhower may have sprung from recent events. Decolonization had accelerated by the early 1960s, especially in Africa, while countries in the nonaligned movement such as India and Indonesia continued to keep both superpowers at bay. The Kennedy Administration became increasingly embroiled in South Vietnam only as the threat of communist subversion to the regime of Ngo Dinh Diem worsened in the early 1960s.

The capstone of Kennedy's criticism of the Eisenhower record was that his predecessor's lack of vigilance had led to the missile gap, a claim discredited in the first few days of the new Administration. The incoming Administration would not ignore the role of nuclear deterrence, and in fact it would accelerate the development of Minuteman and the deployment of Polaris. But the Administration wanted to revise the assumptions of deterrence from the Eisenhower era, a fresh thinking that evolved into the doctrine of flexible response. Members of the new Administration like Defense Secretary Robert McNamara, who had just been named CEO of Ford Motor Company, argued that massive retaliation was too heavy handed, too simplistic, and not even credible. Any apparent Soviet transgression along the Iron Curtain could not possibly be met with an offensive bombing campaign against Russia, while even tactical nukes like the "Atomic Annie" nuclearized shells were of marginal value. Localized Soviet aggression such as over Berlin needed to be met by a correspondingly localized Western response. Both sides would gradually escalate their deployment of conventional forces until finally resorting to nuclear weapons. Flexible response was therefore envisioned to broaden the range of options available to NATO, especially during hostile yet confusing situations in which Western leaders could not immediately discern Soviet intentions.

The shift to flexible response did not imply the Kennedy Administration's comfort with rising deficits as a tradeoff for a retooled defense budget. Bringing corporate experience to the Pentagon, McNamara argued strongly for cutting costs and eliminating wasteful spending. Yet by the same token he and Kennedy also agreed that arbitrary budget ceilings should be discarded. The Defense Department needed to contain costs through what they considered more intellectually honest means founded upon systems analysis, which brought a quantitative approach to procurement. McNamara indeed wanted to overhaul the budget process by implementing a Planning-Programming-

Budgeting System (PPBS). The civilian leadership had until now mainly worked to reconcile the at times highly divergent service budgets. This process had to be brought up to date to reflect the evolution of warfare as the services increasingly melded their aerial, seaborne, ground, and amphibious capabilities in the carrying out of joint operations. The new leadership at the Pentagon wanted to use PPBS to base its budget estimates upon discrete functions, such as general purpose forces, strategic retaliatory forces, research and development, continental defense, sea and airlift, among other categories.[1]

While the Administration used PPBS to reform the Pentagon's budgetary techniques, on a broader level it did abandon Eisenhower's demand for spending restraint year in and year out. In an address to Congress in March 1961, Kennedy stated, "Our arms must be adequate to meet our commitments and ensure our security, without being bound by arbitrary budget ceilings. This nation can afford to be strong—it cannot afford to be weak." This bold assertion prefaced his request for an extra $650 million in defense spending for FY 1962, even before the Berlin crisis.[2] Flexible response and its budgetary implications were never reduced to NSC codification. The Kennedy White House rejected the Eisenhower Administration's last official Basic National Security Policy statement before eventually discarding the very idea of a BNSP. The JCS had been working on a new BNSP for a few years by the time the White House concluded in January 1963 that defense policy would more loosely emanate from the "policy statements" of high-ranking officials instead of bureaucratic formulae drafted by NSC and other interdepartmental staff.[3]

Before implementing substantive changes, Kennedy tasked McNamara with carrying out a review of the current defense posture. McNamara completed his review by late February 1961 and submitted a report to the White House, which included underlying concepts and recommendations for amending the FY 1961 and 1962 budgets. McNamara wrote expansively of flexible response as a framework applicable to various scenarios of minimized armed conflict. Flexible response in no way conveyed a repudiation of nuclear deterrence. On the contrary, it applied to situations of "uncertainty" where caution needed to reign over questions of unleashing nuclear weapons. A new focus on conventional capabilities applied not only to Europe but to "limited war" scenarios in the Third World, including mainland Southeast Asia, warranting an expansion in Special Forces. McNamara recommended a 3,000 manpower increase in Special Forces for this purpose, consistent with Kennedy's own globalist mantra. He also wanted more authority to spend on enhanced air and sealift capabilities.[4]

The Administration still oversaw and even expedited important trends in the strategic arsenal, specifically the transition in procurement from manned bombers to solid fueled missiles. This transition did not mean that bombers would be gutted from the arsenal as a relic of the past. Bombers would continue to fulfill a key part of the nuclear Triad along with land and sea-based nuclear missiles, but the Pentagon was increasingly allocating funds towards missile production instead of new bombers. McNamara, for instance, noted in his report that under current plans the total number of B-52s would plateau at 630 bombers during FY 1963 and 1964. The Pentagon had similarly planned to keep the medium range B-58 at 72 in number during 1962–1964. The older B-47, meanwhile, would be cut from 720 in 1962 to 450 by 1964. Total Atlas missiles, on the other hand, would rise from 72 in 1962 to 129 in 1963, where that number would then be held, with other missiles programmed for larger-scale increases. More advanced Titan missiles would go up from 45 in 1962 to 126 two years later. Even larger increases were reserved for Minuteman and Polaris, with 540 Minuteman and 256 Polaris missiles planned for 1964. McNamara wanted to accelerate these trends, including spending to enable doubling the monthly production rate of Minuteman from 30 missiles to 60. He also wanted to program funds for another ten Polaris subs during FY 1962.[5]

McNamara could achieve minor cost savings by eliminating weapons systems no longer holding any clear utility to the defense establishment. For instance, he advised getting rid of the subsonic Snark cruise missile right away. He also dropped the idea of putting Polaris missiles on surface ships as not worth the cost. McNamara tended to convey a dubious tone on the Nike-Zeus ABM. While fully supporting its continued development to counter similar Soviet initiatives, it would not be ready for years, and by then it could easily be outpaced by ICBM advances. Finally, McNamara advised relegating the B-70 Valkyrie bomber to only prototype development. The B-70 had been designed to replace the B-52 as the Air Force's long-range heavy aircraft, but with the advent of ICBMs the need for this bomber was now clouded in doubt. The B-70 offered no advantages not shared with ICBMs, and as a manned aircraft flying within the atmosphere it suffered from inherent weaknesses.[6]

McNamara reiterated these recommendations when testifying before the Senate Armed Forces Committee in early April. In his prepared remarks he emphasized the shift from the increasingly archaic Atlas and Titan platforms to the more advanced Minuteman and Polaris, urging Congress for an additional 10 Polaris sub construction starts in FY 1962. On Nike-Zeus McNamara cautiously adopted a stance of supporting the ABM's further development while still resisting completion and deployment of the system, possibly in part out of fear that this would cause the Soviets to build more missiles to overwhelm it. McNamara also proposed a multi-purpose aircraft to be developed for all three services. This fighter would be intended for a diverse range of combat scenarios and therefore adaptable to the needs of the Air Force, Navy, and Marines alike.[7] Kennedy expressed similar views only days earlier in his own address before Congress. His request for an additional $650 million in defense spending was not enormous, about $5.5 billion in 2019 dollars, but it still indicated the Administration's somewhat more lenient attitude towards the budget. Kennedy also sought new obligational authority for the solid fueled Skybolt, a ballistic air to surface missile (ASM) with a range of 1,000 miles. He above all espoused a doctrine of flexibility, emphasizing more money for airlift, helicopters, and counterguerrilla activities in the Third World.[8]

This evolving doctrine of flexible response was shaped by real world events, particularly in the center of Europe. For all of Kennedy's attention to the threat of communist activity in Africa, Asia, and Latin America, and in spite of the turmoil in Laos, Europe still served as the pivotal front of the Cold War in 1961, above all the isolated city of Berlin, and the Administration's continuing formulation of flexible response was bound to be affected by Soviet actions in Europe. Moreover, while McNamara identified a few areas for cuts in the defense budget, the deployment of more troops, tanks, and other weaponry to Europe, along with the continued modernization of the strategic arsenal, would clearly entail higher spending. Members of the Administration and outside advisers soon reached the consensus that NATO needed stronger conventional forces in Europe. Elder statesman Dean Acheson submitted a memorandum containing prescriptions easily compatible with flexible response. Describing the possibility of a limited conflict igniting in Europe, Acheson wrote that NATO needed "to smother the conflict as quickly as possible and to handle any spread of the conflict, up to and including the involvement of all readily-available Soviet non-nuclear forces, without recklessly raising the ante." Acheson advised increased defense spending in the U.S. and Europe to both modernize conventional capabilities and to raise force levels. He did not provide specific cost estimates for higher force levels, but he thought $14 billion per year paid by the Europeans would be necessary for funding this buildup, which probably meant other spending would have to be cut.[9]

Kennedy approved the memo as a directive in early April. With the new policy template in place, the Administration prepared to enhance its capacity for conventional conflict in the event of renewed belligerence on the part of Khrushchev. Such belligerence again manifested itself at the Vienna summit in June. With Kennedy plagued by backpain and feeling unwell during the proceedings, Khrushchev returned to his familiar gambit of ultimatum, giving Kennedy six months to withdraw from the "free city" of West Berlin, just as he had for Eisenhower, before handing it over to the East German government. In this highly charged environment, the Administration had to determine the extent to which conventional and nuclear forces would play in defending West Berlin against anticipated Soviet military moves at the end of the six-month deadline around the new year.

At an NSC meeting on July 19, Kennedy reached the decision to prepare for the overseas deployment of six regular Army divisions and two Marine divisions, facilitated by new spending of up to $3.2 billion. This readiness in the active duty Army would require reserve and National Guard units to secure the home front while regular forces could be deployed to Europe during or shortly before the breakout of armed conflict. When discussion during the meeting turned to the question of whether a buildup would weaken the credibility of the West's nuclear deterrent, multiple officials indicated that they did not share these concerns. In their view, the buildup and possible deployment of such additional forces adhered to the policy framework now in place, which was gradual escalation until the reliance on nuclear weapons could not be avoided. Kennedy also broached the subject of public finance, indicating reluctance to pay for an additional $3.2 billion through deficit spending. He decided to hold off on asking for a tax hike until recovery from the 1960 recession had reached a more mature stage.[10] While he also did not preclude the possibility of a tax hike in his national address on July 25 regarding Berlin, Kennedy still expressed confidence that the "improved business outlook means improved revenues," hopefully boding well for a balanced budget in the coming fiscal year.[11]

Kennedy soon after obtained supplemental funding of $3.45 billion from Congress to strengthen conventional capabilities, including larger personnel numbers and more ammunition and hardware.[12] Ground forces played a visible role in ratcheting up the pressure on the Soviets, particularly after the communists began building the Wall separating East from West Berlin in mid-August. The president authorized an armored convoy up the autobahn to probe Soviet intransigence on ground access to West Berlin. The convoy moved along 100 miles of highway behind the Iron Curtain largely without incident until reaching the city. In early September, Kennedy approved McNamara's request to send 37,000 troops to Europe, who would be incorporated into the Seventh Army in West Germany. A frightening moment occurred later in October when U.S. and Soviet tanks faced off at Checkpoint Charlie, the only access point now allowed between the Eastern and Western sectors, before Khrushchev pulled back the Soviet armor. But by then the crisis had turned a corner after McNamara strongly implied in a public statement on September 28 that the U.S. was committed to using nuclear arms if necessary in defense of West Berlin. These kinds of statements perhaps more effectively smoothed concerns among allies about the seriousness of the U.S.'s security guarantee than the overseas deployment of relatively small numbers of troops.[13]

Khrushchev had been driven to test Kennedy over Berlin because of the ailing East German economy, which starkly contrasted with the now prosperous West Germany. The flood of refugees from East to West Berlin had become a great embarrassment to the East German authorities, but it also threatened to unhinge their grip on power, which would have only further destabilized relations between the two superpowers. By erecting the Wall, the East Germans and Soviets stopped this human tide while also gauging American resolve. Neither side wanted to wage nuclear war over Berlin, and as the Soviet leadership began to understand that any military encounter might quickly escalate into such an exchange, they backed off from their earlier demands. Khrushchev de facto ended the crisis when he conceded that the political future of Berlin did not need to be determined by the end of the year, which at least reduced anxiety over the impending deadline. The Berlin crisis of 1961 was the last time the Soviets threatened to cut off Western access to the city, and after 1963 attention on both sides shifted to the Third World, where proxy states and counterinsurgencies became fodder for East-West antagonism.

The Berlin crisis nonetheless served as a clear test case for conventional deterrence. The Administration had needed a force in being of up to eight active Army and Marine divisions and adequate air and sealift for the troops and their hardware across the Atlantic. Kennedy learned the lesson, at least as he saw it, that conventional forces had to be expanded to facilitate a timely response to any similar emergency. In his budget request for FY 1963 submitted just after the crisis wound down, Kennedy asked for two additional Army divisions, which would bring the total number of active Army divisions to sixteen, noting further that "[i]f we are to retain for ourselves a choice other than a nuclear holocaust or retreat, we must increase considerably our conventional forces."[14] Congress authorized the funds, and the Army expanded by two divisions, which relieved reserve and National Guard units that had been called up for active duty. Kennedy also sought to increase spending on air and sealift forces from $1.1 to $1.3 billion, including funds for purchasing new C-130E Hercules transports, the latest version in that line of aircraft. In modernizing the surface fleet, he planned to upgrade 24 destroyers while building another 29 ships.[15] In all, Kennedy planned for $52.7 billion in expenditures for FY 1963, an increase of $5 billion from 1961.[16] Congress enacted defense appropriations of $48.2 billion for FY 1963.[17]

McNamara agreed to the reemphasis of conventional forces in terms of both more troops and enhanced logistics for transporting those troops to regional hot spots. The Cuban missile crisis of October 1962 looked to have justified flexible response as a strategic doctrine. The "excom" principals of the NSC explored plans for airstrikes against the missile sites in Cuba set up by Soviet personnel while Kennedy authorized the building up of conventional forces for an amphibious assault on the island. The quarantine announced by Kennedy in his October 22 address increased the pressure on the Soviets, and the U.S. agreed to dismantle its Jupiters in Turkey in exchange for the dismantling of their own missiles in Cuba. A military confrontation was fortuitously avoided at the last minute, but the crisis still proved the wisdom of flexible response to many officials. The Administration had been on the cusp of ordering airstrikes and a possible invasion, actions that in the absolute best case scenario would have confined armed conflict only to Cuba, not triggered Soviet reprisals against Berlin, and not caused general nuclear war. McNamara later remarked that had Kennedy not requested two additional divisions for the FY 1963 budget, the Army probably would have lacked the means to invade Cuba.[18]

The attention given to flexible response, airlift, and sealift, magnified by the crises in Berlin and Cuba, was still consistent with the long-held view that NATO ground forces needed to be heavy enough to hold back a general Soviet thrust. The Army developed and acquired a series of new weapons in the 1960s for use in Europe, even as the front-page news shifted to other parts of the world. The M60 medium tank first rolled onto the frontlines in 1960, beginning a long service life as the premier battle tank, followed by the Sergeant SSM, Chaparral short-range SAM, TOW anti-tank missile, and the installation of a Shillelagh missile onto a Sheridan light tank. Even though the Davy Crockett miniaturized nuclear platform was canceled for its apparent instability, NATO continued to rely on tactical nuclear weapons. NATO's leadership maintained an adaptable stance on these weapons, determining that they should be used on the battlefield based on changing conditions instead of any fixed rule. At the same time, the Military Committee allowed little room for error. Local actions involving smaller contingents of communist troops would very well not warrant a nuclear response, but a Soviet breakthrough of NATO defense lines left the alliance with limited opportunity for relying entirely on conventional forces. The Soviets, in any case, would likely not launch a conventional offensive without recognizing the strong possibility of a Western nuclear retaliation, which cast doubt on the viability of a purely conventional offensive from the East. The one constant in NATO deliberations was the continued utility of nuclear deterrence.[19]

NUCLEAR CONSIDERATIONS: COUNTERFORCE, MLF, SKYBOLT

The Administration brought a nuanced approach to defense policy, with the formulation of flexible response serving as an example of this nuance. The Administration sought to improve its ability to contend with specific contingencies in Europe and elsewhere, even if the U.S.'s military forces remained substantially the same in composition. The Administration briefly tried to advance a similar framework for the use of strategic weapons as well. At a conference of NATO defense ministers in Athens in May 1962, McNamara introduced the idea of counterforce, which was that the West should use nuclear weapons only to target the Soviet arsenal in the hope that this would best protect the home front against incoming enemy missiles and bombs. In that respect, McNamara regarded nuclear forces in ways very similar to conventional forces. Both were mainly intended to destroy enemy capabilities instead of reducing strategically unimportant urban areas to rubble and killing millions of innocent civilians. McNamara considered the latter outcome futile and not determinative of winning a nuclear war. He foresaw a gradual escalation in the nuclear exchange, much like the escalation inherent to conventional flexible response. McNamara still foresaw that if the Soviets did attack Western cities, the U.S. would in turn respond by striking Soviet cities and killing up to 100 million of their civilians. This second strike would rely upon a mixed arsenal of ICBMs, SLBMs, and bombers that survived the first strike and could be utilized in a timely manner.[20]

As with conventional flexible response, counterforce and nuclear flexible response did not overturn existing deterrence doctrine or the Triad structure first conceived under Eisenhower. McNamara explained that the U.S. still needed to hold overwhelming strategic forces in reserve in order to deter a general Soviet nuclear offensive against urban areas. Yet counterforce as an intellectual doctrine also proved to be short-lived, however much it might have enjoyed appeal for its "no cities" protocol. No one could really predict how a nuclear war would unfold, especially as both sides worked to ensure the survivability of their nuclear weapons after a first strike. Both sides planned to install their new ICBMs in hardened, underground silos hopefully secure from penetration by enemy warheads, while SLBMs were even more effectively hidden beneath the waves of the ocean. Members of the Administration could not escape the horrifying prospects of nuclear war with the Soviet Union, whatever their doctrinal efforts in mitigating damage and loss of life in such situations. McNamara's viewpoint soon graduated to assured destruction, which more realistically foresaw destruction of the opposing state's political, economic, and social foundations. As the U.S. and the Soviet Union proliferated their ICBMs in the 1960s, assured destruction became synonymous with the view that general nuclear war would largely doom human civilization, if not necessarily wipe out all humans living on the planet. In that sense, the use of strategic nuclear weapons in a general war could not be considered a veritable military option that brought any appreciable gain to the side using them.

For the Atlantic alliance, core strategy had not changed. The emerging doctrine of assured destruction only reinforced the assumption that nuclear weapons were the absolute safest bet in keeping Western Europe safe from invasion. Now the question turned to allocating nuclear weapons technology within the existing security framework. Having become increasingly stable and self-sufficient in the postwar era, the Western European allies were naturally going to demand a greater right of control over the use of nuclear force, while the British and French already had their own nuclear programs.

In a first step in the direction of multilateral control over nuclear weapons, Kennedy pledged to attach five Polaris subs to NATO forces, along with an unspecified number of additional subs over the longer-term, in an address before the Canadian Parliament in Ottawa in May 1961. He then went on to propose a possible "sea-borne missile force, which would be truly multilateral in ownership and control."[21]

The Administration wanted to coopt Western European nuclear programs by offering an alternative multilateral model. This multilateral model involved the manning of ships and bases with personnel of different nationalities, entailing a level of integration not envisioned since the Pleven Plan from the early 1950s for intermingling French and German combat units. The Administration's scheme might have been even more devious. By going through the motions of unveiling and seemingly attempting to implement an unworkable plan, the Administration could finally persuade the Western Europeans into abandoning their own nuclear programs and returning to the status quo of dependence on the U.S.'s nuclear umbrella for protection. The Europeans could then focus on strengthening their conventional forces, which was what the Administration wanted all along.[22] Whether or not this was actually the end goal, Administration policymakers, especially those in the State Department, argued that this Multilateral Force (MLF) be naval in character instead of land-based. Proponents of the plan offered several reasons for a seaborne force, as Kennedy had initially proposed it, instead of land-based missiles. The country hosting land-based missiles could easily seize untoward control over them during a crisis, while MLF ships operating in open water would not be susceptible to these interferences, especially when manned by multinational crews. Land-based missiles might also endanger nearby civilians during a Soviet retaliation.[23]

An Administration white paper moved the project along by determining that the MLF should consist of surface ships instead of subs, with Polaris or other IRBMs installed onto guided missile destroyers, a curious idea instead of the more expedient option of simply expanding the Polaris sub fleet under some international guise. A surface Polaris program had already been rejected for the U.S. Navy because subs guaranteed a second-strike capability in a way that surface ships could not. Yet so-called missile ships served NATO's interests in other ways, both political and strategic. Surface ships were more conducive to the internationalist bent of the project, which had been the impetus behind the MLF in the first place. Because sub operations were extremely complex, mixed manning might be impossible for certain assignments aboard submarines, while all Western European navies, including those of the smaller countries, could contribute trained seamen for surface ships. Surface ships would also not necessarily be easy prey for Soviet aerial or naval attack, especially if positioned deep within NATO defense lines in the coastal waters off Norway, Britain, and France. The Soviets could only with great difficulty pierce NATO's protective air screen, and the MLF surface ships would be able to outpace Soviet subs at sea.[24]

While guiding the MLF towards some distant outcome, the Administration inadvertently complicated the project's support among the Europeans by canceling the Skybolt ASM. The Pentagon had designed the ballistic Skybolt missile for compatibility both with its B-52s and British Vulcan bombers. Skybolt had become a key point in Anglo-American dialogue about improving the British nuclear deterrent. In strictly military terms, the decision to cancel appeared to have been a sound one. As Harold Brown, at the time serving as director of defense research and engineering, recounted, Skybolt was technically superior to the Hound Dog ASM, but a combined complement of Hound Dogs and Minuteman negated its particular usefulness. The cancellation might have also reflected assumptions at the time that manned, long-range bombers were becoming outmoded.[25]

The Administration would hold on to the existing fleet of B-52s, but it was no longer interested in expanding this fleet, while it had decided to forgo full-scale development and production of the B-70. With new advances in Minuteman on track, Skybolt's utility looked increasingly tenuous, whatever the ramifications for trans-Atlantic relations. The Skybolt cancellation could not have come as a complete shock to the British, and in any event Kennedy and British Prime Minister Harold MacMillan worked out a compromise at the Nassau conference in December 1962. Under the new agreement, the U.S. sold Polaris missiles to Britain, while Britain funded the costs of the warheads and construction of the new subs. According to the communique, American and British Polaris subs would also "be made available for inclusion in a NATO multilateral nuclear force," but the drafters did not otherwise explain what was meant by this "multilateral nuclear force."[26]

The Skybolt "crisis" had upset expectations of shared deployment of an ASM. It might also have caused consternation among Europeans about the earnestness of the Administration's commitment to the MLF. If Kennedy wanted to cancel Skybolt, then perhaps he would do the same to the MLF, especially if U.S. and British subs were going to be ambiguously joined into a "NATO multilateral nuclear force" that might void the need for a surface ship MLF including personnel from other countries. Perhaps aware of these concerns, the Administration continued to formulate the MLF after the Skybolt cancellation. It opted for surface ships instead of subs in early 1963, and it wanted to experiment with mixed manning by putting a multi-national crew on board a missile guided destroyer as a sort of test case.[27]

In trying to reconcile national nuclear programs with the MLF, the Administration proposed a package for France similar to the one reached with the British at Nassau. French President Charles de Gaulle, however, spurned the offer, wary that the purchase of Polaris missiles from the U.S. would unduly restrict France's scope of action in a national emergency. De Gaulle had already decided to exclude the U.K. from the European Economic Community (EEC), so in some sense a rejection of the American terms was necessary to present a consistent front. But from a technical standpoint the French nuclear capability was not as advanced as that of the British. Since the British could already build warheads and subs, the U.S. only needed to provide them with missiles. The French lacked any comparative capabilities, and whether the Kennedy Administration would furnish the French with this advanced hardware when it had explicitly not done so for the British was unclear. Any agreement between Kennedy and de Gaulle over nuclear weapons looks in retrospect futile, all the more so given de Gaulle's obstinance on British entry into the EEC. Perhaps fittingly, and in a foreshadowing of France's withdrawal from the NATO force structure three years later, de Gaulle rejected the U.S.'s offer for nuclear assistance in the same press conference in which he denied Britain admission into the common market.[28]

Holding down defense costs over the long-term depended upon a stable NATO. The MLF idea served as a superficial response to the deeper danger of European nuclear programs causing fissures within the Atlantic alliance, which might have thrown cost projections out of whack. In that regard, Kennedy proposed the MLF in response to problems that might have become evident within only a few years, and policymakers soon lost interest in the MLF as their attention became overwhelmed by Vietnam. The reactive tendencies of the Kennedy Administration bore similarity to those of the Truman Administration, except Kennedy worked to maintain the international architecture that Truman helped create. Kennedy's legacy took less of a concrete form and was more tied to his personal handling of some of the most dangerous moments of the Cold War. He repudiated austerity to engender a sense of separation between his defense policies and Eisenhower's, but his crisis-laden presidency also did not lead to a full-scale arms buildup.

The Administration instead oversaw a steady, undramatic increase in the defense budget, a trend that continued into FY 1964. The decision to cancel Skybolt had been partly motivated to eliminate costs of just over $500 million, and McNamara wanted to impose the F-111 Aardvark on the Air Force, Navy, and Marines, irrespective of their different tactical needs, in order to streamline development funding. The McNamara Pentagon clearly supported cutting costs where it could. It had to because of the inherent constraints on strategic planning. The drafting of the PPBS now included the formulation of five-year projections to better estimate the military's functional needs. In a document discussing FY 1964 budget requests as part of a five-year projection, McNamara concluded that conventional forces could successfully hold back a Soviet attack in any one of a handful of specified theaters—the Middle East, Southeast Asia, and Northeast Asia—but that multiple Soviet or other communist assaults in these regions necessitated a response partly conventional and partly nuclear. An entirely conventional response in Europe was still most likely unrealistic. McNamara could not ignore the dilemmas about where troop reinforcements should be sent and the extent of reliance on nuclear weapons in a worldwide conflict. The bulk of reinforcements would probably be deployed to Europe in the event of global hostilities, with NATO contingency plans assuming the U.S. field 17 of the 54 NATO divisions in the weeks after mobilization. McNamara approved the adequacy of the Army's 16 division structure, but he also raised the idea of mustering another 15,000 air assault troops, in addition to increasing Air Force fighter wings from 17 to 21.[29]

The report regarding FY 1964 budget options perhaps reflected the influence of the recent Cuban missile crisis on planning, during which these capabilities would have been useful. The Pentagon, meanwhile, did not deviate from its central goal of modernizing nuclear forces. The inventory of remaining Atlases and Titans, along with improved Minuteman and Polaris missiles, were expected to total 2,812 through 1968 compared to the plateauing bomber force of 630 B-52s and 66 B-58s.[30]

By early CY 1963, Kennedy wanted to moderate the growth in defense spending, which still counted for a little under 50% of total outlays. The Administration had already endured a pitched fight over the B-70 cancellation on Capitol Hill, and now it was likely to encounter resistance on the size of the defense budget in general. Facing these political obstacles, Kennedy requested funds to cover, among other items, another six Polaris subs and the tentative air assault division that McNamara had outlined in his report. He planned for $56 billion in defense expenditures for FY 1964, a $10 billion increase from 1960.[31]

This not insignificant growth in defense expenditures coincided with a moment of relative stability in international affairs. As tensions with the Soviets began to subside in 1963, the Administration could focus on arms control negotiations, especially now that the U.S.'s strategic arsenal had reached a more advanced stage of technological capability. Unable to conclude an agreement on atmospheric testing, Eisenhower had ordered a voluntary moratorium on testing in 1958 along with the Soviets and British. Kennedy wanted to adhere to this moratorium, but the Soviet detonation of the "tsar bomba" thermonuclear weapon in October 1961, the largest manmade explosion in history, among other actions forced him into resuming testing, even as he still sought an agreement. Negotiations led by veteran diplomat Averell Harriman stalled as the crises between the two powers reached a new intensity during 1961–1962. Harriman was only able to secure a draft treaty in 1963 after both sides agreed to exclude underground testing from the negotiations, which would have required an elaborate inspections regime. Covering only atmospheric, space, and oceanic testing, the Limited Nuclear Test Ban Treaty nonetheless allowed the Administration to come away with a tangible diplomatic achievement and a first step in arms control. But with both sides rapidly modernizing and expanding their arsenals, the nexus between arms control and reduced defense costs already looked weak.

The Administration had explored a number of ideas relating to conventional and nuclear forces. Flexible response offered a possible way to escape nuclear holocaust, while counterforce lacked plausibility in its attempt to calculate the incremental escalation of strategic strikes in a general war setting. The MLF and post-Skybolt compromises, meanwhile, served as constructive ideas for mitigating disagreements over nuclear policy within NATO. Yet the Administration could not turn back the clock on the arms race. The McNamara Pentagon continued to fund the buildup in the Minuteman arsenal. The proliferation of strategic arms on both sides necessitated a recognition of assured destruction. Without really changing the country's military posture, the Administration was far less emphatic on keeping defense spending to a necessary minimum. As a result, the defense budget in these years steadily increased in dollar expenditures under conditions of low inflation.

TAX CUTS PROPOSED

Kennedy took office two years after current accounts in goods and services turned fully convertible under the Bretton Woods system, in which the U.S. held a central position. Only its dollar was directly linked to gold, and the dollar had also replaced pound sterling as the world's reserve asset. The abnormal trade situation after the end of World War II had ended, and the U.S. sustained three annual current account deficits during the 1950s. Yet the return to fully functioning trade networks could not in any way be described as necessarily disadvantageous. The current account reflects both the competitiveness of a country's exports and the cost-efficient import of merchandise and commodities from abroad. The rebuilt economies in Europe and Japan exported manufactured goods to the U.S., while U.S. companies could tap into bigger markets overseas. U.S. companies did just that, initiating higher rates of long-term direct investment in Europe that sent the capital account into deficit, pulling the overall balance of payments into deficit as well, while the current account stayed positive, at times substantially so, through the 1960s. The capital account went negative during the convertibility phase of the Bretton Woods era because the flow of long-term investable funds out of the country exceeded the inflow of funds. The large outflows in the early 1960s were unsurprising since the U.S. still posted current account surpluses in these years, in keeping with the assumption that a negative capital account tends to counterbalance a positive current account.

But the capital outflows still presented an acute problem for the Administration. They threatened to translate into the export of gold as European central banks accumulated dollars, and they had turned the whole balance of payments negative. Only the expedient of a gold pool set up by central banks, which pegged a market price for private buyers of gold, kept the whole system effectively managed. The Kennedy and later Johnson Administration contrived various ways to stem the outflow of gold, whether linking foreign aid to U.S. exports or even taxing the purchase of foreign issued securities, but without positive result. Having done all possible to avoid returning to floating exchange rates, governments now struggled to maintain an artificial system of adjustable pegs with only a partial link to gold. The capital outflows signaled an overvalued dollar as the currency glutted overseas markets, a problem compounded by a diminishing current account surplus in the late 1960s. Devaluation of the dollar was always anathema to U.S. policymakers. Currency devaluation represented defeat and failure, an enormous loss of prestige that would prove only more disastrous if undertaken for the currency, the U.S. dollar, at the heart of the whole system.

The Administration faced the prospects of a more competitive, revived, international economic order. In the late 1800s, a time of relative economic stability, the U.S.'s industrializing economy had been protected by high tariff walls, but the tariff had not impeded robust agricultural exports. Now multilateral trade agreements mandated lower tariffs, with the Administration planning for another round of trade talks. In this more competitive arena, Kennedy faced economic growth as a challenge, something that had to be actively sustained through policies utilizing the tax code. Any such measures would inevitably impact budget balancing.

Kennedy launched this tax agenda in April 1961 with a message to Congress on his ultimate vision of reforming the tax code through base broadening. In more immediate terms he called for an investment tax credit on depreciable machinery and other equipment. He recommended a 15% credit "of all new plant and equipment investment expenditures in excess of current depreciation allowances," with a stepped down 6% credit for expenditures exceeding half of such allowances, and a 10% credit on the initial $5,000 in investment. The credit was tied to only new investment and excluded expenditures on certain forms of real estate, but otherwise it applied to various entities, from small businesses, which would hopefully take advantage of the bottom 10% credit, to large corporations building plants and other forms of fixed capital.[32]

The proposal also included measures to curtail expected revenue losses, such as by more stringently taxing the foreign profits of U.S. corporate subsidiaries operating overseas. The federal government at the time taxed the worldwide profits of U.S. corporations but allowed corporations to defer realized income earned abroad in the form of dividends. The Administration wanted to mitigate revenue losses attributable to deferral by imposing a tax on earnings of foreign subsidiaries not yet distributed through dividends.

This tax would only be limited to earnings in developed economies and not those in the Third World or a state of transition. Kennedy mentioned other ways to generate extra revenue, including a new 20% withholding on interest and dividends to clamp down on unreported income, repeal of the exclusion on the first $50 of dividend income, along with the 4% credit for dividend income over $50 (which dated to the 1954 tax overhaul), and restrictions on claiming deductions for business entertainment expenses.[33]

Kennedy obtained much but not all of what he wanted when Congress finally passed the legislation in October 1962. Instead of tiered credits tied to specific amounts of expenditure net of depreciation allowances, the Revenue Act of 1962 mandated a single 7% investment credit for machinery and other equipment without any link to depreciation allowances and available for carrybacks and carryforwards. For closing loopholes and offsetting revenue losses, the Act did not adopt Kennedy's proposal to tax the earnings of foreign subsidiaries, but it did end deferral for companies with foreign "tax haven income" constituting over 30% of their total income. This "tax haven income" served as a new term of art designating forms of passive income such as royalties, interest, and dividends, or income deriving from licenses, in advanced economies. Without entirely eliminating deferral, the Act considerably narrowed the circumstances under which companies could escape overseas tax liability through their foreign subsidiaries. The Act also modified Kennedy's proposal to mitigate the evasion of taxes on interest and dividends. Instead of imposing a hard-and-fast rule such as a 20% withholding rate, as Kennedy wanted, the Act expanded the requirements for taxpayers to submit information returns detailing their source of income, hopefully bringing greater transparency to the tax collection process. The Act further limited business entertainment deductions by, among other ways, capping deductions on gifts per person at $25. Congress did not act on Kennedy's request to eliminate the $50 exclusion or credit on dividend income.[34]

Kennedy largely won a legislative victory with the Revenue Act of 1962, but this did not stop him from pushing ahead with a plan for more decisive cuts in personal and corporate income taxes. Kennedy now opted to cut income taxes in order to accelerate the expansion that had been building since the economy had last dipped into recession in 1960. This expansion was apparently not strong enough for members of the Administration, including the cohort of "New Economics" academics staffing the Council of Economic Advisers (CEA). An ulterior rationale lay at the heart of cutting taxes. Because of the payments imbalance, the Administration could not as easily rely on loose monetary policy and low interest rates to spur growth. The Treasury and Federal Reserve had begun crafting an elaborate new policy regime for twisting the yield curve on securities, targeting higher yields for shorter dated securities relative to longer dated ones, precisely with the objective of stemming capital outflows. The payments imbalance thus heavily influenced the Administration's economic thinking, and it also provided a clue into its primary goals regarding the tax cut in the first place. In proposing the tax cut, with the top personal income rate dropping to 65%, Kennedy invoked the dual objectives of increased consumption and business investment. Kennedy predicted that in the event of a rate cut lower earners would increase their consumption and higher earners would expand their capital accumulation and investment, the latter scenario prefiguring "trickle-down economics" of the supply side school. A corporate rate cut would also incentivize business investment. As Kennedy pointed out, the Administration needed the tax cut to drive business investment in order to shore up the balance of payments by boosting exports and redirecting loanable funds back into the domestic economy. The cut in personal tax rates would boost consumption, but it would do so for the purpose of greasing investment. A tax cut wholly geared to consumption, under conditions in which plant equipment already operated at full capacity, would have needlessly fueled imports and worsened the payments imbalance. But Kennedy argued that these conditions did not exist and that the tax cut would boost productivity and output, thereby mitigating the effects of increased imports.[35]

The proposal for deep tax cuts radically departed from Eisenhower's relatively more staid pro-growth proposals, which were philosophically intended to return money to the people while still retaining progressive rates of over 90% on the highest earners. The Kennedy tax plan might also have seemed an improbable one by 1962, with the economy already recovering from recession and commencing the early stages of what would turn out to be a decade-long expansion (though admittedly this happened after the tax cuts eventually went into effect). Nor would tax cuts be in any way budget neutral. The Administration had thus far not succeeded in balancing the budget, with a deficit projected for FY 1963. Kennedy had originally planned for an optimally small $500 million surplus in FY 1963 on the theory that a deficit would be inflationary while a more sizeable surplus would only hamper economic growth.[36] Such a surplus never materialized, and in January 1963 the Administration was predicting an $8.8 billion deficit for that fiscal year, on the heels of an actual deficit of $6.4 billion for FY 1962.[37]

Kennedy sought to unfetter the American economy from the shackles of high marginal rates and juice it with even more robust growth. In many ways the tax cut proposal became emblematic of the Administration's idealistic creed of the New Frontier, that it was trying to do better than what it had inherited, and in blunt economic terms that meant higher GDP growth rates. In his address to Congress in January 1963, Kennedy called for slashing the top personal rate from 91% to 65% and the lowest rate from 20% to 14%. He also proposed cutting corporate taxes from 52% to 47%.[38] Even though this proposal included ways to eliminate loopholes, Kennedy had given up trying to balance the budget for the time being. His budget request for FY 1964 conceded a short-term deficit resulting from the proposed tax cuts.[39] Now the effort to pump up the economy and fulfill a greater potential in output and employment overwhelmed any more conventional concerns related to the deficit. Reiterating the arguments laid out in the budget request and in earlier public remarks, Kennedy posed before Congress a new dilemma between "chronic deficits resulting from chronic slack, on the one hand, and transitional deficits temporarily enlarged by tax revision designed to promote full employment and thus make possible an ultimately balanced budget."[40]

Kennedy's outlook on taxes and the budget must be understood in the context of what he inherited. The 1950s had been partly recessionary, with the downturns of 1953–1954 and 1957–1958 casting a shadow over Eisenhower's economic record. Overall, though, this record was not bad. Real GDP posted growth of 7% in 1955 and nearly 7% again in 1959, matched by slower growth of +2% in 1956, 1957, and 1960, the latter of which saw the beginning of a much shallower recession.[41] Growth had been highest in the years immediately following these recessions, while the recessions had in turn helped send the federal budget deep into the red. Kennedy could look to this record and make a reasonable claim that higher rates of economic growth facilitated budget balancing more than counterproductive spending cuts. Whatever the merits of the tax cuts in purely economic terms, however, no one could foresee, not even the highly schooled CEA economists, the extent to which the cuts might over the longer run enable budget balancing. In addition, Kennedy proposed the tax cuts at a time of increasingly robust growth. The economy had already expanded by over 6% in 1962 in real dollars.[42] But Kennedy expressed confidence that the American economy could reach a greater level of potential and that the deficit would eventually be overcome through expanded growth and full employment. For FY 1964, he allowed only a moderate increase in defense expenditures while intending to keep in check the growth in domestic spending.[43]

The Administration envisioned a longer-term plan for safeguarding the government from a destabilizing debt load and the economy from soaring inflation. Yet Kennedy still set in motion a policy shift that was considerably more lenient towards deficits than what prevailed under either Truman or Eisenhower. Trying to fathom how a two term Kennedy presidency might have dealt with rising deficits through the 1960s is beyond conjecture, but Kennedy did make clear in his public statements both that he was not prepared to cut the defense budget simply to curtail spending and that the tax cuts would in the near term lead to deficits.

Kennedy's support for expanding entitlements, especially new programs funded from general revenue, would have also impacted future budgets. He at first proceeded cautiously with Social Security, following in the footsteps of Truman and Eisenhower by marginally expanding coverage in coordination with payroll tax hikes. Kennedy signed into law the Amendments of

1961 that allowed seniors to become eligible for early retirement benefits at age 62 but at a reduced rate than those available at the full retirement age of 65. He also increased benefits for the blind and disabled. As with previous expansions to Social Security, these policies kept the program funded through dedicated sources and did not directly contribute to deficits.

Kennedy did, however, seek to expand the entitlement state in a new way with the creation of what would come to be known as Medicare, the health insurance program for the elderly and run through the Social Security Administration. After Truman's failure to push through national health insurance in Congress, many Democrats began to focus their energies on a program designed specifically for seniors. Kennedy latched on to the idea by the time he was elected president. He saw seniors as an especially needy group who, even if they had accumulated enough savings for retirement, could still be left destitute because of health care costs arising from an unexpected injury or ailment. In his speeches, such as at a rally at Madison Square Garden in May 1962, Kennedy seemed to imply that the new program would be funded through payroll taxes. The address was vague, and in his budget request for FY 1964 he proposed "health insurance for aged persons, to be financed mainly through the social security system, but with benefits for those not covered by social security to be paid from regular appropriations."[44] If Kennedy allowed some leeway in general revenue funding, he at least emphasized payroll taxes in his public remarks. Seniors would pay into the program over their working lives before becoming eligible at retirement age, just as in Social Security. The idea had gained the support of many Democrats, who now thought that the proposal should be tied closely to the popular Social Security program in order to bolster its political appeal.

Before Kennedy's presidency came to a tragically abrupt end, new ideas began to germinate on his watch that implied a growing acceptance of deficits, including more spending on conventional forces, deep tax cuts to boost economic growth over the long-term, and a new entitlement for providing health care to particular demographic groups. He left many of these goals unfulfilled or even only vaguely articulated, with the stage set for the next administration to move ahead on all fronts.

TAX CUTS ENACTED

The next administration belonged to Lyndon Johnson, who vowed to continue the agenda of the Kennedy presidency. True to his word, within months of assuming office he worked to accomplish goals that had eluded his slain predecessor, most importantly legislative backing of the income tax cuts that Kennedy had proposed a year before. With a few exceptions, Johnson also retained key members of Kennedy's Cabinet, including McNamara at Defense, Dean Rusk at State, and Douglas Dillon at Treasury, in addition to McGeorge Bundy as national security adviser. Yet the former Texas Senator and Majority Leader, a consummate political operator who frequently dispensed the "treatment" on those who found themselves useful to him, soon forged his own path on a wide range of issues, notably civil rights, entitlements, and escalation of the Vietnam War.

Johnson expedited legislation of the tax cut that had been stalled for a year on Capitol Hill before pursuing these other projects. He primarily wanted to fulfill the legacy not of John Kennedy but of Franklin Roosevelt, for whose New Deal he had been an ardent supporter since entering politics in the 1930s. Johnson was by background and inclination wholly absorbed with domestic issues and expanding upon the New Deal. That his administration became bogged down in a war in Vietnam raises a number of questions that cannot be easily answered. Johnson may have felt that losing Vietnam to the communists would have imperiled his domestic agenda in Congress and his own political standing. Even if he could not decisively win the war, he could at least temporarily avoid losing and bring the North Vietnamese to the peace table, helping him gain leverage over hawks in Congress and facilitating enactment of the programs that he hoped to define his presidency. Yet growing fiscal overreach came to define the Johnson presidency, that the government all at once attempted to enhance an affluent way of life, permanently expand the size of government, and fight a costly war on the other side of the world. This overreach could not last forever, and by the end of his full term in office Johnson had already set fiscal policy in a different direction while trying desperately to bring some resolution to the fighting in Vietnam.

In striving to enact tax legislation, he prevailed over fiscal conservatives in Congress and had the tax cuts passed as early as February 1964. These tax cuts served as a watershed in the evolution of economic policy. For the first time in recent memory a presidential administration was willing to sustain deficits in order to accelerate an expansion already underway (the 1948 tax cuts had originated in Congress). The Revenue Act of 1964 closely followed Kennedy's original proposal, with the top personal rate falling from 91% to 70%, the bottom rate from 20% to 14%, and the combined normal and surtax corporate rate from 52% to 48%, all told producing an $11.6 billion cut in tax liability, $9.2 billion for individuals and $2.4 billion for corporations. The corporate rate was still bifurcated between a normal tax rate and a surtax, with the surtax rate on corporate incomes over $25,000 raised from 22% to 28%, as opposed to a rate reduction from 30% to 22% in the normal tax bracket. One of the original selling points of the cuts was that it would serve as a reform measure broadening the tax base, and the cuts did eliminate or reduce a number of miscellaneous breaks in the code, including the dividend credit, the exclusion on employer provided group life insurance, and deductions for state and local excise taxes. Yet the legislation mainly reduced taxes instead of reforming the code, such as would have been accomplished through the elimination of tax shelters and other distortions.[45]

In his remarks upon signing the legislation, Johnson noted that the tax cuts would fuel private investment, adding how an expert had predicted that the cuts "will materially stimulate a boom of capital goods expenditures" in the coming years. If anything, Johnson emphasized the tax law's positive implications for business investment instead of full employment and consumption. He claimed that his administration "doubted the wisdom" of pursuing higher spending, opting rather to inject money directly into the private economy through lower taxes. He punctuated the address by personally vowing that the executive branch agencies would reduce their operating budgets to keep spending in line.[46] Johnson knew the Administration needed to rein in spending to appease fiscal conservatives in Congress. His promise of belt tightening facilitated enactment of the legislation barely three months after taking office.

The legislation retroactively implemented part of the cuts to January 1, 1964, in order to immediately stoke the economy, which redounded to Johnson's political advantage heading into the election year, before fully phasing in the cuts the next year. The cuts appeared to work in driving business investment, which rose from 6% growth in 1963 to 9.4% in 1964, then to 19.7% in 1965.[47] Growth in consumption expenditures were comparatively more moderate, rising over the same period by 5.3%, 7.5%, and 7.9%.[48] Consumption still made up the major share of GDP, at about 60% compared to 17% for business investment,[49] but increased growth in the latter boded well for gains in productivity and competitiveness at a time when a robust current account needed to offset the capital outflows and help strengthen the dollar.

The economy very quickly reached a point close to or at peak capacity shortly after the passage of the tax cuts. Real GDP had risen from 5.5% in 1963 to 7.4% in 1964, and then 8.4% in 1965.[50] The unemployment rate had fallen to 4.5%, its lowest level since 1957.[51] Inflation had not yet become a problem, but the shift to full employment quickly led to concerns over inflation, which had stayed below 2% during the early 1960s. Many economists assumed the increasing scarcity of labor would drive up wages and then prices, a result of the unavoidable tradeoff between employment and inflation. Price growth had reached 3% at the peak of the last expansion in 1957. This fear could not be ignored, but for now price growth in consumer spending excluding food and energy had marginally fallen from 1.5% in 1964 to 1.2% in 1965.[52] Thus by 1965 the Administration had succeeded in juicing the economy to the maximum extent without immediately setting off a wage-price spiral.

Congress passed the Revenue Act of 1964 ten years before the economist Arthur Laffer famously drew his eponymous curve on a restaurant napkin, which depicts how a high enough marginal rate eventually disincentives work and reduces revenue. As depicted graphically, a 100% tax on income causes revenue to plummet to zero, and of course the highest marginal rate in the code up until 1964, at 91%, was very close to 100%, which had induced higher earning taxpayers to seek shelters or more favorable capital gains treatment. The proponents of the tax plan could justifiably point to the fact that World War II had originally pushed personal income tax rates over the 90% threshold, the Korean War pushed them back up there, and that now taxes on the highest earners needed to be brought back to a normal rate. The Revenue Act did not start triggering destabilizing deficits. Affecting returns filed from January 1, 1964, the legislation contributed to a budget deficit totaling $5.9 billion for FY 1964. The deficit then narrowed to $1.4 billion the next year before opening once again to $3.7 billion in 1966.[53] As even the proponents of the plan conceded, the tax cuts led to short-term revenue losses, which were later estimated at 1.6% of GDP.[54] Because tax rates had been so high beforehand, the context surrounding the tax cuts offered a case study in whether the boost in growth and employment offset projected revenue losses. In current dollars revenue kept climbing in the mid-1960s, with total on-budget revenue rising from $92.385 billion in 1963 to $96.284 billion in 1964, and then to $100 billion by 1965, in other words a nearly $8 billion gain in current dollar revenue in the first two years in which the tax cuts were phased in.[55] The rise in current dollar revenue occurred under conditions of weak inflation. Revenue as a percentage of GDP, on the other hand, dipped from 16.7% in 1963 to 16.5% in 1964, and then to 15.7% in 1965. It rose again to 17.3% in 1967 after the phase-in of tax hikes.[56]

At the very least, the 1964 tax cuts succeeded in keeping revenue at sustainable levels, consistent with the expectations of Kennedy and his economic advisers. Revenue did not contract in nominal terms. But other factors began impacting the budget within only a few years, including the rise in social welfare spending and escalation of the war in Vietnam. As foreseen by Kennedy, the tax cuts should have caused only a transitory dip in revenue before the return to surpluses through stable economic growth. This economic growth would continue, but it would not be under stable conditions.

VIETNAM

The threat of communist takeover in South Vietnam had heavily occupied the attention of members of the Kennedy Administration by late 1963. In his almost three years in office Kennedy had dramatically increased the U.S.'s ground presence to 16,000 personnel, including Special Forces and military advisers, as well as logistical support for the South Vietnamese regime. Kennedy's escalation in Vietnam conformed to his calls for stopping the spread of communism in the Third World and his attention to the incremental application of conventional forces to limited military contingencies. The Administration did not actively carry out Diem's overthrow in early November 1963. It authorized a military coup to proceed but did not otherwise interfere. It still may have created a sense that the U.S. was now permanently engaged in Vietnam and therefore invested in that country's future, a questionable proposition as the non-communist government steadily lost ground to the Viet Cong insurgents and their North Vietnamese sponsors. Diem had been an autocratic ruler, but his demise signaled a new period of political turmoil in the South as the cabal of generals replacing him oversaw a loss of control to the communists.

In March 1964 McNamara submitted to Johnson a memorandum recounting his impressions from a fact-finding trip to Saigon. The report reaffirmed that the U.S. presence should still mainly take the form of a training and advisory mission, though ominously it also warned that the Viet Cong were now entrenched in about 40% of rural areas. Within only the past few months the government in Saigon had exhibited a perceptible faltering as militias increasingly deserted it and local officials rapidly replaced one another in a number of different posts, hampering the efficient administration of the hamlets.[57] The challenges posed by Vietnam perplexed members of the JCS and the Administration, forcing them to consider a wide range of options for escalation, including commencement of an air war against the North and expansion of the ground presence, which would be needed to protect deployed air assets. Escalation in Vietnam would mark the first overt shooting since Korea, and the geographic and topographic differences between the two battlegrounds were immense. The shape of the Korean peninsula had allowed U.N. forces to strike the North Korean army from the rear with an amphibious assault in September 1950. The local geography later allowed the retreating and disorganized U.N. forces to regroup south of Seoul and start pushing the Chinese back north of the 38th Parallel. The barren landscape had been favorable to concentrated artillery fire and airpower, benefiting the U.N. South Vietnam, on the other hand, shared borders with North Vietnam, Laos, and Cambodia. Along these borders the communists ran guns and supplies through the Ho Chi Minh Trail. Most of all, the jungles of Vietnam eliminated the U.S.'s advantage in superior firepower over the Viet Cong. If the Administration wanted to contemplate the deployment of ground forces to South Vietnam, then it would also have to determine the scope of its theater of operations and whether U.S. troops should be allowed to venture into border areas. Like Vietnam, the Korean War had been a limited conflict, a "police action" sanctioned by the U.N. Security Council. But the very geography of Korea made partial victory in this conflict possible and negated the need to expand it by opening a bombing campaign against China. South Korea shared its only land border with North Korea, while South Vietnam's jungle-clad borders with three other countries had already rendered it extremely vulnerable to enemy infiltration.

The differences in waging these two conflicts also extended to public finance. Truman adamantly vouched for pay-go rules to fund the Korean War, raising taxes in 1950 and 1951, including the imposition of an excess profits tax on companies, which helped turn in a surplus for FY 1951. These surpluses could not be repeated in subsequent years as funding costs climbed and the public clamored for an end to the war, but higher taxes were in place to help fund the added spending. Johnson had just succeeded not only in cutting taxes but in implementing a new economic policy that could not be easily undone. Unless the Administration wanted to rely entirely on deficit spending to fund military conflict, it would have to find means for raising revenue.

The fact that Johnson found himself authorizing a heavier presence in South Vietnam betrayed how much the situation was getting worse, as indicated by McNamara's March 1964 report. A handful of events set in motion the large-scale deployment of ground forces in July 1965. The dispatch of destroyers to the regional waters near Vietnam, codenamed De Soto missions, precipitated two instances of alleged hostile North Vietnamese action collectively known afterwards as the Gulf of Tonkin incident. When Congress granted Johnson sweeping powers for the use of military force in Indochina in August 1964, he had still not been reelected, and nor did he necessarily seem inclined to invoke the resolution for the use of force. The election pitted him against the hawkish Senator Barry Goldwater, and Johnson was not about to call for the deployment of hundreds of thousands of troops to the South before his reelection. But events began to pressure Johnson into taking more active steps towards ground intervention. Viet Cong guerrillas bombarded the airbase at Bien Hoa shortly before the election, destroying or severely damaging U.S. aircraft on the tarmac, followed by more attacks on American servicemen and aircraft in Pleiku province early in the new year.

These actions compelled Johnson to order aerial reprisals, eventually the longer-term Rolling Thunder bombing campaign against North Vietnam, which after a few false starts began in March 1965, and the sending of Marine units to protect the aircraft used for these operations. Johnson was being steadily dragged deeper into a war that he had assumed command of when becoming president, at least in the sense that hawks in the political and military establishment by now felt an obligation to help South Vietnam avoid takeover. A pullout in 1965 would in the eyes of many tarnish the U.S.'s credibility for assisting its non-communist allies. Johnson brooded over the repercussions of such a pullout on his domestic agenda. Deputy national security adviser Francis Bator tellingly recounted how Johnson decided to virtually camouflage his decision to send another 175,000 ground troops to

Vietnam in July 1965 by holding a news conference early in the afternoon while simultaneously unveiling a new Supreme Court nomination.[58]

As the Administration was sucked into an open-ended military commitment, it needed to find ways to fund escalation without disrupting economic growth or endangering Johnson's cherished domestic priorities. When submitting his budget request for FY 1966 in January 1965, Johnson omitted any mention of Vietnam. He in fact estimated only $51.6 billion in defense expenditures for the year, a decrease of over $2 billion from FY 1964.[59] He devoted most of his budget message to the Great Society, but within the next month he would be authorizing Rolling Thunder. With no one able to predict the outcome in Vietnam over even the near term, the Administration started relying on supplemental appropriations to fund escalation at the end of FY 1965 and during the course of 1966 and 1967. The reliance on supplementals was hardly unprecedented, but the nature of the fighting in Vietnam looked much different than in Korea, lacking clear frontlines or even an effective way of measuring victory. McNamara's performances on Capitol Hill during this critical period failed to quell public criticism of a "credibility gap" caused by the Administration's reluctance to discuss the challenges in Vietnam with greater candor. First Johnson asked for $700 million in supplemental spending at the end of FY 1965, even before the major expansion in ground forces that July.[60] Then McNamara estimated the need for a $1.7 billion amendment early in FY 1966. Congress granted both requests.[61] McNamara next sought $12.3 billion in January 1966 to fund a projected deployment of over 300,000 ground troops.[62]

Budget planning was tied to the premise that the war would reach a hypothetical conclusion by the end of each fiscal year. For FY 1966, Pentagon officials intended these planning techniques to keep supplemental requests synched as closely as possible with the needs of the military on the ground.[63] The Administration always presented projected Vietnam-related military expenditures for the following fiscal year as an item distinct from the rest of the budget, including the defense budget. Johnson perhaps hoped that in framing the budget request this way he could demonstrate that Vietnam posed a temporary problem eventually resolvable by applying enough military pressure on the North Vietnamese. For instance, in submitting his FY 1967 budget request, Johnson estimated $50 billion in regular defense expenditures on top of $10 billion for combat costs in Vietnam, not including military and economic aid to the South Vietnamese government.[64] A year later Johnson successfully asked for $12.3 billion in supplemental funds to keep the war funded beyond FY 1967.[65]

These erratic budget dynamics paralleled the lack of clear military movements on the ground. Johnson generally gave the theater commander, William Westmoreland, broad parameters in waging a counterinsurgency based on search and destroy and attrition, provided he restricted his operations to within South Vietnam. U.S. forces successfully fought a few pitched battles against the North Vietnamese Army and Viet Cong, but isolated firefights failed to destroy enemy forces, who were always drawing on new recruits. Westmoreland fought an amorphous enemy that constantly disappeared amid jungle and rice paddies, depriving the Administration the opportunity to tout any meaningful victory except kill ratios, which if high enough might reach a "crossover point" whereby the Viet Cong lost more guerrillas than it could recruit. U.S. forces focused on subduing the Viet Cong from forward bases in the central highlands while the South Vietnamese Army pacified the rural hamlets throughout the country. But trying to rally the peasants into supporting the regime presented a far greater social and political challenge that sheer military advantage could not alone overcome.

The Administration much more closely managed the air war. It forbade Westmoreland from targeting the Ho Chi Minh Trail with airstrikes, which led hawks to criticize Johnson for stifling the war effort and imposing too narrow a strategy on the military. Yet McNamara and Johnson mainly micromanaged the war by carefully controlling the Rolling Thunder campaign. Ongoing until he unilaterally ordered a bombing halt in October 1968, Johnson hoped the campaign would force the North Vietnamese to the peace table and bring about a timely armistice. Fearing that a comprehensive bombing campaign might trigger Chinese intervention and cause further domestic unrest already evident in the unruly college campuses and cities, he at first limited bombing targets to mobile, tactical equipment. Only after a year did he approve targeting storage facilities for oil and lubricants, which in any other war would have been immediately hit. The North Vietnamese capital of Hanoi and other areas near the border with China were off limits to bombing. McNamara and Johnson became so immersed in the details of Rolling Thunder that they approved bombing targets at Tuesday luncheons in the White House.

The war caused a shift in priorities within the defense budget. The Kennedy Administration had articulated flexible response as a doctrine implicitly subordinate to the modernization of strategic nuclear forces, but the war was bound to sap at least some funds from modernization, while flexible response provided an intellectual framework for escalation in Vietnam. McNamara needed to find ways to cut costs as the Pentagon continued development of the Minuteman II and III ICBMs and Poseidon SLBMs, which would in time replace Polaris, as well as the multipurpose F-111. The Pentagon instead began purchasing larger quantities of ammunition, M16 assault rifles, and helicopters. The latter had earlier served as a useful application of flexible response when McNamara wanted to test the idea of an air assault division. The division was ultimately disbanded in favor of bulking up the 1st Cavalry Division with over 400 helicopters. The 1st Cavalry soon saw active duty in Vietnam, with the UH-1 Iroquois fulfilling various combat functions for the

Army. Bell Aircraft Corporation ended up manufacturing nearly 800 UH-1s by 1965, while the Army also procured in large numbers AH-1G Cobra attack helicopters and CH-47 Chinook transports.[66]

The Johnson Administration became bogged down in Vietnam when the president above all wanted to forge ahead with the Great Society. A manipulative and skilled legislator, Johnson had far less experience in foreign affairs. Visiting South Vietnam at one point during his vice presidency and proclaiming Diem the "Winston Churchill of Asia," he relied on outside guidance for managing the region. Had Johnson possessed greater confidence in international relations and in his own political standing he might have felt more secure in scaling back the already robust presence that he took over. He instead massively escalated the air war and ground presence in the hope that this would somehow bring North Vietnam to its knees as quickly as possible. Only this interpretation can help explain Johnson's extraordinary effort to simultaneously engage in a regional shooting war and to permanently expand the reach of government, which inevitably drove bigger deficits.

ARMS CONTROL: THE PARALLEL AGENDA

Even if the Vietnam War only generated short-term costs, it still consumed the Administration's attention and may have impeded its ability to reach a dramatic new agreement on strategic arms with the Soviets as firefights raged in the jungles of Southeast Asia, casualties mounted, and opposition to the war grew more virulent. The arms race had accelerated the development of increasingly destructive weapons. Negotiations with the Soviets potentially provided a way out of this vortex, the added implication being that detente might ultimately help push down defense costs. That was not because of the necessarily exorbitant costs of new weapons. Transitioning from Minuteman I to the heavier Minuteman II and the Minuteman III would carry a hefty but still manageable price tag of $2.9 billion over a four-year period from 1967 to 1971.[67] Rather, detente might lead to a more relaxed international environment in which the seemingly self-propelled rise in total defense costs, including for conventional and nuclear forces, could be more feasibly restrained. The Administration wanted to pick up where Kennedy had left off after signing the Limited Nuclear Test Ban Treaty, which the Senate ratified in the fall of 1963. It sought a more comprehensive agreement on strategic offensive and defense capabilities that might finally end the arms race just as both sides were rapidly building up their arsenals of ICBMs.

Successful arms control diplomacy depended on the development of weapons systems at home and the leverage gained from this at the negotiating table. For better or worse, the Eisenhower Administration neglected an agreement on offensive arms just as it presided over the deployment of the first guided ballistic missiles. Eisenhower seemed to want to reach a grand bargain with Khrushchev in 1960, but sudden misfortune in the form of a downed U-2 deprived him the opportunity to even start a new round of talks. By the time Kennedy came into office ICBMs and SLBMs had been deployed, but he soon found himself boxed into responding to a series of crises before finally reaching an agreement with the Soviets on testing. With Dean Rusk still at State, Johnson wanted to carry forward this agenda, even if burdened by the Vietnam War and the danger that it might again turn relations with the Soviets frigid, made clear by his decision to respond to the Viet Cong attack on Pleiku with air strikes against North Vietnam while Soviet Premier Alexei Kosygin was visiting Hanoi.[68]

ABM systems threatened to upend arms control calculations. McNamara remained dubious of the viability of ABM, a view shared by many members of the scientific community. His thinking having evolved from counterforce to assured destruction, McNamara assumed that a large enough missile attack could overwhelm even the most sophisticated ABM system, rendering the whole undertaking futile, especially as ICBMs and SLBMs became equipped with multiple independently targetable reentry vehicles (MIRVs) containing multiple warheads per missile within the next decade. Nonetheless, he continued to back the ABM effort and in 1963 integrated the Nike-X system into an existing Army project office that had been managing work on the Nike-Zeus missile. The Army set up a test range for Nike-X missiles on Kwajalein Atoll in the Pacific.[69] The Johnson Administration wanted to increase funds for the program, but to put matters in perspective funding for Nike-X came out of an Army R&D budget of $1.4 billion for FY 1964.[70] Eventual deployment would be much costlier, especially if Nike-X were to provide both blanket area defense from coast to coast and point defense over specific cities and missile installations. One Army study projected costs of $9.4 billion only for the initial two phases of deployment for point coverage over 25 cities. If the Pentagon expanded deployment to an additional 26 cities as planned, then total costs for ABM would only rise further.[71]

The Pentagon faced an apparent dilemma of whether to pour money into an ABM system that could be easily penetrated in any event or to veer to the opposite extreme by aggressively MIRVing all of its ICBMs and SLBMs and demonstrating the futility of ABM to the Soviets once and for all. The dilemma was in actuality not quite that simple, and the Pentagon instead tried to adapt to changing conditions over a shorter-term horizon. The Chinese had already tested an atomic device in 1964 and were now developing a thermonuclear warhead. An ABM system could perhaps defend against a more limited Chinese attack or a missile accidentally firing from a Soviet base. The Soviets, meanwhile, started building their own small-scale ABM network around Moscow based upon the new Galosh missile. When at a summit meeting in Glassboro, New Jersey, in June 1967 Johnson and Rusk pressed

Kosygin to desist from these efforts and to hopefully begin discussions that encompassed ABM, Kosygin refused and implied that ABM would not destabilize the arms race. It was, in his words, purely defensive. The failure to reach an understanding on ABM at Glassboro forced McNamara's hand. Only a few months later he announced Sentinel, a smaller ABM designed specifically against Chinese attack, which would initially provide point defense for up to ten cities. It could then be expanded to include additional cities and offensive missile silos.[72]

Even while under the stresses of the Vietnam War, Johnson made a last-ditch effort to achieve a breakthrough agreement on offensive and defensive systems in 1968, coming surprisingly close to reaching this goal. Congress's vote to appropriate funds for Sentinel along with the successful testing of Minuteman III and Poseidon may have compelled the Kremlin to keep talks alive. Such an achievement could have built upon the success of the Nuclear Weapons Nonproliferation Treaty, which Johnson and Kosygin signed in July 1968 and which still awaited Senate ratification. The signatories of this treaty intended to keep the development of nuclear weapons confined to a small group of countries, which in turn pledged not to disseminate their weapons to non-nuclear countries. The agreement did not entirely succeed in preventing the spread of nuclear weapons technology. Several countries refused to sign it, including China, which had already tested nuclear weapons. But the agreement promised a new era of detente and possibility in East-West dialogue. The agreement also sank the MLF idea, the U.S. would not relinquish its nuclear weapons by law during peacetime, and Britain and France would remain the only Western European nuclear powers. The U.S. might still deploy theater missiles to Europe as part of its commitment to NATO, but these deployments did not breach the terms of the Nonproliferation Treaty, provided the U.S. retained custody and control over its missiles in time of peace.

The Johnson Administration could not quite reach a lasting agreement on strategic weapons in its last year. During preliminary discussions U.S. officials offered a freeze on new offensive missiles and limits on ABM, to which the Soviets appeared receptive. The Soviets had good reason to accept a freeze before the U.S. MIRVed all of its land and sea-based missiles, and they even planned to welcome Johnson for a Leningrad summit. But by late August the Prague Spring movement and the subsequent Soviet invasion of Czechoslovakia muted these deliberations, delaying talks for a few months, by which time Johnson was nearly out of office. President-elect Nixon refused to allow himself to be tied to any agreement signed weeks before his inauguration. The Johnson Administration may have set in motion a new framework for the Strategic Arms Limitation Talks (SALT), but its time had simply run out.[73]

Even had Johnson concluded a momentous agreement on strategic arms, it would have carried minimal budgetary impact with the continuing costs of the Vietnam War. Johnson's efforts still demonstrated the potential for detente and the hope that a thaw in East-West relations could help push down defense costs. Unfortunately, he pursued this agenda at the height of a military conflict that could not be ended quickly enough.

WAR ON POVERTY, GREAT SOCIETY

As the Johnson Administration became drawn into war, the president signed legislation creating new programs that caused a dramatic rise in domestic discretionary and mandatory spending. Johnson focused upon expanding entitlements and welfare. The two terms are sometimes confused, with entitlements occasionally denoting only those programs containing an at least partly pay-in component. Entitlements can be more generally understood as any mandatory spending program for which eligibility is automatically determined through defined criteria. Entitlement and welfare programs overlap, and a pedantic distinction between the two should be avoided. Both are designed to assist the livelihoods of specific demographic groups, and both are governed by uniform rules of eligibility.

Johnson announced the War on Poverty in his address before Congress in January 1964 before reiterating this message from the porch of a dwelling in eastern Kentucky. As indicated by its very name, Johnson spoke of his antipoverty crusade in militaristic terms both as a "war" and an "attack." The objective of this war was the elimination of poverty existing among supposedly 20% of the population, and he conceived of virtual weapons with which to prosecute it. Johnson justified the War on Poverty and the Great Society on the grounds that an expanding economy and growing population, the two of which were interlinked, made it all affordable. He also thought that the expanding economy necessitated additional spending. Projecting population growth of 17% into the mid-1960s,[74] he argued in his budget request for FY 1966 that "[a]s our population increases, as science and technology change our methods of doing things, as our wants multiply with the growth in our incomes, and as urbanization creates new problems, there is growing need for more public and private services."[75] Johnson's whole project depended on robust economic growth, and at least for his purposes he chose the right moment to advance this agenda, since the economy was indeed in the middle of a long expansion. To raise the standard of living among the less fortunate, Johnson described an "all-out attack on the problem of poverty" that relied principally on local community organizing backed by federal grants. He sought $1 billion in funding for programs focused on enhancing the employment prospects of poor youths.[76]

Johnson proclaimed an enormous goal, nothing short of ridding the country of poverty. The means for achieving this was an array of programs that provided training and job opportunities to afflicted youth, especially those in blighted urban areas. The War on Poverty was related to but distinguishable from the Great Society, which Johnson announced as a new national goal in a commencement address at the University of Michigan in May 1964. Johnson here presented the pillars of the Great Society as education, urban renewal, environmentalism, and civil rights. While the phrase Great Society became a catchall for the social welfare programs that Johnson wanted to implement, he did not present it in strictly economic terms in the address. If anything, a strong economy naturally led to the Great Society, "a place where men are more concerned with the quality of their goals than the quantity of their goods[.]"[77]

The War on Poverty and the Great Society led to several new domestic initiatives. In 1964, legislation set up the Office of Economic Opportunity, charged with running programs aimed at reviving the career prospects of poor youths, among them Head Start, Job Corps, and Work-Study. That same year Congress passed legislation creating Aid to Families with Dependent Children (AFDC), a welfare program for families with single parents, and the Food Stamp Act. A connection had long existed between soaking up excess agricultural output, compensating farmers, and doling out food stamps. Congress passed the first farm bill, the Agricultural Assistance Act, in 1933, which required the federal government to purchase agricultural products and redistribute the foods, mostly commodities, to the needy through a network of state and local governments. Food stamps were introduced in 1939 as a better way to streamline the process, but they still constituted only one component of a program intended in macro terms to boost farm prices and mitigate the effects of an oversaturated market. These conditions ceased to exist by the height of World War II, and food stamps stayed on the backburner until Kennedy brought them back as part of a pilot program. The passage of the Food Stamp Act in 1964 marked another step in the expansion of the entitlement-welfare state funded from general revenue. With Johnson's prodding, Congress also established the Departments of Housing and Urban Development (HUD) and Transportation to consolidate federal oversight of housing and infrastructure projects.

Yet Johnson's desire to create new health care entitlements ultimately had a greater effect upon the federal budget sheet. Here he wanted to succeed where Roosevelt, Truman, and Kennedy had fallen short. In his health care proposals, Johnson settled upon hospital insurance for the elderly instead of national health insurance, what became Medicare Part A, much as Kennedy had done. A program limited to hospital insurance could have been conceivably funded entirely through payroll taxes instead of general revenue. In working out compromises between their differing proposals, members of the

House Ways and Means Committee combined the Part A idea with a voluntary Part B program for physicians' services and outpatient care. These compromises inevitably caused the final version to rely on an eclectic group of funding sources. Because most seniors would be automatically eligible for hospital care, Part A Hospital Insurance (HI) relied like Social Security on a new payroll tax with a wage base, while premiums and general revenue paid for Part B Supplementary Insurance (SI). Medicare otherwise incorporated a fee for service payment model. Physicians and other health care providers charged patients for specific services, with Medicare directly reimbursing providers on a reasonable cost basis for medically necessary procedures.

Policymakers would in time deem these standards inadequate and seek more effective cost containment measures. But these policies later pursued in the 1980s did not lead to any significant restructuring of the program. By additionally relying upon general revenue and premiums Medicare lacked the more straightforward funding structure of Social Security. As Medicare continued to evolve, new conflicts emerged over how to fund expansions in the program and make health care for seniors more comprehensive, triggering debate of whether funding should come from payroll tax hikes, higher premiums, or general revenue, or more likely a combination of at least two of these sources. While payroll tax hikes and extensions in coverage enabled Social Security expansion, Medicare expansion did not as clearly implicate a particular funding source because of its more complex design.

The 1965 Social Security Amendments enacting Medicare also included provisions for the creation of Medicaid, a system of health care benefits for low income families. As a joint federal-state program, Medicaid was structured much differently than Medicare. States were granted autonomy in running their own Medicaid programs, with the federal government providing 50% or more in matching funds, all deriving from general revenue. While federal law imposed both restrictions and mandatory requirements for Medicaid eligibility, states could still expand eligibility in certain ways without necessarily sacrificing federal dollars. Federal law originally excluded single, childless adults, even those well below the federal poverty line, from eligibility. At the same time, federal law required that all families enrolled in AFDC be automatically eligible for Medicaid. States, however, could also pay out benefits to "medically needy" families beyond the AFDC limits but that were disproportionately hampered by medical expenses compared to other costs of living. Children of two-parent families were eligible for Medicaid if the family's income stayed within AFDC limits (two-parent families were not eligible for AFDC). Federal matching funds could thus be directed into expanded state Medicaid programs outside the full control of federal authorities.

Now that entitlement programs relied at least in part on general revenue for funding, transfer payments to individuals under these programs started contributing to deficits. Transfer payments under Medicaid rose to $2.3 billion by 1969.[78] Medicare's contribution to deficits rose to the extent of general revenue spending for Part B transfers, which increased to $984 million by 1969 compared to premium income of $903 million.[79] Medicaid spending continued its ascent in the next decade while the federal contribution to Medicare SI overwhelmingly outstripped premium income. Now the federal government could not as easily secure balanced budgets in the near term as transfers under Medicare and Medicaid increased in the aggregate and took up general revenue. Nor were these payments necessarily countercyclical. Unlike unemployment insurance funded through payroll taxes, these transfers cut into the government's revenue in a recession or in an expansion.

The transfer payments under Medicare and Medicaid represented a long-term shift in the budget that played out over decades. Over the shorter-term, Johnson also utilized the discretionary budget to expand upon existing New Deal programs and build up the Great Society. Housing and urban renewal programs were by their very character intended to increase affluence and standard of living. A key barometer, the national homeownership rate, rose slightly from 63.0% in 1965 to 64.3% by 1969 (to put in perspective within the whole last half century it peaked at 69% in 2004).[80] The Federal Housing Administration (FHA) and the Federal National Mortgage Association (Fannie Mae), both established in the New Deal years and grouped within HUD, had helped strengthen a housing market through interventionist mandates. The FHA extended mortgage insurance to borrowers to incentivize lending by financial institutions while Fannie infused liquidity into a robust secondary market by purchasing FHA mortgages from lenders. In reaction to rising deficits, Johnson acted to fully privatize Fannie in 1968, with the institution relying on equity stock instead of appropriations to finance its operations. The FHA, meanwhile, remained largely self-financed within HUD through the collection of premiums from borrowers. Other HUD programs were not self-financed. The Department spent funds on urban renewal, neighborhood facility grants, open space land grants, water and sewer grants, demonstration cities, and public housing. With estimated authority to spend $3.78 billion by 1968,[81] HUD's mandate testified to the sweep of the Administration's concern for broad sectors of the economy, a departure of scale from the "small potatoes" Fair Deal, as Johnson had derided Truman's own iteration of the New Deal. The Great Society legislation initiated a shift in the bulk of expenditures from defense to domestic programs, even in the middle of a long war. 1961, the year of the Berlin crisis, marked the last time defense expenditures made up at least 50% of total outlays. Remarkably, defense spending stayed under 50% of this total, in a range of between 42% and 46%, during the course of the war, when in 1970 its share dropped further to 41.8%.[82]

RECA

Johnson pursued increased social welfare and defense spending after having massively cut taxes. The deficit predictably widened to $8.8 billion at the start of FY 1967, with the Treasury projecting it to balloon further to $25.2 billion by FY 1968.[83] As early as mid-1966 Johnson knew that he was going to have to push for tax hikes to clamp down on the deficits. His economic advisers and Federal Reserve officials counseled him to request tax hikes from Congress, both to mitigate deficits and inflation. Yet members of Congress faced reelection that year and were reluctant to press ahead with unpopular taxes. Moreover, Johnson worried that tax hikes would only further weaken support for his domestic agenda, which was already endangered by the quagmire in Vietnam. He first proposed a very temporary fix, a less than two-year suspension in the investment tax credit and in accelerated depreciation, which seemed like a timely measure amid the continuing economic expansion. Congress acted on the legislation in November 1966 and retroactively imposed the suspension for the month before.[84]

With the mid-term elections over, Johnson next proposed a two-year 6% surcharge on personal and corporate incomes in his state of the union address and in his budget message for FY 1968. He revised his proposal upwards to 10% in August, but fiscal conservatives in Congress like House Ways and Means chairman Wilbur Mills continued to resist large tax hikes without corresponding spending cuts. After months of haggling and delay, the two sides finally worked out a compromise, and the Revenue Expenditure and Control Act (RECA) passed into law in June 1968. As a new form of emergency deficit reduction legislation, the Act contained both tax and spending provisions. It mandated one-year, 10% surcharges on individuals and corporations that Johnson had requested while also delaying designated cuts in excise taxes on automobiles and telephones for another year. On the spending side, the Act imposed a package of automatic spending cuts, related cutbacks in federal workers, and reductions in spending authority. These measures set a precedent for sweeping, blunt, anti-deficit instrumentalities that contributed no constructive change to the budget. For FY 1968 the Act directed a $6 billion cut in federal expenditures, while for FY 1969 it planned for a $10 billion cut in authority.[85]

Several factors forced the government into cobbling together this expedient. Johnson had at first succeeded in what he wanted to do on many different fronts, whether it was enacting tax cuts, deploying forces to Vietnam, or building the Great Society, but now these successes were coming back to haunt him by 1968, with the tax cuts, however beneficial for economic growth, simply incompatible with the trajectory in federal spending after 1964, no end in sight for the Vietnam War, and rising inflation only further constraining his latitude on the budget. In the short-term RECA worked to turn in a small budget surplus for FY 1969 while also possibly contributing to a moderate recession by decade's end. But over the longer-term the Great Society delivered permanent change to the budget, specifically the two new entitlements of Medicare and Medicaid. These programs now locked in a large portion of general revenue through rules of automatic eligibility for designated groups of recipients. The growing dominance of mandatory spending over the federal till would make budget balancing increasingly difficult for future administrations. The balanced budget resulting from the 1968 tax and spending law would be the last one for nearly three decades. Johnson's rejoinder to rising deficits invoked the impressive performance of the economy through the 1960s. His public statements routinely pointed to the economic expansion of this period and the implication that a growing economy required more public services to uphold a better way of life and the "Great Society." And indeed the debt to GDP ratio did fall from 37.5% to 27.3% during his time in office. Yet debt to GDP had been sloping downwards since the end of World War II before this descent stopped in the 1970s.[86]

Goaded by Johnson, Congress had altered the budget by imposing a new funding scheme for mandatory spending programs, and the budget would remain altered even as the population aged and the economy slowed. Vietnam War spending also greatly contributed to deficits and inflation, but withdrawal from the war ultimately allowed the government to return to a relatively more normal defense budget. Nor did the rise in defense spending exceed domestic outlays even during the war. By the time Johnson left office, total defense costs, including Vietnam War spending, had risen by $28 billion compared to an increase in social welfare spending of $37.4 billion.[87]

In Johnson's last year as president, the Vietnam War entered a new, critical phase, with the Viet Cong staging the Tet Offensive deep into Saigon and other South Vietnamese cities while laying siege to the Marine bastion of Khe Sanh in the jungle highlands. In response to these crises, and to the North Korean seizure of the intelligence trawler U.S.S. *Pueblo*, the Pentagon, now in the hands of veteran insider Clark Clifford, sought over $7 billion in supplemental funds for FY 1968, an outcome that McNamara had hoped to avoid when first crafting the budget for that year.[88] Even with the supplemental, the final twist of Johnson's presidency was his ability to secure a balanced budget for his last fiscal year, 1969, extending five months into Nixon's term. As a result of the tax surcharges, Johnson anticipated a small surplus of $2.4 billion for FY 1969.[89] The surplus turned out to be $800 million larger than expected.[90] This last surplus may have sufficed as a veneer of fiscal stability, but in truth it concealed underlying trends that dictated a near unavoidable shift to deficits in the years to come. Johnson expanded the budget in a time of prosperity, and now this expanded budget would be tested in an age of limits.

NOTES

1. President of U.S., *The Budget of the United States Government for the Fiscal Year Ending June 30, 1963* (Government Printing Office, Washington, D.C., 1962), 56–58.
2. The American Presidency Project, "John F. Kennedy: Special Message to the Congress on the Defense Budget, March 28, 1961," http://www.presidency.ucsb.edu/ws/?pid=8554, accessed September 2018.
3. Walter S. Poole, *History of the Joint Chiefs of Staff, The Joint Chiefs of Staff and National Policy, Vol. VIII: 1961–1964* (Washington, D.C.: Office of Joint History, Office of the Chairman of the Joint Chiefs of Staff, 2011), 21.
4. Papers of John F. Kennedy. Presidential Papers. President's Office Files. Departments and Agencies. Defense: FY 1961 and FY 1962 military programs and budgets, 21 February, 1961. JFKPOF-077–002. John F. Kennedy Presidential Library and Museum.
5. FY '61 and '62 military programs.
6. Ibid.
7. Papers of John F. Kennedy. Presidential Papers. National Security Files. Departments and Agencies. Department of Defense: General: McNamara testimony before Senate Armed Forces Committee, 4 April, 1961. JFKNS-273–007. John F. Kennedy Presidential Library and Museum.
8. Kennedy, "Message on Defense Budget."
9. Papers of John F. Kennedy. Presidential Papers. National Security Files. Robert W. Komer Files. NATO, 1961–1963. JFKNSF-439–001. John F. Kennedy Presidential Library and Museum.
10. *Foreign Relations of the United States, 1961–1963, Volume XIV, Berlin Crisis, 1961–1963*, ed. Charles S. Sampson (Washington, D.C.: Government Printing Office, 1993), Document 77, https://history.state.gov/historicaldocuments/frus1961–63v14/d77, accessed June 2019.
11. "Radio and Television Report to the American People on the Berlin Crisis, July 25, 1961." President John F. Kennedy. The White House. July 25, 1961. John F. Kennedy Presidential Library and Museum.
12. Lawrence S. Kaplan, Ronald D. Landa, and Edward J. Drea, *History of the Office of the Secretary of Defense, Vol. V, The McNamara Ascendancy: 1961–1965* (Historical Office, Office of the Secretary of Defense, Washington, D.C., 2006), 67–69.
13. Kaplan, Landa, and Drea, *The McNamara Ascendancy*, 161–62.
14. President, *1963 Budget*, 12.
15. Ibid., 60–61.
16. Ibid., 10.
17. Kaplan, Landa, and Drea, *The McNamara Ascendancy*, 113.
18. Robert S. McNamara, recorded interview, April 4, 1964, 2, John F. Kennedy Library Oral History Program.
19. Military Committee. "Report by the Military Committee to the North Atlantic Council on Military Aspects of the Control of Nuclear Weapons in NATO." MC 0095, Military Committee Series. NATO Archives, Brussels, Belgium.
20. *Foreign Relations of the United States, 1961–1963, Volume VIII, National Security Policy*, ed. David W. Mabon (Washington, D.C.: Government Printing Office, 1996), Document 82, https://history.state.gov/historicaldocuments/frus1961–63v08/d82, accessed June 2019.
21. Papers of John F. Kennedy. Presidential Papers. President's Office Files. Speech Files. Address to Canadian Parliament, Ottawa, 17 May, 1961. JFKPOF-034–027. John F. Kennedy Presidential Library and Museum.
22. Kaplan, Landa, and Drea, *The McNamara Ascendancy*, 398–99.
23. Papers of John F. Kennedy. Presidential Papers. National Security Files. Carl Kaysen Files. NATO: Subjects: Nuclear Force, 1962. JFKNSF-375–007. John F. Kennedy Presidential Library and Museum.
24. Papers of John F. Kennedy. Presidential Papers. National Security Files. Meetings and Memoranda. National Security Action Memoranda [NSAM]: NSAM 222, Security Aspects of

Using Submarines in a Multilateral Force. JFKNSF-340–008. John F. Kennedy Presidential Library and Museum.

25. Harold Brown, recorded interview, July 9, 1964, 8–10, John F. Kennedy Library Oral History Program.

26. Papers of John F. Kennedy. Presidential Papers. National Security Files. Meetings and Memoranda. Staff memoranda: Neustadt, Richard E.: "Skybolt and Nassau," November 1963. JFKNSF-322–020. John F. Kennedy Presidential Library and Museum.

27. Papers of John F. Kennedy. Presidential Papers. National Security Files. Meetings and Memoranda. National Security Action Memoranda [NSAM]: NSAM 253, Re: Use of mixed manned NATO forces for multilateral force. JFKNSF-341–013. John F. Kennedy Presidential Library and Museum.

28. Neustadt, "Skybolt and Nassau."

29. Papers of John F. Kennedy. Presidential Papers. National Security Files. Departments and Agencies. Department of Defense: Subjects: Defense budget FY '64, Vol. I: Recommended General Purpose Forces. JFKNSF-275–011. John F. Kennedy Presidential Library and Museum.

30. Papers of John F. Kennedy. Presidential Papers. National Security Files. Departments and Agencies. Department of Defense: Subjects: Defense budget FY '64, Vol. I: Recommended Strategic Retaliatory Forces. JFKNSF-275–010. John F. Kennedy Presidential Library and Museum.

31. President of U.S., *The Budget of the United States Government for the Fiscal Year Ending June 30, 1964* (Washington, D.C.: Government Printing Office, 1963), 17.

32. Secretary of Treasury, *Annual Report of the Secretary of the Treasury on the State of the Finances for the Fiscal Year Ended June 30, 1961* (Washington, D.C.: Government Printing Office, 1962), 305.

33. Secretary of Treasury, *1961 Treasury Annual Report*, 306–10.

34. Secretary of Treasury, *Annual Report of the Secretary of the Treasury on the State of the Finances for the Fiscal Year Ended June 30, 1962* (Washington, D.C.: Government Printing Office, 1963), 62–66.

35. Papers of John F. Kennedy. Presidential Papers. President's Office Files. Speech Files. Remarks to Economic Club of New York. JFKPOF-042–008. John F. Kennedy Presidential Library and Museum.

36. President, *1963 Budget*, 8–9.

37. President, *1964 Budget*, 9.

38. Secretary of Treasury, *Annual Report of the Secretary of the Treasury on the State of the Finances for the Fiscal Year Ended June 30, 1963* (Washington, D.C.: Government Printing Office, 1964), 294.

39. President, *1964 Budget*, 10.

40. Secretary of Treasury, *1963 Treasury Annual Report*, 297.

41. Federal Reserve Bank of St. Louis Economic Data, "Real Gross Domestic Product," https://fred.stlouisfed.org/ series/GDPC1#0, accessed December 2018.

42. FRED, Real GDP.

43. President, *1964 Budget*, 15.

44. Ibid., 25.

45. Secretary of Treasury, *Annual Report of the Secretary of the Treasury on the State of the Finances for the Fiscal Year Ended June 30, 1964* (Washington, D.C.: Government Printing Office, 1965), 37–39.

46. Secretary of Treasury, *1964 Treasury Annual Report*, 262–263.

47. Federal Reserve Bank of St. Louis Economic Data, "Gross private domestic investment: Domestic business," https://fred.stlouisfed.org/series/W987RC1Q027SBEA, accessed August 2019.

48. Federal Reserve Bank of St. Louis Economic Data, "Personal Consumption Expenditures," https://fred.stlouisfed.org/series/PCECA, accessed August 2019.

49. Federal Reserve Bank of St. Louis Economic Data, "Shares of gross domestic product: Personal consumption expenditures," https://fred.stlouisfed.org/series/DPCERE1Q156NBEA;

"Shares of gross domestic product: Gross private domestic investment," https://fred.stlouisfed.org/series/A006RE1Q156NBEA, accessed August 2019.

50. FRED, Real GDP.

51. Federal Reserve Bank of St. Louis Economic Data, "Civilian Unemployment Rate," https://fred.stlouisfed.org/series/UNRATE/, accessed January 2019.

52. Federal Reserve Bank of St. Louis Economic Data, "Personal Consumption Expenditures Excluding Food and Energy (Chain-Type Price Index)," https://fred.stlouisfed.org/series/PCEPILFE#0, accessed January 2019.

53. OMB, "Historical Tables," 25.

54. Tempalski, "Revenue Effects," 15.

55. OMB, "Historical Tables," 32.

56. Federal Reserve Bank of St. Louis Economic Data, "Federal Receipts as Percent of Gross Domestic Product," https://fred.stlouisfed.org/series/FYFRGDA188S, accessed January 2019.

57. *Foreign Relations of the United States, 1964–1968, Volume I, Vietnam, 1964*, ed. Edward C. Keefer and Charles S. Sampson (Washington, D.C.: Government Printing Office, 1992), Document 84, https://history.state.gov/historicaldocuments/frus1964–68v01/d84, accessed June 2019.

58. Francis M. Bator, "No Good Choices: LBJ and the Vietnam/Great Society Connection," *Diplomatic History* 32, no. 3 (June 2008): 317, JSTOR, https://www.jstor.org/stable/24915871?read-now=1&refreqid=excelsior%3Aceb4b71234efdc05f43cead99acf4eaa&seq=1#page_scan_tab_contents, accessed July 2019.

59. President of U.S., *The Budget of the United States Government for the Fiscal Year Ending June 30, 1966* (Washington, D.C.: Government Printing Office, 1965), 16.

60. Edward J. Drea, *Secretaries of Defense Historical Series, Vol. VI., McNamara, Clifford, and the Burdens of Vietnam: 1965–1969* (Washington, D.C.: Historical Office, Office of the Secretary of Defense, 2011), 89.

61. Drea, *Burdens of Vietnam*, 95.

62. Ibid., 101

63. Ibid., 97–98.

64. President of U.S., *The Budget of the United States Government for the Fiscal Year Ending June 30, 1967* (Washington, D.C.: Government Printing Office, 1966), 19–20.

65. Drea, *Burdens of Vietnam*, 162–63.

66. Walter S. Poole, *History of Acquisition in the Department of Defense, Vol. II, Adapting to Flexible Response: 1960–1968* (Washington, D.C.: Historical Office, Office of the Secretary of Defense, 2013), 165–67.

67. Drea, *Burdens of Vietnam*, 353.

68. Ibid., 56.

69. James Walker, Lewis Bernstein, and Sharon Lang, *Seize the High Ground: The Army in Space and Missile Defense* (Washington, D.C.: Historical Office, U.S. Army Space and Defense Command, 2003), 49.

70. President, *1966 Budget*, 220.

71. Drea, *Burdens of Vietnam*, 352.

72. Walker, Bernstein, and Lang, *Seize the High Ground*, 53–54.

73. Drea, *Burdens of Vietnam*, 339–44.

74. President of U.S., *The Budget of the United States Government for the Fiscal Year Ending June 30, 1965* (Washington, D.C.: Government Printing Office, 1964), 16.

75. President, *1966 Budget*, 10.

76. President, *1965 Budget*, 17.

77. The American Presidency Project, "Lyndon B. Johnson: Remarks at the University of Michigan, May 22, 1964," https://www.presidency.ucsb.edu/documents/remarks-the-university-michigan, accessed January 2019.

78. OMB, "Historical Tables," 335.

79. Ibid., 312.

80. Federal Reserve Bank of St. Louis Economic Data, "Homeownership Rate for the United States," https://fred.stlouisfed.org/series/RHORUSQ156N, accessed August 2019.

81. President of U.S., *The Budget of the United States Government for the Fiscal Year Ending June 30, 1968* (Washington, D.C.: Government Printing Office, 1967), 279.
82. OMB, "Historical Tables," 52–53.
83. Secretary of Treasury, *Annual Report of the Secretary of the Treasury on the State of the Finances for the Fiscal Year Ended June 30, 1968* (Washington, D.C.: Government Printing Office, 1969), 4.
84. Secretary of Treasury, *Annual Report of the Secretary of the Treasury on the State of the Finances for the Fiscal Year Ended June 30, 1967* (Washington, D.C.: Government Printing Office, 1968), 29–30.
85. Secretary of Treasury, *1968 Treasury Annual Report*, 27–31.
86. FRED, Federal Debt as Percent of GDP.
87. President of U.S., *The Budget of the United States Government for the Fiscal Year Ending June 30, 1970* (Washington, D.C.: Government Printing Office, 1969), 27.
88. Drea, *Burdens of Vietnam*, 249–50.
89. President, *1970 Budget*, 10.
90. President of U.S., *The Budget of the United States Government Fiscal Year 1971* (Washington, D.C.: Government Printing Office, 1970), 7.

Chapter Five

Adapting to Limits

Nixon, Ford, and Carter, 1969–1981

The presidential administrations of the 1970s inhabited an era marked by an increasing sense of limitation, of oil shortages, inflation, a weak dollar, threatening economic competition from overseas, and waning military commitments in the Third World. This era was also marked by deficits. The budget failed to balance at any point in the 1970s, but the deficits of this era were not as huge as they would become in the next decade, and the debt to GDP ratio remained under control. Inflation dominated the economic setting until the Federal Reserve finally began implementing disinflationary policies in late 1979. Before then this persistent, building inflation constrained governmental action by compelling tighter fiscal policies, to the point where inflation may have served as a check on excessive spending. By trying to restrain spending while grappling with the inflation conundrum, the Nixon, Ford, and Carter Administrations were not dissimilar in their economic policy outlook. They all relied on modest, pro-growth changes to the tax code instead of radical measures. With the top personal rate staying at 70% until 1981, these administrations instead preferred expanding so-called tax expenditures, isolated breaks within the code, whether for individuals or corporations, as well as moderately reducing corporate rates. All three administrations were of a fiscally conservative bent, but they lacked the political means to bring fundamental changes to the budget that would have made a return to fiscal balance more feasible.

The three administrations also sought arms control agreements with the Soviets to reduce tensions and restore diplomacy as a creative element in world affairs. Whatever the merits of arms control in general, none of the administrations deliberately exploited it in order to slash the defense budget.

Outlays for combat forces declined in the early 1970s with the withdrawal from Vietnam, but even this decline was partly offset by a rise in personnel paychecks to facilitate the shift to an all-volunteer military. Defense spending started rising again in the second half of the decade, not least of which because the defense budget was especially sensitive to inflationary pressures. Detente and arms control may have reduced tensions and ended the brinksmanship that had brought the world to the precipice of nuclear war in the early 1960s, but they did not somehow provide an escape valve from funding a costly defense budget. The Soviets continued to modernize their ICBMs and SLBMs. The Pentagon needed to keep pace with these efforts even within the confines of SALT. Yet the pullout from Vietnam marked the end of an expensive, bloody war and bred reluctance towards any future intervention that might lead to similar battle conditions devoid of decisive victory.

EXTRICATION FROM VIETNAM, BUDGET SYMMETRIES

As the immediate successor to Johnson, Richard Nixon wanted to orchestrate a careful act that all at once revived summitry, triangulated relations with the Soviets and Chinese, extricated combat personnel from Vietnam, and kept U.S. credibility in the world intact. Nixon's ambitions in foreign policy did not really translate in budgetary terms, but they were not inconsistent with his innately cautious instincts in domestic affairs. Having shared the ticket with Eisenhower twice, he wanted to reprise that era but now sealed with greater diplomatic achievements. Improbably, he may also have been the most optimistic of the three presidents in the 1970s for a balanced budget, having inherited one on the day of his inauguration. He hoped to extend balanced budgets for the foreseeable future, estimating small surpluses of $1.5 and $1.3 billion in 1970 and 1971 respectively.[1] The Administration could not bear responsibility for sending the budget back into deficit after Johnson and Congress had finally reached a compromise over taxes and spending that made the surplus possible, and in any event the Administration had to be worried about inflation. Nixon sought to create modest savings by eliminating or restructuring various programs in a changing budget sheet. As he noted after a year in office, "[a]bout 41% of estimated outlays in the 1971 budget will be devoted to human resources—spending for education and manpower, health, income security, and veterans benefits and services," in contrast to a decline in defense spending to its smallest chunk of the budgetary pie since the start of the Korean War. Nixon estimated defense spending to fall to 37% of the budget for FY 1971.[2]

Nixon oversaw the decline in defense spending as he pulled troops out of Vietnam, somewhat similar to how Eisenhower had reduced defense costs after achieving an armistice in Korea. Nixon's defense secretary, Melvin

Laird, a long-serving House member with experience in military appropriations, consistently supported troop level reductions during Nixon's first term. Laird favored such a program on its own merits, provided aid continued flowing to the South Vietnamese, but he also equated the pullout with a downsized defense budget. Troop levels in Vietnam needed to be brought down simply to match the fall in defense spending. He therefore approached the Vietnam War from a budgetary standpoint, while hawks in the White House, like national security adviser Henry Kissinger and his assistant Alexander Haig, were far more reluctant to start unilaterally withdrawing troops simply to cut costs.[3] Laird's views won out, helped along by a more "participatory" management style that turned back McNamara's consolidation of power in OSD to the detriment of the services. Without formally undoing PPBS, Laird increasingly brought the service chiefs into the fold on spending decisions so long as their input conformed to guidelines issued by OSD, which resembled the budget ceilings of the pre-McNamara Pentagon.[4]

In larger terms, Nixon recognized the mounting political odds he faced if U.S. forces remained bogged down in Vietnam by the time his reelection campaign kicked into gear. He also did not want to be the first U.S. president to lose a war and feared electoral repercussions in that regard. I 1969, 536,000 U.S. troops were deployed in Vietnam. Consistent with Laird's recommendations, Nixon started gradually pulling out troops in the tens of thousands before announcing in April 1970 a major cut of 150,000 for FY 1971, which had the effect of temporarily slowing the withdrawal but still committed the Administration over a longer timeframe. Left in-country would be 259,000 troops subject to continued withdrawal.[5] Nixon's path to extrication was not without deviations. He wanted a gap of at least a few years between the U.S. pullout and the probable reigniting of hostilities between North and South. His strategy of forcing concessions from the North Vietnamese did not differ markedly from Johnson's, except unlike Johnson he faced a much tighter timetable and greater political constraints. For all his concern over leaks, Nixon could not really keep his strategy secret. He needed to publicly announce troop drawdowns for political reasons, and his support for Vietnamization implied an ultimate decision to hand over the brunt of the fighting to the South Vietnamese.

Nixon still tried to infuse unpredictability into this process through his much touted "madman theory," that the North Vietnamese should be terrified of his willingness to do anything to bring the war to an end. He did step up pressure in various ways, first by beginning a secret bombing campaign against enemy sanctuaries just inside Cambodia and then later invading the area using South Vietnamese and U.S. troops. He further explored a series of options for escalation codenamed Duck Hook. When the North staged a spring offensive in 1972 after most U.S. combat troops had already left, Nixon resorted to what had been Duck Hook options, including an escalation in bombing of the North and the mining of Haiphong harbor. But these countermoves did not reverse the inevitable troop drawdown, which corresponded with diminishing spending authority for the war. The Administration planned to reduce total defense expenditures to $73.6 billion in 1971 from $81.2 billion in 1969.[6]

In his annual report for FY 1973, Laird wrote of a "National Security Strategy of Realistic Deterrence." He coupled this strategy with the Nixon Doctrine, off-handedly asserted by the president with reporters while embarking on a worldwide tour in 1969. In trying to disassociate himself from future entanglements in the Third World, Nixon indicated that the nuclear umbrella still protected NATO partners but that other regional allies like South Vietnam should expect to assume the burden of fighting. Articulating these abstract ideas for public consumption was relatively easy compared to the actual difficulty of exerting pressure on the North Vietnamese, pulling troops out from the South, and assuaging American public opinion all at once. When Nixon formulated these thoughts, over half a million U.S. soldiers were still fighting in South Vietnam. But by lending the pullout a larger conceptual context Nixon looked ahead to the U.S.'s global security posture after the combat mission in Southeast Asia ended.

Laird incorporated the tenets of this doctrine into his own strategy for deterrence. His framework represented a return to core modes of strategic thinking "in an environment of virtual balance in the strategic nuclear field, and in a period of vigorous Soviet military expansion at sea, on the land, in the air and in space."[7] In contrast to Paul Nitze's broader attention to economic and military factors in NSC 68, Laird conceded that strategic doctrine could not be implemented in a fiscal void, that weapons systems and personnel cost a great deal of money, and that the defense budget increasingly competed with domestic programs for funding. He bluntly stated that "resources are limited" and like Nixon recited the fall in the portion of the budget allocated to defense to as low as 30% by 1973.[8]

Nixon eventually lost confidence in Laird and replaced him with Elliot Richardson at the start of his second term. But during Laird's tenure the Pentagon effectively wound down the U.S.'s combat presence in Vietnam, which Nixon had depended upon in order to win another term in office. The ceasefire reached as a result of the Paris peace talks provided a temporary breathing spell to the decades-long war, so that by early 1973 Nixon was in position to request a more or less peacetime defense budget for the first time since the beginning of 1965.

DEFICITS RESUMED, NEW ECONOMIC POLICY, NEW FEDERALISM

Despite the withdrawal from Vietnam and the corresponding drop in defense expenditures in the early 1970s, Nixon encountered numerous challenges that impeded budget balancing in his first term. Along with economic factors, a looser post-RECA tax policy deserves much of the responsibility for the continuing, at times severe deficits, but the government was also spending more money on domestic programs than it had ten years ago when Nixon served as vice president.

Nixon's first order of business on the domestic front required him to work across the aisle on taxes. He had little choice except to closely cooperate in maintaining a stable tax policy while the fighting wore on in Vietnam. With RECA slated to expire at the end of the fiscal year on June 30, 1969, Johnson, President-elect Nixon, and members of Congress coordinated to extend the legislation. The new Administration proposed retaining the 10% surcharges for the remainder of CY 1969, then continuing the surcharges to the end of FY 1970 at a stepped down 5% rate while repealing the investment tax credit. Repealing the investment tax credit would mitigate the revenue loss from reducing the surcharges by 50% in the first half of CY 1970. Congress went along in enacting these proposals while also introducing a new alternative minimum tax on wealthier taxpayers who could otherwise use a variety of means to eliminate liability.[9] Though the Tax Reform Act of 1969 (TRA-69) incorporated increases in the personal exemption and other tax breaks for lower income individuals, its primary goal was to keep a lid on deficits and contain inflation. The legislation directly followed from RECA in its fiscal impact but to a lesser degree. While RECA led to an averaged 1.09% gain in revenue as a percentage of GDP over a two-year stretch, TRA-69 did so by only .30%.[10]

Extending the tax surcharges allowed a rare moment of non-partisan reprieve in the realm of public finance. But the surcharge extensions were only temporary, and the chances for more budget balancing immediately took a turn for the worse as the economy slipped into recession at the end of CY 1969. Real GDP growth fell into negative territory in the last quarter of 1969 and hovered there in the first quarter of 1970.[11] Recession triggered an unemployment rate higher than what the public had been used to for some time, and it then continued to plague the soft recovery. After staying well below 4% in the late 1960s, by most definitions conforming to full employment, the unemployment rate averaged 6% during 1971, from which point it did not fall swiftly enough for the Administration.[12] With the unemployment rate stubbornly high, the doling out of unemployment benefits overseen by the Labor Department and run by the states increased in near automatic terms to $7 billion by 1972.[13] The rise in unemployment benefits may not have driven deficit spending, given their funding through taxes on employers and state contributions, but it signaled a stalling economy and the weak state of government revenue by the early 1970s. Federal revenue as a percentage of GDP had risen from 16.3% in 1968 to 18.4% in 1969 as a result of the RECA surcharges combined with economic growth at the peak of the expansion. As the surcharges were phased-out under TRA-69 and as the economy contracted, revenue fell to just under 18% of GDP in 1970 before bottoming out at 16% in 1971.[14] The stalling economy and surcharge phase-outs caused deficits to jump from $2.8 billion in 1970[15] to $23 billion by 1971.[16]

Recession and high unemployment did not harmonize with Nixon's ideal budgetary outlook. For the FY 1972 budget request, Nixon economists concocted the idea of the full employment budget, which measured the appropriate level of spending based on estimated full employment revenue, or in other words the amount of revenue if the economy were hypothetically running at full employment. The budget message released in late January 1971 tried to distinguish the full employment budget from the loose fiscal policies of Nixon's predecessors by implying that estimated full employment revenue provided a kind of check on excessive spending. While Kennedy and Johnson may have been willing to spend beyond the limits of full employment revenue, the Nixon Administration indicated that it would refrain from doing so. But in a Keynesian add-on, the message went on to say that "[t]he full employment budget idea is in the nature of a self-fulfilling prophecy: By operating as if we were at full employment, we will help to bring about that full employment."[17] For instance, while the Administration projected a large deficit of $18.6 billion for FY 1971, full employment revenue generated a hypothetical surplus of $1.4 billion.[18] The full employment budget served entirely as a gimmick. By the time the drafting of the budget request had been completed in early 1971, the economy was no longer operating at full employment. The unemployment rate would stay on average at 6% throughout the year, and the economy had not yet robustly recovered from recession, having again nose-dived into negative growth territory in the last quarter of 1970.[19]

The idea of the full employment budget revealed the Administration's sudden tolerance of lax fiscal policy and bigger deficits in response to worsening economic conditions. CY 1971 turned into a tumultuous time as multiple economic challenges came to a head. In addition to high unemployment, real GDP posted an anemic .18% growth for all of 1970.[20] The Administration needed to jolt the economy to start a sustainable expansion. Vietnam War and Great Society spending, meanwhile, had already driven accumulating inflation, with consumer prices excluding food and energy reaching over 4% growth in every year since 1968.[21] Even before the first oil shock of the 1970s, price growth had significantly outpaced real growth, so the Administration needed to find a way to stunt inflation while boosting the economy, especially business investment. Disinflation through tighter monetary policy was off the table, with unemployment already high and GDP growth wobbly. Policymakers would have to find alternative means for stifling inflation, while changes in the tax code continued to offer tools for boosting real growth.

Beneath these domestic challenges lurked another more peculiar problem, that the Bretton Woods exchange rate system underpinning the world economy no longer worked properly. Operating within narrow adjustable pegs, it had become too inflexible and incompatible with the flow of global trade. The U.S.'s current account in goods and services turned negative in the second quarter of 1971, the first time this had happened since 1959, when the whole system formally commenced, sending a clear signal of the dollar's overvaluation. The dollar thereafter plunged in the international markets, forcing European central banks to purchase huge quantities of the currency. As the dollar fell, European central banks threatened to turn in their mountainous dollar reserves at the Treasury's gold window. Tight monetary policy might have saved Bretton Woods for a few more years, but it, like devaluation, had become alien to the Administration.

Nixon ironically found these issues substantively boring and preferred to conduct free ranging discussions on foreign policy with Kissinger. But fated by history with an array of economic challenges, he decided that he had to act in one fell swoop to shock markets, galvanize his supporters, and confound his detractors, and that is exactly what he did on August 15, 1971. In a single televised address he announced the termination of gold payments at the Treasury, the imposition of a ninety-day wage and price freeze under authority already granted to him by Congress, and an import surcharge. The most consequential component of this New Economic Policy from a budgetary standpoint was the proposal to reinstitute the investment tax credit. The Administration's decision to restore the tax credit that it had so recently worked to repeal crystallized the priority now given to the overall state of the economy instead of the deficit. The Administration wanted to drive up tax expenditures to boost business investment. Nixon proposed a 10% credit for investment in machinery and other equipment that would then be automatically reduced to 5% the next year. When writing the Revenue Act of 1971, Congress instead legislated a permanent 7% credit for investment in new machinery and other equipment, along with the repeal of a 7% excise tax on motor vehicles and marginal increases in the personal exemption and standard deduction.[22]

The Revenue Act led to revenue losses as the Administration transitioned into easing the economy. Shortly after Congress passed the legislation, Nixon estimated a $38.8 billion deficit for FY 1972.[23] The Administration's pivot to expansion appeared timely, with the economy rebounding robustly during 1971–1973, even as inflation continued to gain steam. The deficit briefly closed to $3.5 billion for FY 1974, marking the furthest point in Nixon's agenda for fiscal stabilization.[24] Nixon had to contend with war and recession, the same obstacles that lay between Eisenhower and a normal budget setting early in his first term. But the Eisenhower Administration had gone on to secure three surpluses in the wake of the armistice in Korea and two economic expansions. The Nixon Administration faced a litmus test of whether it could turn in a surplus under similar conditions of peacetime expansion by 1973, and it had not quite succeeded, temporarily narrowing the deficit rather than eliminating it.

Great Society spending had an undeniable effect on growing deficits. Transfer payments under Medicare and Medicaid remained relatively modest in the early 1970s, but they continued an upward climb. Spending for domestic discretionary programs likewise rose. For instance, spending on education, training, employment, and social services rose by $8 billion from 1969 through 1975 to a total of $15.2 billion, while spending on natural resources, environment, and energy increased in the same period by over $5 billion to $9.5 billion.[25] Underlying differences still existed between the rise in discretionary and entitlement spending. Entitlement transfers, for instance, could not be easily reformed or changed because they benefited specific groups of people, and they were also affected by larger demographic trends. With the spending locked in, they automatically increased as more people became eligible for benefits.

Whatever Nixon's personal views on the role of government, he lacked the support to in any way dismantle or substantially reform the Great Society. Republicans failed to ride his coattails for a takeover of at least one of the houses of Congress in the close 1968 presidential election or even his landslide reelection victory four years later. Forced by circumstance to work with Democratic majorities, his domestic agenda of the New Federalism promoted devolution of money and power from Washington, D.C., back to the state governments, in turn reflecting his belief that the federal budget would generate surpluses at least part of the time in the 1970s, much like it had in the 1950s. Nixon bundled together his domestic agenda into a single address in August 1969, similar to the announcement for the New Economic Policy two years later. The idea to convert the AFDC welfare program into a form of basic universal income called the Family Assistance Plan (FAP) bore the influence of White House poverty czar Daniel Patrick Moynihan. Nixon wanted to set up payments under this plan to families that included a working father, with an annual base figure of $1,600 per family. To incentivize work, the father could keep the benefits while earning outside income. After earning $60 per month, the family would still be able to receive 50% of the benefits. Nixon sought to impose other work requirements, but by his own admission the program would cost up to $4 billion. He planned to delay FAP's start date until FY 1971, hopefully by which point a larger budget surplus would sustain the program. Nixon's other idea of revenue sharing between the federal government and the states, a central feature of the New Federalism, in principle but not in effect depended on budget surpluses. As with FAP, Nixon wanted to appropriate $500 million in startup funds for revenue sharing in FY 1971 when hopefully budget trends would be more auspicious.[26]

The House passed a bill for FAP, but it died in the Senate. While Nixon succeeded in getting revenue sharing off the ground, the federal government did not once share surplus revenue until the program's demise in 1986. Nixon's domestic agenda early in his first term provides a glimpse into how he hoped the budget and economy would turn out in the next few years. His expectations were not wholly unjustified. RECA seemed to have put a halt to the preceding years of growing fiscal excess. As the government more frequently balanced the budget, the Administration could pursue constructive reforms for the welfare state and federal-state relations. In actuality, Nixon's legacy took a different course with the continued rise in inflation and deficits. Ad hoc benefit increases for Social Security were no longer adequate. Automatic cost of living adjustments (COLAs) now needed to prevent inflation from eating away at benefits. Nixon also signed legislation reorganizing aid to the needy, blind, and aged into a new Supplemental Security Income (SSI) program managed by the Social Security Administration but funded through general revenue. Hampered by Watergate in the waning days of his presidency, Nixon even reached out to Democrats in Congress in hopes of collaborating on a plan for comprehensive health insurance but to no avail.

Nixon in his public statements reiterated the importance of lean deficits to counter rising debt and inflation. He increasingly resorted to impounding money, which did not per se violate the Constitution, but it did finally cause Congress to pass the Congressional Budget and Impoundment Control Act of 1974, establishing the House and Senate Budget Committees and the CBO for non-partisan research while restricting the president's authority to impound money. The authors of the legislation intended for it to facilitate the more effective assigning of priorities through a new budget and appropriations process and give Congress, aided by its intellectual appendage of the CBO, added weight in the formulation of long-term policy options. Yet whatever its merits, the 1974 Budget Act did not lead to balanced budgets in the short or long-term. The factors propelling the ongoing deficits had little to do with process and everything to do with substantive spending and tax policies. Decisions over defense spending and the tax code had long determined an administration's ability to turn in surpluses. Now entitlement transfer payments also took up revenue, in addition to a host of other discretionary programs. The problem lay with substantive policy and whether the president and Congress had the will to stanch the overflow of red ink, not the process of passing an annual budget. The seemingly less proximate but substantive outlying factors, those related to arms, revenue, and entitlements, kept driving deficits and needed to be comprehensively addressed in order to get the budget back into surplus.

DETENTE AT ITS ZENITH

Nixon's engagement in the area he deemed most important, foreign affairs and the fostering of a less rigid diplomatic arena, may have had a more remote bearing upon rising deficits, but defense policy and to a lesser extent arms control still factored into the budget outlook. The withdrawal from Vietnam did not cause a long-term decline in defense costs. The switch to an all-volunteer military in 1973 necessitated higher pay and better benefits to induce recruits to join than with a conscript force. The military expended $5 billion more in compensation to active duty members than in the late 1960s, even with an over one million cut in personnel, while benefits for former members had already risen by almost $5 billion for over a decade.[27] The Pentagon was also bound to reassess the military's conventional strength in the center of Europe after the long interval of preoccupation with Southeast Asia. Nixon for his part succeeded in reducing the number of regular Army divisions to 13 from 19 in 1968.[28] Defense expenditures as a percentage of GNP fell to under 6% by 1975 after reaching a high of 9% in 1968.[29]

The resumption of SALT negotiations with the Soviets afforded the opportunity to place upper limits on strategic forces. The picture on future defense costs was otherwise unclear. The withdrawal from Vietnam had pushed down the costs of general purpose forces from $30.4 billion in 1968 to $25.8 in 1973. But even this latter figure still stood over three times higher than the costs of strategic forces at $7.2 billion for that same year.[30] Continuing the negotiations gave advantages to the Administration's political and diplomatic position, but it also had to decide on the extent to which it wanted to MIRV the nuclear arsenal. Unless the Pentagon completed these transitions, the Soviets might surpass the U.S. in strategic capabilities. Leonid Brezhnev, who as communist party chairman emerged as the dominant figure on the Politburo, at the very least sought parity with the U.S. The only question was whether the Soviets would in fact take the lead. As Laird recounted in his report for FY 1971, the Soviets had started nothing short of an arms buildup, with the number of ICBM launchers in their arsenal rising from 250 in 1966 to now 1,100, higher than the U.S. total of 1,054. The Soviets also rivaled U.S. capabilities at sea with the deployment of Y-class subs, which each carried sixteen ballistic missiles. Laird feared that within a few years up to 50 Soviet Y-class subs would outnumber the aging Polaris fleet of 41 subs.[31]

Yet if the Administration wanted leeway on offensive MIRVs, any agreement with the Soviets would have to address defensive ABM systems. The continued work on ABM forced a number of questions over whether it was even feasible, whether the Pentagon should simply focus on offensive missile strength to overwhelm a rival ABM, or alternatively if implemented whether ABM should provide area defense or limited protection against accidental launches. Many scientists and defense academics opposed ABM on the grounds that it would destabilize the arms race as nuclear powers rushed to increase their ICBM launcher counts to render any such system impotent. McNamara had mainly considered ABM an unrealistic capability subject to negotiation, but after the inconclusive Glassboro summit he had little choice except to move ahead with the Sentinel program. At Glassboro Johnson's negotiating team could not really offer anything substantive to Kosygin beyond the vague hope that both sides might reach an understanding on ABM. McNamara's announcement of Sentinel seemed to have helped prod the Soviets into entering talks the next year, but by the time Nixon took office this ABM program had become deeply unpopular among members of Congress and their constituents. Nixon decided to revamp the program with the renamed Safeguard, focused on protecting military sites distant from heavily populated urban areas. The Administration started planning construction for the first two sites, with overall costs about the same as Sentinel at $6 billion.[32]

The potential costs of Safeguard were not necessarily of overriding concern for the Administration since it still considered the program mainly a negotiating tool. The Pentagon was invested with planning and implementing Safeguard, while Congress assumed responsibility for its funding. Laird knew that Congressional approval of Safeguard in the form of authorization and appropriations was crucial in turning the system into a legitimate threat in the eyes of the Soviets. Only a well-funded and well-planned Safeguard could strengthen the bargaining position of U.S. negotiators in Helsinki. Members of Congress, however, were not privy to these negotiations, and Nixon and Laird remained steadfast in their public support for ABM on its own terms as a technology without divulging its real utility for negotiations. Trying to persuade the Senate to go along with ABM was especially difficult for the Administration. The Senate had authorized the first two ABM sites at air force bases, but a subsequent vote authorized only one additional site and not protection for Washington, D.C. Kissinger worried that skepticism in the Senate diminished Safeguard's credibility, but at least the Pentagon had succeeded in jumpstarting ABM.[33]

Negotiations meanwhile continued in Helsinki. Any agreement had to be broad enough to reflect the dissimilarities in the U.S. and Soviet strategic force structures. The U.S. had over the span of a few decades built up a diverse Triad of bombers, ICBMs, and SLBMs. Lagging in the arms race, the

Soviets had concentrated on expanding their force of much heavier ICBMs, most of all the massive SS-9s. Yet Soviet modernization was already starting to blur these basic differences. In addition to Y-class subs, the Soviets had deployed the Backfire medium bomber, which with technical enhancements could be extended to intercontinental range. At the same time, U.S. negotiators heeded Nixon's admonition that any agreement must not apply to intermediate range missiles or tactical nuclear weapons in Europe. The agreement would only cover strategic offensive arms, eventually defined to mean weapons with a range greater than the distance between the most northeastern part of the U.S. and the most northwestern part of the Soviet Union.

In Moscow in May 1972, Nixon and Brezhnev signed an ABM Treaty and an Interim Agreement on offensive arms. The ABM Treaty restricted missile defense only to the protection of a missile installation and the national capital. Since the Pentagon had just begun building the first two Safeguard sites using funds appropriated by Congress, the treaty did not disrupt ABM planning. As Laird and Nixon had hoped, the Administration instead managed to push Safeguard ahead far enough along to gain leverage in the Helsinki talks. The Pentagon would now be obligated to abandon the full twelve site system. The Interim Agreement on offensive arms, meanwhile, prohibited construction of new land-based ICBM launchers while capping SLBMs, essentially freezing offensive arms at existing levels. An attached protocol to the agreement directed that the U.S. maintain no more than 710 SLBMs and 44 ballistic missile subs, while the Soviets were limited to 950 SLBMs and 62 such subs. The agreement did not address MIRVs and in effect allowed the Navy to replace Polaris with Poseidon, which would increase warhead counts, even as the number of SLBMs and subs stayed within the SALT limits. Nonetheless, the agreement did not especially favor the American side, especially since the Soviets threatened to MIRV their huge ICBMs and gain a tremendous advantage. In retrospect the Moscow summit and the signing of SALT I marked the zenith of detente, from which point it would only face heavier criticism and steadily lose its influence over public opinion, but at the time the Administration urgently needed to reach a new agreement to resolve lingering uncertainties.

Nixon thus departed from the scene after having secured a notable accomplishment in diplomatic affairs but with a great deal more work ahead. At the same time, the budgetary ramifications of arms control could not be easily comprehended. The ABM Treaty had saved the U.S. from having to spend huge amounts of money on blanket anti-missile coverage, while the interim ceilings on offensive arms in principle held down what might have been an unstoppable arms race in ICBMs. Yet both sides were still unhindered in MIRVing their missiles.

WOES AT THE SUCCESSION

Gerald Ford assumed office just as the economy entered a stagflation tailspin, fomented by the combination of high inflation and economic contraction. Stagflation was first apparent when inflation stayed over 4% through the 1969–1970 recession, which admittedly lasted only two quarters. The oil shock of 1973–1974 then exacerbated the whole monetary and economic setting after OPEC, the club of Middle Eastern oil exporters, cut output and embargoed oil exports to the U.S. in retaliation for its support to Israel during the 1973 Arab-Israeli conflict. Besides geopolitical animosities, OPEC was motivated to reduce output and recoup lost revenue in response to the dollar's continued slide in the world markets under the new floating exchange rates. Oil was priced in dollars, and a depreciating dollar crimped profits for the exporters. The Nixon Administration had imposed price controls on crude oil and gas along with general goods and services. By the end of April 1974 it had lifted the non-energy controls, after which consumer prices shot up by 7.9% for the rest of that year and then peaked at 8.4% the next year.[34] At the same time, the economy floundered through a long, two-year recession, also the first time the economy posted annual negative growth since 1958. While the conditions underlying stagflation were first observable as early as 1970, then temporarily forestalled by high rates of real GDP growth, they blew out into the open four years later. Under no circumstances could the new Administration hope to balance the budget when encountering these economic headwinds. It projected a deficit of $34.7 billion for FY 1975, almost ten times that of the year before.[35]

Yet Ford's background suited him for these challenges. His membership on the House Appropriations Committee for over two decades before his elevation to minority leader and then vice president made him unusually knowledgeable of the budget. As president he formed an Economic Policy Board among trusted advisers to thrash out policy options. His conservative inclinations first led him to formulate policies for checking inflation instead of fomenting growth. Drawing a page from the playbook of 1968, Ford proposed in October 1974 temporary surtaxes to regain revenue and slow inflation. He wanted the 5% surtaxes to be levied on individuals and corporations only during CY 1975. To ameliorate the effects of new taxes in a recession, Ford proposed that the surtax only apply to individuals with incomes above designated limits. Depending on whether they filed jointly as a married couple or as a single person, taxpayers earning at or below $15,000 and $7,500 respectively could expect relief from the surtax. The surtax would meanwhile be imposed on all corporations. Except for permanently increasing the investment tax credit up to 10%, Ford intended for most of his proposals to be implemented within a temporary timeframe.[36]

Ford unveiled various other proposals as part of his Whip Inflation Now (WIN) agenda, which beneath the sloganeering and memorabilia of pins and hats mainly relied on tight fiscal policy to rein in prices. Ford abstained from calling for a disinflationary monetary policy, which in any event lay within the purview of the autonomous Federal Reserve, and he was saddled with a long recession. The worsening contraction indeed forced the Administration into making a U-turn on fiscal policy by the time Ford submitted his budget request for FY 1976. Now the Administration pivoted from counteracting inflation to pushing the economy out of recession, with Ford proposing tax cuts of one year's duration in the form of 12% refunds up to $1,000, a temporary cut in corporate taxes from 48% to 42% for incomes over $25,000 also for one year, and an equally temporary increase in the investment tax credit up to 12%. His proposals included a permanent feature for expanding the standard deduction, but otherwise he intended these measures to foster recovery over the short-term. The final legislation passed by Congress, the Tax Reduction Act of 1975 (TRA-75), retained the transitory aspects of these policies. With Ford's signature, Congress legislated a 10% rebate on last year's returns within a narrow band of $100 to $200, a 10% investment tax credit for a two-year period, a $30 credit for 1975, a 10% refundable earned income credit also for 1975, and an expanded standard deduction again for 1975.[37]

The Administration would not be able to submit a balanced budget for the foreseeable future, but nor did its top officials presume that economic conditions justified increased spending. Ford indicated in his budget message that "tax relief, not more Government spending, is the key to turning the economy around to renewed growth."[38] He frequently relied on his veto power to block attempts by Congress to raise spending. He even vetoed a bill that included another round of tax cuts but not offsetting spending cuts. He still managed to compromise over extensions for TRA-75.[39] The modest, temporary tax relief passed by Congress helped revive the economy from its slump, if not entirely subdue inflationary pressures. Real GDP posted growth of 5.4% by 1976.[40]

Ford successfully pushed through timely anti-recession measures, but the longer-term outlook still looked grim. Even after OPEC ended the embargo the U.S. remained dependent on reduced output of foreign oil, while the world had already endured a global food crisis wrought by poor harvests and distortionary government policies, only putting further upward pressure on inflation. On energy Ford listened to his advisers and proposed a plan to drive domestic production by imposing a tariff on oil imports and decontrolling oil and gas prices. The program was purely economic, at its heart a recognition that the price controls stifled domestic production of oil and natural gas and had to be lifted to incentivize investment in the energy sector. But Ford could not sell the plan to Congress precisely because it would have hurt consumers over the short-term. Subsequent legislation instead focused on energy price controls, conservation, and fuel economy standards. Ford's overarching domestic concern continued to be deficits, which in his view were interrelated with inflation. Cutting down on deficits had to be undertaken not only for its own sake, to mitigate future debt burdens, but to force a return to price stability, while on the other hand rampant inflation only drove higher deficits.

TOWARDS SALT II: OPPORTUNITY AND INTRANSIGENCE

Nixon had bequeathed to Ford an unfinished SALT, with various obstacles stalling the progress of talks. The arms race between the two sides had now come full circle and reaped a forum for highly arcane discussions. Arms control suffered from criticism that it was arbitrary and superficial. Like an ancient rune its lexicon for non-experts could be indecipherable. Negotiators struggled to define weapons systems in a certain way and how these weapons could be counted under particular requirements. Yet the substantive complexities obscured the core reality of the process, which was to compress tensions by keeping the two sides talking amenably to one another in hopes of arriving at some workable settlement governing nuclear weapons. The talks had definite goals, in the nearer term capping MIRVs and perhaps over the longer-term eliminating whole classes of weapons systems. The U.S. and Soviet Union also had unrelated economic and political issues to discuss through their interlocutors, such as trade in wheat and grain and European security, but the two sides had become locked into the arms control puzzle precisely because of the weapons they now aimed at each other. Despite the at times seemingly convoluted nature of the deliberations, the U.S. and Soviets lacked an alternative modus operandi unless they wanted to return to a dangerously unregulated arms race.

The Soviets planned to MIRV their land-based ICBMs of up to 360 in number compared to 550 for the U.S., and a framework needed to be devised for capping MIRVs in a way agreeable to both sides. By the time Ford took office, the Soviets had rejected most of the U.S. proposals, including a freeze on MIRVs at currently deployed levels, a cap on MIRVs linked to missile throw weight, a new ceiling of 1,150 U.S. MIRVs against 700 Soviet MIRVs, and a prohibition of heavy missiles equipped with MIRVs. For their part, the Soviets offered a ceiling of respectively 1,100 U.S. MIRVs and 1,000 Soviet MIRVs, but U.S. negotiators could not accept a ceiling so low that it would stifle the further development and production of Trident SLBMs, which would be phased-in after Poseidon.[41]

Any workable SALT II agreement probably could not forever cement the U.S.'s lead in MIRVs, whether land or sub-based. The Soviets clearly had no interest in an agreement that limited their heavy missiles, while U.S. negotiators bristled at Soviet attempts to restrict Trident. Kissinger still crafted new proposals early in the Ford Administration that aimed to stop a Soviet build-up of MIRVed heavy missiles. In addition to outright prohibiting MIRVed heavy ICBMs, he offered in his dialogues with the Soviets the idea of subjecting both sides to equal aggregate limits of 2,200 on all types of strategic nuclear delivery vehicles over a ten-year span until 1985. This ceiling further entailed a sublimit of 1,320 MIRV-equipped missiles. The sublimit was ostensibly high enough to cater to the U.S.'s Trident program while also allowing the Soviets to continue building MIRVed ICBMs. To lessen the sting of banning MIRVed heavy missiles, Kissinger further offered to limit the range on air to surface missiles. From the U.S. perspective, any such limitation served as an important concession. If the new agreement disadvantaged the Soviets' propensity for big, land-based missiles, it also disadvantaged the U.S.'s over three-decade lead in bombers. The Kremlin twisted the notion of equal aggregate limits somewhat when counteroffering 2,400 delivery vehicles for the Soviets as opposed to 2,200 for the U.S. while still accepting the necessity of a separate MIRV sublimit. The Soviets also sought to limit the U.S. advantage in ASM technology by requiring that ASMs loaded onto new bombers not exceed a range of over 4,000 kilometers. And consistent with this requirement they wanted ASMs to count as a type of nuclear delivery vehicle under the equal aggregate limits.[42]

In October 1974, Ford and other top Administration officials toured the Far East, with stops in Japan, Korea, and Siberia. Ford greeted Brezhnev for the first time at the Siberian city of Vladivostok on the Pacific coast before their entourages traveled by railway to the smaller resort town of Okeanskaya. By this point Brezhnev seemed to have embraced the idea of equal aggregate limits and now agreed to a 2,400 ceiling on all strategic nuclear delivery vehicles—ICBMs, SLBMs, and heavy bombers—along with a 1,320 sublimit on MIRVs. Ford and Kissinger responded with the same approach of conceding limits on U.S. air and naval power while still trying to put a halt to Soviet construction of MIRVed heavy missiles. Without rejecting the ceilings on all delivery vehicles and on MIRVs, Ford counteroffered with additional ceilings on ICBMs, SLBMs, and bombers. In exchange for the Soviets agreeing to limit their heavy SS-18 ICBMs to only 180 in number, with or without MIRVs, the U.S. would maintain a fleet of only 250 bombers and keep its total SLBM count at or under 288. In trying to push back against Brezhnev, Ford and Kissinger wanted to ensure the deployment of the B-1 and Trident while also keeping a lid on the mainstay of Soviet nuclear deterrence. Not surprisingly, Brezhnev recoiled at the proposal. He wanted a flexible arms control regime that did not impede the Soviet missile buildup that had started when he took the helm as party chairman. Brezhnev also wanted limits on ASMs. Designating ASMs as a nuclear delivery vehicle under the SALT rules served as a far more modest workaround than outright range restrictions. The two leaders eventually reached an understanding on this more modest concession of incorporating "Skybolt-type" ballistic ASMs into the equal aggregate limits, which had largely been the position of U.S. negotiators all along.[43]

But talks continued to stall over the Backfire and another type of ASM, cruise missiles, during the remainder of Ford's presidency. While the Soviets argued that the Tupolev Tu-22M "Backfire" should be classified as a medium bomber not capable of striking targets in the U.S., with technical improvements such as midair refueling it could conceivably fly two-way missions of intercontinental range. In this scenario it should have counted as a nuclear delivery vehicle subject to the equal aggregate limits. The Soviets, meanwhile, demanded that air launched cruise missiles (ALCMs) with a range of over 600 kilometers, an ASM that could be equipped with a nuclear warhead, be included in the equal aggregate limits. The distinction between ALCMs and air launched ballistic missiles in the mold of Skybolt, over which little dispute remained, was pertinent because ALCMs, even if launched hundreds of miles from Soviet air defenses, still flew within the atmosphere and might not warrant inclusion as a strategic delivery vehicle, especially if the Soviets were not interested in conceding limits on the Backfire. U.S. officials broached various ways to bridge the divide. For instance, the Pentagon formulated a negotiating position that started counting the Backfire under the equal aggregate limits only after the Soviets had produced and deployed 100 of the aircraft, while from its end the U.S. would refrain from deploying more than 100 F-111s. Another option restricted the production of tanker aircraft, which would have been necessary for refueling the Backfire in midair.[44]

U.S. negotiators also tried to link an agreement on the Backfire to concessions regarding sea-launched cruise missiles (SLCMs), where they were more malleable. For instance, when visiting Brezhnev in Moscow in January 1976, Kissinger offered to cap the number of surface ships armed with SLCMs at only twenty-five over the course of five years ending in 1982. The Soviets would in exchange agree to only produce 275 Backfires during this same period. But most importantly, Kissinger conceded to counting bombers carrying ALCMs with a range of over 600 kilometers as MIRVed vehicles under the equal aggregate limits, which went a long way to meeting Soviet demands. It also showed how much the U.S. side wanted to control the production and deployment of the Backfire, now the major stumbling block in negotiations.[45]

The U.S.'s need for a heavy, mobile ICBM further affected the calculations of arms control negotiators. Pentagon planners increasingly worried that the Soviets could in time wipe out the Minuteman arsenal in a first strike. The U.S. might still rely on bombers and SLBMs in a reprisal attack, but the growing vulnerability of the Minuteman missiles endangered the country's means for nuclear deterrence. Such a weakness in land-based nuclear forces could not be permitted. For FY 1978, Donald Rumsfeld, Ford's chief of staff who took over as defense secretary after a Cabinet shakeup in October 1975, sought nearly $300 million in developmental funds for the heavy MX missile to accelerate its readiness by the mid-1980s. By the time he submitted this annual report the Ford Administration had entered its last days, but decisions on the MX were not about to go away with it. Rumsfeld envisioned deploying the MX through a "survivable basing mode" that relied principally upon mobility and concealment.[46] Deployment of the MX still waited a decade into the future. Kissinger, meanwhile, ruminated that a ban on deploying mobile ICBMs under SALT II was not necessarily detrimental to national security. The U.S. could deploy the MX when it was ready by the time the next arms control agreement expired in the mid-1980s. Yet he also recognized concerns that such a ban on deployment might weaken the Pentagon's hand in securing funds from Congress for continued work on the missile.[47]

In the end, influenced by skepticism among top defense officials towards the SALT process, Ford refrained from pushing for a deal during the 1976 election cycle, especially with his foreign policy under attack from the left and right. The arms control discussions on strategic nuclear weapons also magnified the importance of conventional forces, and the Administration was not prepared to reduce defense costs in a time of high inflation. Ford requested $8 billion more in defense spending for FY 1976. But inflation aside, the Administration also wanted to forge ahead in heavying up regular forces and returning to the core task of defending Europe. While Ford outwardly held out hope for mutual drawdowns in NATO and Warsaw Pact forces, he planned to harden the Army's combat capabilities through an increase in the number of active divisions from thirteen up to sixteen while keeping personnel levels the same.[48] In the same vein, Rumsfeld noted the important development of a new medium tank and a mechanized infantry combat vehicle to replace the M113. These projects worked on the future M1 Abrams tank and the M2 Bradley fighting vehicle.[49]

Ford failed to secure SALT II, with ambiguous consequences for the budget, though the negotiations at least steadied the military's strategic framework at a time when inflation and high nominal interest rates meant the government could ill afford a full-scale arms race.

TRANSITION, GROWING OVERSTRETCH

The beginning of CY 1976 marked a moment when the budget under older assumptions looked like it should have returned to surplus. Economic recovery had begun by the second quarter of 1975 and continued without interruption. Yet when Ford submitted his budget request for FY 1977, the Administration estimated a deficit of $43 billion for the year, the same as in FY 1975 and a decline from $76 billion expected for FY 1976.[50] The rebounding economy could no longer automatically propel the budget back into surplus territory. The last time these circumstances helped produce surplus revenue, however minimal, had been in 1960, which was right on the cusp of a comparatively mild recession, while tax hikes generated the 1969 surplus. Ford instead vowed in his message that, under the Administration's plan for reducing the annual growth in federal spending to 5.5%, the budget could be balanced by 1980.[51]

This projection depended upon external economic factors, while the inability to fully extinguish inflationary pressures might have necessitated tight monetary policy in the future. Ford's budget request, which boldly planned for surplus in three years, really signified the government's increasing loss of control over its own budget. It could no longer anticipate a surplus even in a peacetime expansion, now with the Vietnam War over, the first oil shock in the past, a revived economy, and a president who did everything he could within his constitutional powers to cut spending. No single reason fully explained why the Administration now needed a three-year window to plan for a surplus, but transfer payments under Medicaid and Medicare were consuming ever larger chunks of revenue. In actual expenditures for 1977, Medicaid paid out $9.9 billion[52] and the federal contribution to Medicare Part B rose to $5 billion.[53] The on-budget deficit ultimately reached $50 billion for that year,[54] so that the combined general revenue expenditures for Medicaid and Medicare equaled 29% of the deficit. Tax expenditures, old and new, also drove the rise in deficits, with the Administration predicting that the expanded investment tax credit would lead to over $9 billion in revenue losses for that year alone if made permanent, while deductions for mortgage interest and homeowner property taxes would total $7.7 billion in lost revenue.[55] Nor was the Administration predisposed to drastically cutting defense spending to offset rising entitlement transfer payments and tax expenditures. It instead planned for a $9 billion increase in defense outlays for FY 1977.[56]

The Ford Administration could not avoid fiscal overstretch. The government was committed to increasing defense spending even in an age of detente, boosting economic growth through tax breaks, and transferring payments to eligible beneficiaries under mandatory rules. Ford still conveyed a well-earned record of achievement to the public as he fought for nomination and then reelection in 1976, having worked to rescue the economy from stagflation while restoring confidence in government after Watergate. Yet foreign policy had turned into a weak point for Ford during the election cycle. The Ford foreign policy record came under assault from conservatives, who lambasted detente as weak and feckless, and liberals, who castigated the amorality of realpolitik and its lack of attention to human rights. The Ford-

Kissinger foreign policy also suffered blows from a third group, neo-conservatives, domestic liberals who wanted to toe a hard line against the Soviets. In 1974, Senator Henry Jackson of Washington State, a leading neo-conservative in Congress, demanded an amendment to a trade bill that required Moscow to ease restrictions on the emigration of its own citizens. The Administration eventually worked out a deal with Jackson, and Congress passed the trade bill, but by then the Soviets were uninterested in applying for most favored nation status, one of the original aims of the bill.

Detente began to encounter a higher level of criticism by late 1974, especially with SALT II on hold. Then in the summer of 1975 Ford, along with thirty-four other world leaders, signed the Helsinki Final Act, which concluded the Conference on Security and Cooperation in Europe. The Helsinki Accords were organized functionally into a series of baskets that addressed a range of issues affecting the peoples of Europe, including the ratification of political borders, trade, human rights, and cultural exchanges. The agreement represented another milestone for detente and a concrete diplomatic achievement for Ford, even if it did not carry the force of a binding treaty. Yet depending upon one's perspective, the Helsinki Accords either held the communist governments to account for their actions in repressing dissent or it legitimated Soviet suzerainty over Eastern Europe. The latter view benefited from the fact that the Warsaw Pact had long promoted the idea of such a conference, while NATO, and the U.S. especially, had only cautiously accepted the start of talks.

The former California governor and Hollywood actor Ronald Reagan entered the primary race in late 1975 mainly to attack Ford's foreign policy record, which he vociferously opposed. He also leapt onto the Panama Canal as a campaign issue after the Administration agreed to enter negotiations with the Panamanian government over future rights to the canal. Ford held off Reagan to win the nomination before going against Jimmy Carter in the national election. A former Navy officer, peanut farmer, and governor of the state of Georgia, Carter denounced the "Ford recession" that had already come to pass, and he also vowed to balance the budget by 1980. Carter positioned himself as an outsider who proverbially ran against Washington, which as a catchphrase carried as much resonance as it ever would in the post-Watergate political environment. He wanted to base foreign policy upon a new avowal of human rights without undoing the arms control framework. The race tightened in the autumn, but detente and Helsinki spelled trouble for Ford after he fumbled an answer during one of the presidential debates on Eastern Europe. He appeared unwilling to acknowledge that the Soviets in any way dominated the region, perhaps to express his belief that one day these states would be free of foreign subjugation, but to many observers the gaffe came across as sheer ignorance.

Carter's narrow electoral victory did not in the end significantly alter the course of taxes and spending from the Ford or Nixon years. Carter favored incrementally expanding entitlements, but in practice his administration's fiscal posture did not differ hugely from Ford's. He gravitated to lean budgets, even as an actual balanced budget did not enter the near term picture. Presiding over a $45 billion deficit for FY 1977, the incoming Carter Administration estimated it to climb to $61 billion by 1979. When proposing $25 billion in tax cuts, Carter noted the viability of "a path that will permit a balanced budget in the future if the private economy continues its recovery over the coming years."[57] The Carter Administration resisted coordinating spending and tax cuts as Ford wanted by 1975. Yet with his technical background in engineering Carter still sought to eliminate waste and inefficiency in government operations. He directed that the federal government adopt zero-base budgeting in order to instill a fresh reappraisal of spending year in and year out.[58]

However beneficial zero-base budgeting may have been, the Administration would have to be much more aggressive in its approach to spending cuts if it wanted to turn in a surplus within the next few years. But like its predecessors the Administration was beset with a multitude of commitments that could not be easily compromised.

DETENTE ENDS, DEFENSE TURNAROUND

The Pentagon budget served as an obvious target for cuts, and the Administration focused on ways to reduce defense costs in its first year. These initial cutbacks relied on cancelling a few big-ticket items and curbing Navy spending. With the Administration bound to the Army's 16 division structure and bulking up combat forces designated for Europe, it instead devoted its cost cutting energies to two expensive and controversial weapons systems, the MX missile and the B-1 bomber. As costly as the MX missile might be once deployed—perhaps as high as $33 billion, double the costs of strategic forces at the time—Carter and his defense secretary, Harold Brown, could not realistically forgo further development and eventual production of the missile. The danger of an eviscerating Soviet first strike on the vulnerable Minuteman silos seemed increasingly likely in the next decade, and a large, mobile missile provided the deterrent power necessary to eliminate the feasibility of such a preemptive attack from behind the Iron Curtain. Only after this preliminary decision did the Administration confront the real challenge of trying to persuade members of Congress on the merits of its mobile basing scheme. MX missiles would be deployed into arteries of racetracks and shelters across a swathe of the Southwest. Local politicians and environmental activists united to stop the plan, and Carter failed to deploy the missile by the time he left office.[59]

Unlike the MX, the decision on the B-1, a high-altitude supersonic bomber, resulted in a conclusive outcome on Capitol Hill, at least during Carter's term. The B-1's estimated costs ran as high as $100 million per aircraft. ALCMs fired from B-52s flying hundreds of miles from the Soviet border represented a viable alternative, especially as improving air defenses in the U.S.S.R. threatened to decimate B-1s streaking into Soviet airspace. Having answered inconclusively when asked about the subject on the campaign trail, Carter at last decided to cancel the B-1 while going forward with the MX. But the B-1 dilemma had not been easily resolvable. Some experts argued that arming B-52s with ALCMs might eventually cost more than a stretched out procurement schedule for the B-1, which was expected to successfully get through Soviet air defenses at least for the next ten years. As a gesture to B-1 advocates like Barry Goldwater, Carter agreed to fund development costs for a few prototypes while otherwise canceling the project.[60]

Not prejudiced by his background as an Annapolis midshipman, Carter wanted to further maximize cost savings by cutting the Navy's budget. The Administration reduced the procurement of ballistic missile submarines, decided against another *Nimitz* class nuclear powered carrier (to the point where Carter vetoed an authorization bill for such a carrier), and wanted to replace more F-14 Tomcats with new, less costly F/A-18 Hornets. The dispute over F-14s versus F/A-18s revealed differences in naval strategy. The F-14 performed as an aggressive fighter to facilitate offensive aerial operations against the Soviet Union. The F/A-18, on the other hand, served as a multipurpose aircraft of limited range, a function more consistent with a passive naval posture of defending sea lanes. The cost of the F-14 compelled Brown to push for procuring a larger number of F/A-18s, even as this policy ran into opposition in the Navy and Congress.[61] The Administration's economizing on naval expenditures inevitably affected the shipbuilding program begun under Ford, which now needed to be downsized. It planned to reduce naval procurement to only fourteen ships and even investigate the advantage of obtaining more aircraft carriers in general, whether conventional, nuclear, or vertical takeoff and landing.[62]

The Administration foremost wanted to retool the FY 1979 defense budget by heavying up the Army and improving its combat mission in Europe. Ford had begun this process by increasing the Army's divisions from thirteen to sixteen, but now Carter wanted to address underlying weaknesses in this mission through the procurement of new weapons systems and bulking up existing units. For the first time, the Administration ordered M-1 Abrams tanks and Patriot SAMs into production. It also increased procurement of the new A-10 "Warthog," an anti-tank dive bomber, along with fighter aircraft like the F-15 Eagle and F-16 Fighting Falcon. In all, the Administration planned to spend an additional $5 billion on forces designated for NATO.[63] It strengthened ground forces in other ways. Brown intended to convert one of the light Army infantry divisions into a heavy mechanized division, bringing the total number of heavy divisions, both mechanized and armored, up to ten, compared to six light divisions, whether infantry, airborne, or air mobile.[64] Another project in development could not be publicly disclosed, stealth technology. The Pentagon increased funds for working on the future F-117 Nighthawk stealth fighter, which with its jagged edges was designed to evade radar and drop in unnoticed into enemy airspace.[65]

The Administration beefed up NATO forces as it also worked to conclude the SALT II agreement with the Soviets. The same obstacles slowed progress at the next round of talks in Geneva, but the groundwork had been laid for breaking the impasse. The Soviets were clearly not interested in incorporating the Backfire into the equal aggregate limits. Any deal negotiated between the two sides would have to separate the Backfire from the main agreement, and this is what happened when Carter and Brezhnev finally signed SALT II in Vienna in June 1979. The SALT II treaty text turned out being far longer and more complicated than the one for the Interim Agreement of 1972, with each article containing a series of agreed statements and common understandings. The agreement restricted all strategic delivery vehicles to between 2,400 and 2,250 in number and MIRVed vehicles to 1,320 over a five-year period. A bomber capable of carrying a cruise missile with a range in excess of 600 kilometers counted as a "heavy bomber" included within the equal aggregate limits, along with ICBMs, SLBMs, and ballistic ASMs, but the treaty did not otherwise impose range restrictions on ALCMs. Only an attached protocol prohibited both parties from deploying land and sea-based cruise missiles with a range in excess of 600 kilometers for a two-year period. As an addendum to the agreement, Brezhnev submitted a statement to Carter clarifying the Soviet guarantee to cap Backfire production at thirty aircraft per year.

The next major challenge was in compelling Congress to go along with the Administration. The Senate remained reluctant to ratify the treaty for the rest of 1979. Critics had already argued that detente made the U.S. look weak and the West divided compared to the rising Soviet military threat, and these fears were compounded by communist takeovers in several countries in Asia, Africa, and Latin America in the 1970s. This series of events did not signify a worldwide conspiracy directed by the Kremlin, a misconception dating to the 1950s. But the Soviets were ready to exploit upheaval wherever it existed, and upheaval broke out in areas that had before been relatively stable. In Ethiopia, mutinying soldiers formed the Marxist-Leninist Derg group and overthrew the emperor in 1974. Four years later, they repulsed Somalian forces in the Ogaden border region after a bloody war. The Soviet and Cuban-backed MPLA organization took over north and central Angola when the

Portuguese ended colonial rule and withdrew their last garrisons. Communist army officers staged a coup in Afghanistan in 1978, and a year later the left-wing Sandinistas brought down the Somoza dictatorship in Nicaragua. Among the most despairing of these communist victories had occurred in Southeast Asia a few years earlier. When hostilities between the North and South Vietnamese resumed in 1975, Ford, after unsuccessfully requesting an aid package from Congress, stated in a public address that the war was effectively over for the U.S., a great relief to the public at home but a clear signal that little could stop communist troops from entering Saigon. Across the border in Cambodia the doctrinaire Khmer Rouge overthrew a U.S.-supported military dictatorship and sent the country into a wave of unrest and mass execution so extreme and brutal that it came to be regarded as genocide.

These takeovers fueled the perception that around the world the communists were on the march. The Soviets took full advantage of the opportunities before them by sending in arms and equipment to support their new proxies. In East Africa, for instance, they shipped arms by air and sea to aid the Derg, including artillery and tanks, while Soviet military advisers along with Cuban ground troops established a presence in Ethiopia and Angola. Only in Afghanistan did the Soviets intervene directly when, in December 1979, KGB commandos and other special forces stormed the palace of the Afghan premier to assassinate him and secure the rule of a more compliant puppet ruler. The Kremlin then swiftly deployed troops, armored vehicles, and gunships to the country to begin a decade-long war against the Mujahedeen. The next year Soviet troops conducted exercises to simulate an invasion of Iran that briefly brought panic to the Carter Administration. Even in Afghanistan, however, the Soviets blundered into a protracted counterinsurgency that sapped their resources and manpower instead of staging a premeditated drive to the Indian Ocean.

The Soviet invasion of Afghanistan ended any hope of Senate ratification of SALT II, and Carter withdrew it from consideration the following January. But SALT II did not turn out to be a total failure. Both Carter and Brezhnev pledged to adhere to its terms, helping to fulfill the predictability and stability sought through the arms control process in the first place. The Administration now faced the larger challenge of responding to the image that detente had only led to U.S. military weakness against a resurgent Soviet Union. That was not really a fair assumption. With SALT keeping in check strategic weapons proliferation, the Pentagon had introduced or was in the process of developing sophisticated new weapons systems for conventional ground contingencies, NATO's historical Achilles heel, including the Abrams tank, the Bradley fighting vehicle, the Blackhawk helicopter, the Cobra and Apache attack helicopters, and the Nighthawk stealth fighter, not including strategic assets such as Trident SLBMs and air-launched cruise missiles. Yet in the face of new pressures, the Carter Administration began a five-year stretch out in increased defense spending that eventually morphed into the Reagan buildup. Carter requested $158.2 billion in defense spending authority for FY 1981 and planned for expenditures of $142.7 billion, translating into 5% and 3% real growth in the defense budget respectively.[66] Carter wanted to divert the extra funds into NATO forces and Trident.[67] The Administration had comparatively little trouble in pushing through this program in the increasingly hawkish atmosphere, with Congress appropriating $5 billion more than Carter had outlined in his supplemental.[68] By the time Carter submitted his budget for FY 1982 he was a lame-duck, but his requests were still consistent with the stretch out. He wanted $200 billion in spending authority to accommodate $184 billion in expenditures for that year, which were in turn planned to rise to $237.8 billion over the next three years.[69]

The defense stretch out coincided with a shift towards a more forcefully articulated foreign policy. In his state of the union address in January 1980, Carter ordered an embargo on all grain shipments to the Soviet Union. Policymakers had long seen the U.S.S.R.'s dependence on grain imports as a potential vulnerability through which concessions could be extracted, and Carter decided to use this economic leverage for all it was worth after the invasion of Afghanistan. He also proclaimed the aforenamed Carter Doctrine, the Administration's prerogative to repulse outside aggression against countries in the Middle East. The doctrine provided a ready-made framework for responding to emerging problems in an area that national security adviser Zbigniew Brzezinski dubbed the "arc of crisis" stretching from South Asia to the Horn of Africa. With the Soviet invasion of Afghanistan, the toppling of the Shah of Iran by radical dissidents, the taking of U.S. hostages at the embassy in Tehran, and a second oil shortage following the Iranian revolution, the Administration most of all wanted to assert its hegemony over this turmoil-ridden but strategically important area. Applying to a specific geopolitical context rather than serving as an abstract statement of principle, the doctrine led to the highly tangible idea of a Rapid Deployment Joint Task Force. As Brown explained in his report for FY 1981, the military would station transport ships and equipment at a specific point near the Middle East and any other strategically important region. In the event of a crisis, combat units could be swiftly airlifted to the prepositioned ships before starting military operations.[70] How this new capability would be employed and to what effect was not entirely clear. Airlifted Marines were not heavy enough to fight Soviet ground forces in the Middle East, but they could possibly secure oil facilities on the Arabian peninsula in the event of local unrest. The Pentagon created a command headquarters for the task force in North Carolina, with the prepositioned ships located at the Diego Garcia base in the Indian Ocean rented from the British. Troops detailed for the command carried out exercises in the Egyptian desert. The Reagan Administration turned the task force into the interservice Central Command, headquartered out of Tampa, Florida, in 1983.

Carter had never planned to start a mini arms buildup, even in conventional forces. Only world events transpired to force a new shift in this direction. The end of detente and calls for ramped up defense spending demonstrated the difficulty of trying to connect a moderate national security posture to a fiscally conservative budget approach. Even with the U.S. avoiding involvement in another shooting war, turmoil abroad triggered fiscal aftershocks at home.

DOMESTIC MISERIES

Consistent with his campaign pledge, Carter had hoped to eventually balance the budget as the economy improved, but he never achieved this goal. He took office at a time of solid economic growth nonetheless marred by a high unemployment rate, persistent inflation, and rising nominal interest rates. After reaching over 5.4% in 1976, real GDP growth fell to 4.6% the next year before rising again to 5.5% in 1978.[71] The unemployment rate, meanwhile, had fallen from a high of 8.5% in 1975 to 5.9% by 1979.[72] After hitting 8.4% in 1975, inflation in consumer prices excluding food and energy fell to the still problematically high 6% the next year. From that point on prices advanced steadily before jumping by 9.2% in 1980.[73] The recession of 1974–1975 had not wringed out inflation from the economy. While price growth had dropped by 1976, inflationary pressures accelerated again when Carter took office.

This misery index of inflation and unemployment put the Administration in a bind. Tight fiscal policy might have helped quell building inflation, but Carter also had to answer to constituencies affected by the unemployment rate. He ended up adopting a program of moderate tax relief for lower income individuals and for corporations that boosted economic growth but, like his predecessors, left inflation only getting stronger. The Tax Reduction and Simplification Act of 1977 (TRA-77) narrowly followed Carter's proposals of converting the percentage standard deduction, 16% of adjusted gross income bounded by minimum and maximum amounts, into a flat standard deduction of $2,200 and $3,200 for single and married filers respectively. The legislation also temporarily renewed the life of the refundable earned income tax credit for those with dependent children and a nonrefundable general tax credit for providing marginal assistance per capita.[74]

Carter proposed a more robust package for 1978. He wanted tax cuts tied to offsetting reform measures in order to forestall revenue losses. He sought to reduce the top personal rate from 70% to 68% and the bottom rate from 14% to 12%, while other brackets would receive a cut as high as 7%. His proposal also permanently kept the investment tax credit at 10% and expanded it to include structures instead of only machinery and other equipment. To offset revenue loss, the Administration planned to curtail deductions for medical expenses and political contributions while repealing altogether deductions for local taxes and an exclusion for up to $5,000 in death benefits.[75] When Carter signed the Revenue Act of 1978 into law in November, the legislation contained unmistakably expansionary features, such as a 10% increase in the capital gains exclusion, a $250 increase in the personal exemption (replacing the general tax credit), an increased and modified earned income credit, a restructuring of personal rates into fifteen brackets, a restructuring of corporate rates from three to five brackets, with the top rate falling from 48% to 46%, and a permanent 10% investment tax credit. All told, the Act generated $34.8 billion in new and extended tax cuts. The offsetting tax increases were by contrast minimal at only $1.4 billion.[76]

The Revenue Act of 1978 led to revenue losses of over $20 billion in the second year after its enactment. A 1980 windfall profits tax on oil producers offset much of these losses through over $15 billion current dollar revenue gains several years in a row.[77] The budget registered a deficit of $59.6 billion for FY 1980,[78] with rising prices inflating the deficit and distorting the revenue effects of tax legislation, but inflation also pushed incomes into higher brackets and boosted revenue. In real terms the deficit as a percentage of GDP stabilized for a while during the Carter era to 1.55% by 1979 after having risen to 3.9% in 1976.[79]

The Administration could not generate a budget surplus in these years, even with a strong economy and with Congress having yet to appropriate funds for deploying the MX missile. Slumping economic growth in the latter half of Carter's tenure provides one causal explanation by 1979–1980. But the fundamental reasons remained the same, a budget now organized into funding an array of commitments, whether for defense, tax expenditures, or the entitlement state. As Carter expanded government with the creation of the Departments of Energy, Health and Human Services, and Education (the latter two the result of a split up of Health, Education, and Welfare), defense and transfer payments consumed a massive portion of spending year in and year out. For FY 1979, defense costs climbed to $117.7 billion compared to $259.4 spent on human resources, which included Medicare, Medicaid, and veterans' benefits. Circumstantial factors also impacted the budget. Veterans' benefits, for instance, were bound to rise after a long shooting war and large-scale conscription. At the same time, inflation pushed up the government's nominal borrowing costs. Net interest payments (excluding interest earned from government trust funds) totaled $42.6 billion for 1979, $16 billion more than in 1976.[80]

Even as the Administration struggled to tighten spending, Carter was not entirely averse to funding expansion of the entitlement state at least partly from general revenue. Automatically indexing Social Security benefits for inflation had threatened to open a gap in the coming years between benefits and payroll taxes. Carter primarily wanted to raise the wage base, which cut off liability for payroll taxes at specified limits in income, in order to eliminate the impending shortfall. But he also proposed that under given economic conditions, such as high unemployment, general revenue funding kick in to help pay Social Security benefits. The funding scheme would have supposedly operated countercyclically in response to contracting payroll tax receipts in a slower economy, but it would have also turned Social Security away from exclusive reliance on payroll taxes for funding. Congress refused to incorporate the general revenue measure into the 1977 Amendments and instead raised the wage base and payroll taxes. A hike in payroll taxes from 5.85% to 6.7% was slated to go into effect in 1982, with the wage base increased from $16,000 to $31,000.[81]

On health care, however, Carter's proposals appeared more cautious compared to the calls for universal health insurance coming from the Senate. Carter elaborated on his national health care plan in a June 1979 address to Congress. The plan was designed to expand coverage among specific groups of people, such as seniors, those below a certain income level, those facing catastrophic expenses, and terminated employees. It was not universal in scope in the sense of mandating that every working adult hold health insurance. But Carter still planned for the federal government to pay out $18 billion in subsidies to these groups, over twice as much what employers and employees would in the aggregate be expected to pay in premiums. In addition to including a hospital cost containment measure, Carter wanted to hold off on implementing these subsidies until 1983, when hopefully the economy would be stronger and revenues larger.[82]

Carter's plan never carried much support in Congress. If anything, his disagreements over health care with Senator Edward Kennedy ignited a split in the Democratic Party and Kennedy's insurgent presidential campaign. Even with large Democratic majorities in Congress, Carter held off from more ambitious legislation for a single payer health care system. Though he did not succeed in actually balancing the budget, his record demonstrated a clear intention to keep spending in line and reflected a modicum of fiscal respectability. Deficits remained a prominent political issue and fed into the growing anti-government mood by 1980, but now they competed with other pressing problems for public attention, including high unemployment, double digit inflation, gas lines resulting from the 1979 oil shock, and the hostage crisis in Tehran, all contributing to a "crisis of confidence" that Carter warned of in one of his most notable addresses. Revolution had temporarily shut down Iran's oil production. The subsequent speculative hoarding of oil combined with meddling Energy Department policies produced a full-scale shortage in the U.S., which did not occur in Europe or elsewhere. Carter thus faced a wide range of problems by 1979–1980 and could not have been expected to remain fixated on balancing the budget. But Reagan's candidacy in the general election did put the budget squarely back into the public discourse.

Over the course of the 1960s and 1970s government debt to GDP had fallen and then plateaued, remaining generally stable except for a spike during the recession of 1974–1975. Yet stability in the ratio of public debt to GDP should not belie the fact that the government had now entered an era of deficit normality. The presidential administrations of the 1970s were cognizant of these fiscal challenges, but they could not effectively rein in deficits. They instead kept looking ahead to some distant future when economic growth would be robust enough to again help bring the budget back into surplus. In time that future became the present, and it would be defined by only bigger deficits.

NOTES

1. President, *1971 Budget*, 7.
2. Ibid., 20.
3. Richard A. Hunt, *Secretaries of Defense Historical Series, Vol. VII, Melvin Laird and the Foundation of the Post-Vietnam Military: 1969–1973* (Washington, D.C.: Historical Office, Office of the Secretary of Defense, 2015), 129–30.
4. Hunt, *Melvin Laird*, 8.
5. Ibid., 133.
6. President, *1971 Budget*, 81–82.
7. Secretary of Defense, *Annual Defense Department Report FY 1973* (Washington, D.C.: Government Printing Office, 1972), 22.
8. Secretary of Defense, *1973 Defense Annual Report*, 31.
9. Secretary of Treasury, *Annual Report of the Secretary of the Treasury on the State of the Finances for the Fiscal Year Ended June 30, 1969* (Washington, D.C.: Government Printing Office, 1970), 24–26.
10. Tempalski, "Revenue Effects," 17.
11. FRED, Real GDP.
12. FRED, Civilian Unemployment Rate.
13. President of U.S., *The Budget of the United States Government Fiscal Year 1974* (Washington, D.C.: Government Printing Office, 1973), 141.
14. FRED, Federal Receipts as Percent of GDP.
15. President of U.S., *The Budget of the United States Government Fiscal Year 1972* (Washington, D.C.: Government Printing Office, 1971), 10.
16. President of U.S., *The Budget of the United States Government Fiscal Year 1973* (Washington, D.C.: Government Printing Office, 1972), 15.
17. President, *1972 Budget*, 7.
18. Ibid., 10.
19. FRED, Real GDP.
20. Ibid.
21. FRED, Consumer Prices.
22. Secretary of Treasury, *Annual Report of the Secretary of the Treasury on the State of the Finances for the Fiscal Year Ended June 30, 1972* (Washington, D.C.: Government Printing Office, 1972), 36–39.
23. President, *1973 Budget*, 15.

24. President of U.S., *The Budget of the United States Government Fiscal Year 1976* (Washington, D.C.: Government Printing Office, 1975), 3.
25. President of U.S., *The Budget of the United States Government Fiscal Year 1977* (Washington, D.C.: Government Printing Office, 1976), 57.
26. The American Presidency Project, "Richard Nixon: Address to the Nation on Domestic Programs, August 08, 1969," https://www.presidency.ucsb.edu/documents/address-the-nation-domestic-programs, accessed January 2019.
27. President of U.S., *The Budget of the United States Government Fiscal Year 1975* (Washington, D.C.: Government Printing Office, 1974), 67.
28. President, *1975 Budget*, 64.
29. OMB, "Historical Tables," 61.
30. President, *1975 Budget*, 63.
31. Secretary of Defense, *Fiscal Year 1971 Defense Program and Budget* (Washington, D.C.: Government Printing Office, 1970), 35–36.
32. Hunt, *Melvin Laird*, 398–99.
33. Ibid., 417–18.
34. FRED, Consumer Prices.
35. President, *1976 Budget*, 3.
36. Secretary of Treasury, *Annual Report of the Secretary of the Treasury on the State of the Finances for the Fiscal Year Ended June 30, 1975* (Washington, D.C.: Government Printing Office, 1975), 43.
37. Secretary of Treasury, *1975 Treasury Annual Report*, 43–45.
38. President, *1976 Budget*, 4.
39. Secretary of Treasury, *Annual Report of the Secretary of the Treasury on the State of the Finances for the Fiscal Year Ended June 30, 1976 and Transition Quarter* (Washington, D.C.: Government Printing Office, 1977), 52–53.
40. FRED, Real GDP.
41. Folder: "NSC Meeting, 9/14/1974." NSC Meeting File. Box 1. Gerald R. Ford Presidential Library.
42. Folder: "NSC Meeting, 12/2/1974." NSC Meeting File. Box 1. Gerald R. Ford Presidential Library.
43. 12/2/1974 NSC meeting.
44. Folder: "NSC Meeting, 7/25/1975." NSC Meeting File. Box 2. Gerald R. Ford Presidential Library.
45. Folder: "NSC Meeting, 7/30/1976." NSC Meeting File. Box 2. Gerald R. Ford Presidential Library.
46. Secretary of Defense, *Annual Defense Department Report FY 1978* (Washington, D.C.: Government Printing Office, 1977), 129–30.
47. 7/25/1975 NSC meeting.
48. President, *1976 Budget*, 70.
49. Secretary of Defense, *Annual Defense Department Report FY 1977* (Washington, D.C.: Government Printing Office, 1976), 142–43.
50. President, *1977 Budget*, 2.
51. Ibid., M3–M4.
52. OMB, "Historical Tables," 335.
53. Ibid., 314.
54. Ibid., 25.
55. President, *1977 Budget*, 58–59.
56. Ibid., 61.
57. President of U.S., *The Budget of the United States Government Fiscal Year 1979* (Washington, D.C.: Government Printing Office, 1978), 3–4.
58. President, *1979 Budget*, 6–7.
59. Edward C. Keefer, *Secretaries of Defense Historical Series, Vol. VIII, Harold Brown, Offsetting the Soviet Military Challenge: 1977–1981* (Washington, D.C.: Historical Office, Office of the Secretary of Defense, 2017), 176–79.
60. Keefer, *Harold Brown*, 48–57.

61. Ibid., 222–23.
62. President, *1979 Budget*, 72–73.
63. Ibid., 70–72.
64. Secretary of Defense, *Department of Defense Annual Report Fiscal Year 1979* (Washington, D.C.: Government Printing Office, 1978), 141.
65. Keefer, *Harold Brown*, 577.
66. President of U.S., *The Budget of the United States Government Fiscal Year 1981* (Washington, D.C.: Government Printing Office, 1980), M4.
67. President, *1981 Budget*, 91.
68. Keefer, *Harold Brown*, 565.
69. President of U.S., *Budget of the United States Government Fiscal Year 1982* (Washington, D.C.: Office of Management and Budget, 1981), 93.
70. Secretary of Defense, *Department of Defense Annual Report Fiscal Year 1981* (Washington, D.C.: Government Printing Office, 1980), 115–16.
71. FRED, Real GDP.
72. FRED, Civilian Unemployment Rate.
73. FRED, Consumer Prices.
74. Secretary of Treasury, *Annual Report of the Secretary of the Treasury on the State of the Finances Fiscal Year 1977* (Washington, D.C.: Government Printing Office, 1978), 46–47.
75. Secretary of Treasury, *Annual Report of the Secretary of the Treasury on the State of the Finances Fiscal Year 1978* (Washington, D.C.: Government Printing Office, 1979), 57–61.
76. Secretary of Treasury, *Annual Report of the Secretary of the Treasury on the State of the Finances Fiscal Year 1979* (Washington, D.C.: Government Printing Office, 1980), 51–53.
77. Tempalski, "Revenue Effects," 16.
78. President, *1982 Budget*, M3.
79. FRED, Federal Surplus or Deficit as Percent of GDP.
80. President, *1981 Budget*, 78–79.
81. Secretary of Treasury, *1978 Treasury Annual Report*, 64.
82. The American Presidency Project, "Jimmy Carter: National Health Plan Message to the Congress on Proposed Legislation, June 12, 1978," https://www.presidency.ucsb.edu/documents/national-health-plan-message-the-congress-proposed-legislation, accessed January 2019.

Chapter Six

Deficit Horizon

Reagan and Bush, 1981–1991

The Reagan Revolution took full aim at the perceived excesses of government. Its titular leader personally cultivated the image of the natural kind of leader to downsize administration, de-regulate, cut back spending, and usher in a new era of consistently balanced budgets that had been out of reach for decades. Reagan had a penchant on the campaign trail and in meetings for telling jokes and anecdotes about the absurdities of bloated government bureaucracy. His unusual background made him completely different from almost all other politicians, and the evident preference for a course correction among the public carried him to decisive electoral victory in 1980. Reagan set an optimistic tone in office, which many argued was an achievement in itself. Yet Reagan's optimism would be tested by the challenge of putting his principles to practical effect.

From very early on, Reagan's presidency was also tested by disinflation. The Volcker Federal Reserve had already changed its operating procedures in October 1979 to facilitate monetary tightening, a blunt approach for squeezing inflation from the economy through open market operations. The Fed quickly retreated from this posture in early 1980 after the start of a new recession and decided to wait out the presidential campaign. But after Reagan assumed office the Fed renewed its tightening even at great economic cost until it determined that the inflation picture had settled back to normal. Disinflation was bound to be costly after years of wage-price spirals. Prices remained obstinately high during the trough of stagflation in 1974–1975, and now only an even worse recession finally altered the economic environment away from a widespread belief in advancing, unstoppable prices. Negative real GDP growth hit 1.8% in 1982 compared to .54% in 1974.[1] Post–World

War II unemployment peaked at 9.7% in 1982, more than the 8.5% rate sustained in 1975 and just barely exceeding the 9.6% rate in the wake of the Great Recession almost thirty years later. Unemployment thereafter fell during the remainder of the Reagan presidency, eventually coming to 5.5% in 1988, its lowest level since 1973.[2] Yet the Fed extinguished the specter of invincible inflation, cutting consumer price growth by over half from 9.2% in 1980 to 4.1% by 1984.[3] Reagan presided over the end of a long inflationary era, even as inflation still ticked up for the rest of the decade, and he provided support for the Fed's disinflationary policies against fierce political opposition. Tax cuts, which had previously been thought to cause or at least exacerbate inflation, took on new meaning as the Fed simultaneously tightened the screws on its monetary policy. Yet with disinflation came new problems, including an appreciating dollar and a bulging trade deficit, which hit a high of $154 billion in 1987.[4]

The Reagan Administration pursued an agenda of cutting taxes, reducing domestic spending, and expanding the defense stretch out begun under Carter. Policies in the 1980s did not follow a linear progression. Rising deficits compelled pushback in Congress for tax hikes and deficit control legislation, while the entitlement state became an arena for modification if not total restructuring. In the end, debt to GDP spurted up to its highest level since World War II, an unprecedented trend during a peacetime economic expansion.

TAX CUTS, TAX HIKES, TAX REFORM

Reagan entered office having embraced the supply side theory of income tax cuts to drive capital accumulation and investment. It was predicated on the Laffer curve that lower rates incentivize work and, if not entirely capable of paying for themselves, at least offset some of the expected revenue shortfall. Republican Senator William Roth and Congressman Jack Kemp backed legislation for these across the board supply side cuts in 1978 after California passed a referendum that reduced property taxes without cutting spending or in any other way mitigating revenue losses. The Roth-Kemp plan called for cutting income taxes by 33%, inviting the criticism that it would do nothing but worsen inflation and the deficit. The proposal seemed ill-timed to many. In its report on the plan, the CBO conceded growth effects over a five-year period while acknowledging the danger of exacerbated deficits and inflation. Though advocates of Roth-Kemp emphasized its incentives for capital investment, the CBO report noted broader repercussions for the economy, including effects on aggregate demand and the production process that might ultimately hinder the efficient allocation of goods and services, contrary to what the backers of the plan wanted. The tax law could, for instance, cause the economy to heat up to an unsustainable level and "strain the total productive capacity of the nation[.]"[5]

Versions of the Roth-Kemp plan closely resembled the Kennedy-Johnson tax cut of 1964, with the top personal income rate now to be lowered from 70% to 50%. The supply siders faced a preliminary question of whether a sweeping new tax law would constitute reform or whether it would only deepen the rate cuts from the 1964 Revenue Act. Such a comprehensive reform bill would have overturned the shift to isolated tax breaks during the 1970s in the form of an expanded investment tax credit, the earned income credit for the working poor, and credits for investment in alternative energy sources. In the end, however, support in Congress coalesced around an all-out revenue loss bill that not only lowered the top personal rate to 50% but also added in a new Accelerated Cost Recovery System (ACRS) that substantially shortened the depreciation schedules for equipment and other capital assets, allowing companies to capitalize these assets within a time frame of three to fifteen years. Instead of eliminating tax breaks to offset revenue losses, the Economic Recovery Tax Act (ERTA) expanded the breadth of tax expenditures with new credits for R&D and child-care, among other interests. Above all, ERTA indexed the personal rate cuts for inflation once the new rates took effect. The rate cuts would be phased in over a three-year period. After that, the brackets would be adjusted for inflation. Had ERTA not contained the indexing provision, then inflation would have lessened revenue loss over the longer-term through bracket creep by pushing incomes into higher brackets. Indexing changed all that, with Reagan coming out in support of indexing at a fairly late stage in the effort to pass the bill. When ERTA passed in August 1981, attention focused very quickly upon the revenue effects of the law and the need to make up the impending shortfall in revenue.[6] That ERTA produced huge revenue losses in the years ahead in retrospect vindicated this knee-jerk response. In real terms ERTA's revenue loss equaled 1.2% of GDP within a year of enactment and then rose to 4% four years later.[7]

ERTA's passage did not signify the triumph of an idea, whether it be the elegant but unsubstantiated arguments of the supply side school or the auxiliary, somewhat contradictory "starve the beast" theory positing that the public would not tolerate rising deficits caused by tax cuts and demand restraints on spending. In short order momentum grew in Democratic and Republican ranks for tax hikes to stem the flow of red ink, even during a recession. Congress acted by passing the Tax Equity and Fiscal Responsibility Act (TEFRA) of 1982 and the Deficit Reduction Act (DEFRA) of 1984. Neither legislation seriously undid the major components of ERTA. They retained the statutory rate cuts, bracket indexing, and ACRS (with a few modifications), relying instead on closing loopholes and raising excise taxes to bring in revenue. TEFRA, for instance, strengthened the alternative minimum tax, imposed cigarette taxes, and reduced the cost basis of depreciable property by 50% of the investment tax credit, which limited allowable deductions. A broad 10% withholding on interest and dividend income, among TEFRA's most notable provisions, lasted only a year on the books.[8] Averaged over four years, TEFRA triggered a $37.5 billion revenue gain in current dollars per year while DEFRA's gain over the same period came to $17.9 billion. These gains compared to ERTA's revenue loss of $111.4 billion per year within the first four years of its enactment even before bracket indexing went into effect.[9]

The seesawing between tax cuts and tax hikes stabilized into an effort for tax reform during Reagan's second term. The ensuing Tax Reform Act of 1986 (TRA-86) turned out to be the most sweeping tax reform overhaul in decades, with personal income taxes reduced to two rates, 15% and 28%, while the legislation further transferred $120 billion in tax burden from individuals to corporations.[10] This turnabout was in response to a decades long drain in corporate tax revenue, which had fallen to only 6.2% of total federal receipts by 1985.[11] Even though TRA-86 lowered the top corporate rate to 34%, it increased the tax burden on corporations in various ways, such as by repealing the investment tax credit for good and effectively lengthening depreciation periods. TRA-86 further eliminated distortions by raising the rate on long-term capital gains for individuals from 20% up to 28%, the same upper rate on ordinary income. TRA-86 also tackled a long-standing problem, the widespread and abusive use of tax shelters in order to avoid paying personal income tax. Taxpayers had long resorted to limited partnerships used to deduct losses, but new rules effectively ended these practices. Deductions taken for these shelters had to be directly tied to passive income realized, while taxpayers also had to be materially involved in partnership activity in order to be eligible for deductions.[12] The legislation contained an increasingly controversial "bubble rate," a 5% surtax on middle incomes, which put the maximum rate at 33% for these taxpayers. Taxpayers hit with the 33% rate earned less than those paying the statutory rate of 28%. While occasionally an object of political scorn, the bubble was offset by other measures that reflected overall progressivity in the tax code. Lower income taxpayers, for instance, could take advantage of the personal exemption unlike the highest earners, while the highest earners were also subjected to a phase-out of the 15% rate for the lowest part of their income and instead paid a flat 28% rate. Moreover, the proponents of TRA-86 sold the legislation as budget neutral. Within four years of enactment it had achieved total minimality in its effect on the budget, with a revenue gain of only .01% of GDP.[13]

The Administration followed a circuitous route to tax reform, first with drastic cuts, then marginal hikes. The victory for tax reform in 1986 had been a surprising one, with a more efficient code that taxed individuals at a lower top statutory rate than corporations and cracked down on shelters. But in terms of revenue the net effect of the Administration's tax policy had been a loss, and if it wanted to balance the budget or at least restrain the growth of debt to GDP it would have to look elsewhere.

ENTITLEMENTS AND WELFARE

A balanced budget was nowhere in sight during Reagan's first term. The president's budget message for FY 1983 did not mince its words, conceding outright that "the effects of recession, higher interest rates, declining inflation, and incomplete congressional action will mean high, continuing, and troublesome Federal budget deficits."[14] The message might also have included ERTA tax cuts and a defense buildup as contributing factors. The deficit yawned to $185.3 billion by FY 1984, a time of rising purchasing power.[15] In the first term the Administration had to focus on cutting domestic spending because defense cuts were not to be contemplated. The Administration did not bring about any significant restructuring or elimination of entitlement programs, but Reagan came into office committed to cutting entitlement and welfare spending where possible.

The Administration first proposed to cap federal matching funds for Medicaid, producing savings of $9 billion over the next few years. Members of Congress reacted negatively to the proposal, but the Administration did succeed phasing-in temporary cuts of 3% to 4.5% in federal Medicaid spending until 1984.[16] It even wanted the federal government to assume full responsibility for Medicaid (perhaps to expedite future spending cuts) while transferring control over welfare and food stamps to the states. Little came of this idea, and the Administration's subsequent proposals for generating savings were met with a similar lack of enthusiasm in Congress. In submitting his budget request for FY 1983, Reagan introduced a new "Budget Deficit Reduction Program" that planned for $51.6 billion in entitlement savings over three years. Most of the proposed changes for Medicare marginally cut payments to physicians and hospitals, the latter only temporarily at 2%. The program also would have brought federal workers into Medicare, imposed a fee on Medicaid beneficiaries for eligibility, attached work requirements to welfare, and more stringently adjusted food stamps to income levels.[17]

For FY 1986, the Administration again proposed a large cut to entitlements, this time targeted at $59.8 billion over four years. The package included a sundry list of items, such as temporary freezes of Medicare reimbursement rates and of COLAs for retired government workers and military personnel. Another idea would have required Medicare beneficiaries to pay 10% more on their premiums for Part B coverage (from 25% to 35%), but general revenue would have covered the remaining 65%. The Administration balanced these narrow proposals with other far-reaching ideas like converting welfare, food stamps, and Medicaid into federal block grants.[18]

Medicare cost containment measures helped restrain program spending. Legislation passed in 1983 replaced the reasonable cost standard governing reimbursement rates to hospitals providing inpatient care under Part A with a new Prospective Payment System (PPS), which designated predetermined rates for hospital services. The PPS also applied to non-physician services under Part B. Congress thereafter imposed a freeze on Medicare physician fees, an expedient that was eventually replaced by a formal physician fee schedule, which like PPS ended the reasonable cost standard and replaced it with a predetermined pricing system. Cost containment measures like PPS served as constructive prescriptions, while the freeze on physician fees helped steady Medicare spending funded from general revenue. By 1988, the federal contribution to Medicare Part B had risen to $25.4 billion.[19] Medicaid spending, meanwhile, had reached $30.5 billion.[20] With an on-budget deficit of $192.265 billion for that year,[21] general revenue spending on Medicare and Medicaid equaled 29% of the deficit.

Among the more forgotten laws affecting entitlements that Reagan signed was the 1988 Medicare Catastrophic Coverage Act (MCCA). A proposal for expanding hospital insurance and prescription drug benefits funded through premium hikes on wealthier seniors started within the Administration. The law very quickly became unpopular among seniors for its tax increase in the guise of higher premiums, especially as the higher premiums started causing Medicare to run a surplus. Seniors began demonstrating against the law, at one point even besieging a car driven by House Ways and Means chairman Dan Rostenkowski. They complained of the higher premiums for their existing benefits as totally needless. President Bush, who had initially supported MCCA, felt bound to sign its repeal only a year later. The failure of MCCA indicated the inherent difficulty of finding practical ways to fund expansions in Medicare. A later expansion in 2003 formally established an entirely new component of Medicare devoted to prescription drugs while dividing funding between premiums and general revenue.

On Social Security, an impending funding shortfall necessitated immediate action. A commission headed by former CEA and future Fed chairman Alan Greenspan returned a report concluding that the funding structure for Social Security should remain largely intact but that certain changes be made to avoid both short and long-term financing problems. The report's recommendations followed from the expansions to Social Security since the early 1950s, with extensions in coverage and tax hikes providing enough revenue to keep the program adequately funded. For instance, the commission proposed increasing the payroll tax on self-employed workers to equal that of the combined tax on employers and employees. The taxes on employers and employees would in turn be raised to 6.2% each by 1990 for a combined

12.4% rate. The commission also recommended bringing non-profit and new federal workers into the program and taxing Social Security benefits for higher incomes. Reagan, who had all along pledged not to dismantle Social Security, signed legislation that incorporated most of these proposals. The Social Security Amendments of 1983 had no immediate impact on the deficit, in large part because the commission's proposals did not deviate in any significant way from the program's core mode of financing through dedicated revenue sources.

ARMS BUILDUP, GRAMM-RUDMAN

The Administration's decision to undergo a military buildup larger than the stretch out already planned under Carter further exacerbated the deficit. How the Reagan Administration approached the relation between defense spending and the larger budget differed significantly from that of its predecessors, especially Eisenhower. The Eisenhower Administration had implemented a national security policy that conformed to its cautious budgetary outlook, in that it articulated strategic doctrines and prescribed levels of defense spending that were largely consistent with its fiscal policy goals. In the 1950s defense spending took up a much larger portion of total outlays than it did in the 1980s, but the Eisenhower Administration still regarded the military as fiscally equivalent to other government operations and therefore subject to the same budget scrutiny. The Reagan Administration, by contrast, refrained from linking defense spending to its larger fiscal imperatives. Passage of ERTA did not cause the Administration to scale back its plans for increasing military forces. During Reagan's first term defense spending usually rose by at least $20 billion per year, at times $25 billion or higher. And while these are nominal figures, the higher spending occurred at a time of expanding purchasing power. Defense spending reached nearly 6% of GDP in FY 1983, up from 4.8% in 1980. But it also stayed well below 30% of total outlays throughout the Reagan era.[22]

The Reagan Administration reversed some of Carter's major decisions. It ordered the production and deployment of a new version of the B-1 bomber, the B-1B, redesigned for radar evasion and low-altitude penetration, while it also continued work on the MX missile but not as a mobile system. Most of all, it diverted money into the Navy to begin a huge shipbuilding program to last at least five years. It added two new carriers, bringing the total number up to fifteen, while reactivating four *Iowa* class battleships and arming them with Tomahawk cruise missiles. In all, the Administration planned to construct another 133 ships through 1987 at a cost of $96 billion.[23] It did not quite fulfill its pledge of building a 600 ship Navy, but it put naval forces on a more aggressive footing, with NATO subs conducting exercises in the Arctic just off the northern coast of Russia.

By the time Reagan started his second term, members of Congress were demanding a change in the trajectory of spending. As in the 1960s, rising deficits sparked a backlash on Capitol Hill. In 1982, the Senate had proposed with a two-thirds vote a balanced budget amendment to the Constitution, but votes came up short in the House and the amendment was never formally sent to the states for ratification. Three years later Congress devised a new deficit control mechanism. Reagan obligingly signed the law in December 1985, called Gramm-Rudman-Hollings (GRH) for its co-sponsors. The legislation served as an emergency measure for reducing the deficit. It specified deficit targets for the next six years, starting at $171.9 billion for 1986 and falling eventually to zero by 1991.[24] GRH was therefore intended to balance the budget over the mid-term, but it did not assign priorities in spending or in any other way implement substantive changes to the budget. It instead allowed maximum flexibility for the government to come up with alternative paths for meeting the deficit targets per fiscal year. It also allowed maximum flexibility for the government to essentially avoid meeting the deficit targets per fiscal year.

GRH may have looked like a gimmick, but it was reinforced by the threat of sequestration, draconian, across the board spending cuts allocated evenly between defense and domestic spending. While exempting a few big items such as Social Security, anti-poverty, and interest on the debt, the cuts were designed to inflict maximum pain and therefore discipline the government into keeping its spending within the prescribed limits. The sequester could not be avoided for FY 1986, the fiscal year in which Reagan signed the legislation. Pursuant to the legislation, staff from the OMB and CBO submitted a report with recommended spending cuts to the Comptroller General, who reviewed them before giving his go-ahead.[25] The Supreme Court ruled the provision granting the Comptroller General review and approval authority unconstitutional for violating separation of powers on the rationale that the Comptroller General, as an official removable by Congress through joint resolution, could not be vested with executive functions. The seemingly unforeseen unconstitutionality of GRH reflected its novelty and the scope of its extraordinary emergency measures to tackle growing deficits. The Court's ruling did not stop Congress from amending the legislation and transferring final responsibility over sequester options to OMB, situated right within the White House and beyond Congress's removal powers not arising to the level of impeachment. A more troubling concern was Congress's ability to contrive various ways of avoiding full compliance with its own law. The original act included some leeway for fiscal years after 1986 by permitting spending within a $10 billion limit in excess of the deficit target. Critics argued that, even more problematically, Congress could use various tricks for getting around the legislation and meeting short-term deficit targets in only the most technical way possible, such as by transferring certain items off-budget sheet or retroactively designating current expenditures for a past fiscal year. While Congress relied on all these methods to in some way or another jettison GRH, the legislation was not a total failure. It created real pressure for Congress to reduce spending. After staying at 4.89% in 1985, the federal deficit as a percentage of GDP briefly shrunk to 2.7% by 1989, helped along by robust economic growth.[26] GRH nonetheless invited criticism for its neglect of delivering meaningful change to the budget. It relied on expedients to close deficits, and in turn loopholes could be used to undermine it. And the deficit as a percentage of GDP rose again markedly after 1989, further exacerbated by bailouts to savings and loan organizations. While supportive of GRH, Reagan still found it inadequate and hoped for more lasting answers in the form of a balanced budget amendment and a line item veto.[27] Even so, keeping up austerity measures fulfilled the longer-term goal of stabilizing the debt to GDP ratio, which had spiked from 24.6% in 1981 to 38.8% by 1989.[28]

GORBACHEV, REYKJAVIK, COLD WAR WIND-DOWN

Reagan still promised to adhere to the unratified SALT II as Carter had done, which in practice secured ceilings on strategic forces, but this self-imposed obligation did not affect the costly buildup in conventional forces. Momentum had shifted against engagement with the Soviets even before Reagan won the 1980 election. He deigned not to meet with the three ailing Soviet leaders of his first administration, Brezhnev, Yuri Andropov, and Konstantin Chernenko, all of whom died in relatively quick succession from late 1982 to early 1985. As the Soviet old guard died off, Reagan assailed the U.S.S.R. as an "evil empire" while proposing the Strategic Defense Initiative (SDI), an expensive space-based system for intercepting enemy ballistic missiles. Reagan's SDI proposal and his rhetorical crusade against the Soviets may have been suitably timed as he awaited more propitious changes in the Politburo before reviving diplomatic contacts at the summit. Yet he did not conceive of SDI in the same way Nixon regarded Safeguard or Johnson Sentinel, as just another extravagant ABM program to be used as a bargaining ploy in the lead-up to negotiations with the Soviets. Reagan by all accounts actually believed that SDI could best fulfill his ultimate goal of ridding the world of nuclear weapons. This conviction put him at odds with members of his own Administration and the new leaders who emerged in the Kremlin. It also impeded the progress of arms control negotiations in his second term. Soviet leaders took SDI seriously and tried desperately to limit the Administration's funding for it, which only further emboldened Reagan to insist upon its continued development.

Not all of the Administration's policies on nuclear weapons were this radical. Reagan inherited Carter's "dual tracks" approach for theater ballistic missiles in Europe. In response to the Soviet deployment of intermediate range SS-20 missiles to Eastern Europe, the U.S. military planned to deploy new Pershing II ballistic missiles to West Germany, which could hit Moscow in a matter of minutes. In an eventual "zero option" agreement, the two sides would mutually withdraw their missiles and save Europe the risk of obliteration from these types of weapons. The deployment of the Pershing II missiles in 1983 briefly set off a "Euromissile" crisis as activists took to the streets in protest. Reagan received criticism for the supposedly confrontational deployments, but he was only following established policy. The Pershing II deployments conformed to NATO's reliance on theater missiles dating to the first Thor and Jupiter IRBMs from the early 1960s and the later Pershing Is. Nor did Paul Nitze, enlisted again as an arms negotiator by the Administration, break the deadlock with his "walk in the woods" proposal at Geneva, in which the U.S. would have canceled its Pershing II deployments if the Soviets limited their SS-20 launchers west of the Urals to only 75 in number. The U.S. would have in turn been permitted 75 cruise missile launchers in Europe. Such a compromise was not appealing. If the Administration were going to cancel the Pershing II deployments, then it would have to be as part of the zero option. By the time Reagan began his second term the Administration's policy on nuclear arms was thus well settled. It still abided by the SALT II ceilings and had deployed the Pershing IIs, with Reagan injecting into the mix his own personal contribution of SDI. How any of these factors might influence arms control negotiations in the near future depended on who became the new leader of the communist party in the Soviet Union upon Chernenko's death in March 1985.

Mikhail Gorbachev took the helm as party general secretary that month, a not wholly surprising turn of events. Gorbachev was a generation younger than his predecessors and had harbored reformist instincts throughout his career. He had already made a good impression on audiences in his travels to Western Europe and Canada, and his prior experience as secretary for agriculture on the Politburo informed him of the inefficiencies of the Soviet command economy. Troubles were mounting for the Soviet Union by the 1980s, as Gorbachev well knew, some structural and others circumstantial. Soviet troops were bogged down in an unwinnable war in Afghanistan, forcing the Kremlin to desperately seek a multilateral framework for extrication. The high oil prices of the 1970s that had kept Soviet coffers flush with cash and helped bankroll the U.S.S.R.'s military buildup had now plummeted. The rigidities of the command economy were also making life difficult for the proletariat, with the Soviet economy experiencing chronic shortages of grain, wheat, and most of all consumer goods. Faced with these enormous challenges, Gorbachev stoked the Kremlin with a reformist spirit if not necessarily a clear agenda. He initially announced an anti-alcohol campaign that became the butt of jokes from Reagan on down. But his reformist views portended crucial changes in Soviet society, such as an increasing acceptance of public discussion over contentious subjects and even plans to hold relatively freer elections not monopolized by the communist party. Without abandoning Leninism per se, Gorbachev seemed to want to direct the Soviet Union towards a more social democratic model even before instituting large-scale economic reforms.

Both Reagan and Gorbachev shared a desire to reduce tensions and rid their countries of their offensive nuclear arsenals. While many members of the Administration doubted Gorbachev's sincerity to implement both arms control and political reforms at home, Reagan enthusiastically collaborated with the general secretary. At a "working summit" in Reykjavik in October 1986, the pair came almost surreally close to reaching an agreement for eliminating all nuclear weapons within a ten-year period. Such an agreement would have entailed substantial defense cuts on both the U.S. and Soviet side, albeit potentially offset by increases in conventional forces. Yet the talks foundered due to disagreements over SDI. Reagan would not relinquish his commitment to large-scale development and eventual deployment of SDI, which Gorbachev wanted confined to laboratory testing. The two leaders were unable to break the impasse, and both walked away disappointed. Only a few weeks later the Administration decided to officially breach the SALT II limits with the deployment of an additional cruise missile-equipped B-52, an order that was soon after rescinded.

Yet Reagan and Gorbachev eventually returned to the "dual tracks" approach for theater missiles in Europe. By detaching negotiations on theater weapons from SDI and intercontinental arsenals, the two leaders signed the Intermediate-Range Nuclear Forces (INF) Treaty in December 1987 that for the first time eliminated an entire class of weapons, land-based cruise and ballistic missiles with a range of between 500 to 5,500 kilometers. The INF Treaty initially provoked a doubtful reaction in Western European capitals. It after all overturned decades of NATO conventions in nuclear deterrence, but its ratification was premised on the assumption that Gorbachev genuinely wanted to reform the Soviet Union and end the Cold War.

Stunningly, the end of the Cold War became unmistakable in the next few years. The rapid breakdown of the Iron Curtain amid nationalistic stirrings in Eastern Europe and within the U.S.S.R. swept up even Reagan's cautious successor, George H.W. Bush, who announced a "strategic pause" before further pursuing arms control talks with Gorbachev. Soon the strategic pause gave way to the declaration that the government had earned a "peace dividend" in the new international environment. The brief war in the Persian

Gulf did not turn back these trends. Bush and Gorbachev signed the Strategic Arms Reduction Treaty (START) in July 1991, substantially reducing their nuclear arsenals and eliminating the entire force of Minuteman II missiles. Later that year Bush went further in announcing the unilateral cancellation of a mobile version of the MX missile, the disarming of ships and aircraft previously equipped with nukes, and de-MIRVing the remaining Minuteman missiles, professing little doubt that the Soviets, soon to be Russians working with the other former socialist republics, would follow suit.[29]

When detente crumbled at the end of the 1970s, the U.S. had seemed to enter a grave new era in which communism showed few outward signs of weakness. Yet this perception did not really stand up to reality. Communist forces took over countries in Asia and Africa, though much of the Soviet involvement in Third World countries betrayed weakness rather than strength. Even when oil profits were high, the Kremlin was forced into paying out assistance to its proxies around the world, including the Eastern European satellites and the Cubans, a constant strain on its financial reserves. The Soviet military threat had become nothing short of monolithic on land and increasingly at sea. But at the same time the government in Moscow could not provide basic goods and services to its people. The invasion of Afghanistan was ominous. But Soviet troops, mostly corralled in cities, towns, and other fortified points, could not win a decisive victory over the amorphous guerrillas, and their alienating presence in no way served as a launching pad for incursions deeper into Southwest Asia. Perhaps the greatest threat by 1980 was more unseen, the obliteration of the Minuteman arsenal in a first strike unless the Pentagon resorted to a hair-trigger response based on possibly inaccurate information. Yet even this threat needed to be assessed in light of new Trident subs and cruise missiles, which strengthened the aerial and naval elements of the Triad, not to mention the technical feasibility of a mobile MX, whatever its unpopularity in Congress and among the public.

Soviet belligerence was nonetheless deemed extreme enough to warrant increased real defense spending starting in early 1980. This buildup was probably not sustainable over the long-term, with members of Congress insisting on budget cuts well before anyone could claim an end to the Cold War. National debt continued to climb for the rest of the decade, but the promising signs from the Kremlin soon turned into a full-fledged breakdown of the old order dividing Europe. The Western alliance had outlasted the Soviet Union at no small cost. The end of the Cold War was above all important for the peace and security of the world, but it was also important for the financial state of the federal government.

Neither Reagan nor anyone in his administration could have possibly known the Cold War would end within roughly ten years of his taking office in 1981. He mocked a supposedly bankrupt detente and supported an arms buildup. Some factors existed largely beyond his control, such as disinflation, an appreciating dollar, and the growing trade deficit. But in the 1980s deficits were always on the horizon, a normality in the fiscal picture. The end of the Cold War potentially beckoned a return to surplus normality, but this was not certain.

Reagan's successor, George H. W. Bush, was predisposed to a budget agreement that could bring lasting answers to the rising deficits. He had criticized Reagan's supply sider views as "voodoo economics" in the 1980 presidential campaign before inevitably siding with the tax cut orthodoxy prevailing in the Republican Party during his eight years as vice president. He went so far as to dare his audience at the Republican national convention in 1988 to read his lips when vowing not to raise taxes. But Bush had uniquely positioned himself more as a steward of the national interest and less as an ideological warrior, having served in a series of appointed posts earlier in his career, including ambassador to the U.N., emissary to the People's Republic of China, and director of the CIA. In the face of deficits, Bush reached out to the Democratic Congress for ways to compromise in mid-1990, impliedly retracting the "read my lips" pledge on taxes, something he considered an unfortunate breach of his word but a necessary step to avoid $100 billion in sequester cuts. With tepid support from the right-wing of his own party, Bush conceded to "tax revenue increases," which were meant to take the form of higher excise taxes, along with spending cuts. After a budget summit at Andrews Air Force Base just outside Washington in September, the president seemed to have secured a grand bargain, except that the bill went down in a vote in Congress, fueled by resentment among some Republicans towards the excise tax hikes. The vote only forced Bush to buckle down and concede to income tax hikes, including marginally raising the top statutory rate back up to 31% (erasing the bubble from TRA-86) and hiking the wage base on Medicare taxes.

In imposing spending cuts, the Omnibus Budget Reconciliation Act (OBRA) incorporated new deficit control measures codified as the Budget Enforcement Act (BEA). The BEA turned out to be effective deficit control legislation because it contained more clear-cut rules than GRH. While GRH addressed spending in the seemingly most aggressive possible way by laying out deficit targets per year, it still left sizable room for Congress to get around its own rules. The BEA could not be so easily manipulated. It mandated pay-go rules for both entitlements and changes in the tax code, which prevented Congress from relying on borrowing to finance increased transfer payments or tax cuts. The legislation further imposed fixed caps on discretionary spending, whether for defense, domestic programs, or international affairs. The caps were twice annually adjusted for inflation, so that in current dollars spending continued to rise in most years for the rest of the 1990s. But tax revenue also rose with inflation. The BEA included a loophole for Congress to grant supplemental appropriations for unforeseen emergencies outside the parameters of pay-go. This provision was timely, giving the Administration leeway on deploying ground troops, aircraft, and combat ships to the Persian Gulf after the Iraqi invasion of Kuwait. Bush's successful marshalling of an international coalition to expel the Iraqi forces after one hundred hours of ground fighting bolstered the claim of a new world order not divided between East and West but founded upon the inalienability of national sovereignty and the timely response to regional crises.

In a very similar vein, behind the improved budget mechanics the Administration and Congress had made substantive decisions for cutting spending and reassigning priorities. With the conclusion to the Persian Gulf War, Bush announced the "peace dividend," that the post–Cold War order permitted reduced military spending, enabling both stabilization in the national debt and the diversion of public moneys to pressing domestic needs. As the FY 1993 budget request noted, the nation's defense posture had radically changed in a short period of time, from defending the western side of the Iron Curtain to rapidly deploying forces to regional hot spots such as in Panama and the Persian Gulf. A smaller defense budget could accommodate leaner but nimbler capabilities. The budget request backed up this language with action. The Administration had already been pushing for lower spending in current dollars, and it planned to maintain this trend with a further $9.9 billion cut in military spending for the fiscal year.[30]

Bush's effort to reach a budget agreement with centrist members of Congress in 1990, even at great political cost, in retrospect marks a rare moment of non-partisan statesmanship. At the time, OBRA did not look like it would necessarily lead to a balanced budget anytime soon, and it did not, even with projected savings of $500 billion over five years (the 1990–1991 recession also factored into deficits). The Administration was preoccupied with putting together an international coalition and deploying forces to the Gulf for a conflict that many feared would be protracted and bloody. The surprisingly quick end to military operations then gave way to domestic challenges as the economy sank into recession for the first time in eight years. Pay-go rules bound the Administration's hands and prevented it from jolting the economy with temporary tax cuts, contributing to Bush's loss in the 1992 election. Over a longer span of time defense cuts and moderate tax hikes, reinforced by the provisions of the BEA, boded well for budget balancing, and the budget would balance by decade's end. Yet in final perspective, from the viewpoint of today, this brief shift to surpluses in the late 1990s could not turn back the long-term trend of deficit normality. The imperatives of global military commitments, a tax code necessarily instrumental for economic growth, and a robust and expanding entitlement state exerted greater pressure on the budget and overturned the fragile underpinnings of fiscal stability in the early 2000s. The deficit normative state temporarily relapsed at the turn of the new century, but looked at from a distance it has continued unendingly from the Cold War to today.

NOTES

1. FRED, Real GDP.
2. FRED, Civilian Unemployment Rate.
3. FRED, Consumer Prices.
4. Federal Reserve Bank of St. Louis Economic Data, "Balance on Current Account, NIPA's," https://fred.stlouisfed.org/series/NETFI, accessed August 2019.
5. CBO, *An Analysis of the Roth-Kemp Tax Proposal* (Washington, D.C.: Congressional Budget Office, 1978), x.
6. Don Fullerton, Charls Walker, and Russell Long, "Tax Policy" in *American Economic Policy in the 1980s*, ed. Martin Feldstein (Chicago: University of Chicago Press, 1994), 180–85.
7. Tempalski, "Revenue Effects," 17.
8. Fullerton, Walker, and Long, "Tax Policy," 186–87.
9. Tempalski, "Revenue Effects," 16.
10. Alan J. Auerbach and James M. Poterba, "Why Have Corporate Tax Revenues Declined?" in *Tax Policy and the Economy, Vol. I*, ed. Lawrence H. Summers (Cambridge, MA: MIT Press, 1987), 15.
11. Auerbach and Poterba, "Corporate Tax Revenues," 3.
12. Andrew A. Samwick, "Tax Shelters and Passive Losses after the Tax Reform Act of 1986," in *Empirical Foundations of Household Taxation*, ed. Martin Feldstein and James Poterba (Chicago: University of Chicago Press, 1986), 193–94.
13. Tempalski, "Revenue Effects," 17.
14. President of U.S., *Budget of the United States Government Fiscal Year 1983* (Washington, D.C.: Government Printing Office, 1982), M15.
15. President of U.S., *Budget of the United States Government Fiscal Year 1986* (Washington, D.C.: Government Printing Office, 1985), M6.
16. Diane Rowland, Barbara Lyons, and Jennifer Edwards, "Medicaid: Health Care for the Poor in the Reagan Era," *Annual Review of Public Health* 9 (1988): 430.
17. President, *1983 Budget*, (3–7)–(3–10).
18. President, *1986 Budget*, (2–6) – (2–8).
19. OMB, "Historical Tables," 316.
20. Ibid., 335.
21. Ibid., 25.
22. Ibid., 54–55.
23. President, *1983 Budget*, (5–13).
24. President of U.S., *Budget of the United States Government Fiscal Year 1987* (Washington, D.C.: Government Printing Office, 1986), (2–14).
25. President, *1987 Budget*, (2–14) – (2–15).
26. FRED, Federal Surplus or Deficit as Percent of GDP.
27. President, *1987 Budget*, (M-9) – (M-10).
28. FRED, Federal Debt as Percent of GDP.
29. The American Presidency Project, "George Bush: Address to the Nation on Reducing United States and Soviet Nuclear Weapons, September 27, 1991," https://www.presidency.ucsb.edu/documents/address-the-nation-reducing-united-states-and-soviet-nuclear-weapons, accessed February 2019.
30. President of U.S., *Budget of the United States Government Fiscal Year 1993* (Washington, D.C.: Government Printing Office, 1992), 239.

Chapter Seven

Overstretch in the Twenty-First Century

The budget turned deficit normative over the long period of time coinciding with the Cold War from 1945 to 1991. As with the passage of human events in general, the shift took place not so much gradually as it did episodically. Arguably the deficit had already turned normative as early as 1931, when the budget started registering a continuous string of deficits during the Great Depression and World War II. But the postwar situation might have engendered a new era of fiscal stability resembling that of the 1920s, and for a brief moment this seemed possible. Truman did succeed in demobilizing the military and sending the budget back into surplus in the fiscal years 1947, 1948, and 1949, even while aiding reconstruction in Europe and building a new Western defense system. The reflexive response to North Korean aggression in June 1950 testified to the threatening environment of the time. Truman had suddenly sent U.S. troops just days before on occupation duty back into a real, shooting war, and the austerity that he had so staunchly maintained through the years of rising tensions with the Soviets could no longer survive. Eisenhower, uniquely positioned given his background as Allied supreme commander, was never going to single-handedly demobilize most of the armed forces in 1953 after concluding an armistice with the North Koreans and Chinese. The armistice ended the fighting and the casualties on the Korean peninsula, but the world looked no safer than before the war started. The arms race had entered a more serious and dangerous phase with hydrogen bomb proliferation and the miniaturization of warheads onto ICBMs. Eisenhower made important decisions first on continental defense and then ICBMs, keeping spending for those capabilities under control. Defense overwhelmingly impacted the budget during this era. Eisenhower faced the challenge not only of carefully managing a new military, scientific, and industrial colossus, or "complex" as he termed it, but also of contending with the same swings in the business cycle that had traditionally sent budgets into the red. He secured balanced budgets in 1956, 1957, and once more in 1960, impeded in part by two recessions and rising nominal defense costs. Truman and Eisenhower occupied different points of the ideological spectrum, but they shared a similar, rigid outlook on the budget. Spending cost money and needed to be paid for in taxes.

Circumstances began to change as the revived global trade arena brought about greater concern at home for economic growth. The Kennedy Administration started a policy shift that signaled a more lenient attitude towards deficits. Kennedy wanted to expand the entitlement state, carrying uncertain implications for the general fiscal till, while decisively cutting income taxes without major offsetting cutbacks in defense spending. As he bluntly put it, he would not reduce the defense budget simply in order to cut spending. Yet like Truman and Eisenhower he presided in an ever more dangerous world. The U.S. and Soviet Union came to the brink of nuclear war not once but twice during his short presidency, first over Berlin and the next year over missiles in Cuba. Kennedy had little credible basis for cutting defense spending even if he had wanted to, having to answer both to the public and hawks in Congress. After the succession in presidential leadership, Johnson acted quickly on a number of fronts, fulfilling Kennedy's goal of cutting taxes, escalating in Vietnam, and pursuing the Great Society that left the budget permanently expanded. Entitlement transfer payments funded from general revenue produced long-term changes. These payments and their effect on deficits were bound to grow in future years as more people became eligible based on designated criteria. Johnson notably achieved a budget surplus for FY 1969 through tax hikes while these transfer payments were still comparatively modest.

Nixon, Ford, and Carter all failed to balance the budget as the government diverted increasingly more spending into so-called human resources instead of defense. But after the withdrawal from Vietnam this trend did not imply cutbacks in defense spending. Nominal defense spending had to keep pace with inflation in the mid-1970s, which was exacerbated by oil shocks. Nor did detente sufficiently stabilize world conditions to warrant defense cuts. Detente and the SALT agreements considerably relaxed tensions, bringing a respite in inter-bloc antagonism at the very least saving the federal government dollars from an unnecessary defense buildup. SALT on some level restrained spending for strategic weapons, but those limits only underscored the importance of conventional forces. The Helsinki Accords did not proximately lead to mutual drawdowns in NATO and Warsaw Pact forces on the continent of Europe. If anything, the Ford Administration hardened the all voluntary military with more Army divisions, and the Carter Administration pushed for a "NATO budget" further strengthening ground and close air support capabilities. Yet the impact of detente on the budget came clearest into view only after it ended, when the Soviets invaded Afghanistan and Carter transitioned to a defense stretch out. With Cold War temperatures dropping back into a deep freeze, policymakers once again witnessed, and actively participated in, a budget highly sensitive to adverse developments overseas, which translated into more real defense spending than during the detente years.

Persistent inflation and deficits in the 1970s would have justified austerity, a mix of higher taxes and lower spending, but none of the administrations of this period came close to successfully implementing such a program. Nixon impounded money while also, along with Ford and Carter, cutting taxes through new tax expenditures, avoiding the full-scale repercussions of disinflation. Even without tax hikes, the economy tumbled into a long recession after the first oil crisis in 1973–1974. Deficits had clearly become normal by the mid-1970s, caused by rising defense spending, a tax code cluttered with a growing number of breaks, and entitlement programs increasingly consuming general funds. Debt to GDP remained stable, but the shift to deficits on a year by year basis had already occurred.

Bearing superlative credentials as a fiscal conservative, Reagan's legacy took a different course with another round of income tax cuts, a massive expansion of the defense buildup begun under Carter, a series of tax hikes, and Social Security reform that kept the program intact, offset by only modest reductions in entitlement spending. Cost control measures for Medicare and temporary cuts to Medicaid kept transfer payments in line, but Reagan did not bring about any significant restructuring of the federal government. Instead debt to GDP rose to almost 40%. The debt overload of this era triggered alarm on Capitol Hill and paved the way for extraordinary deficit control legislation, first GRH and then the BEA. Members of Congress and the Reagan Administration had not necessarily given up on balancing the budget, at least not overtly, but now the government required its own self-imposed apparatus, backed up by the ultra option of the sequester, to keep spending and deficits under control. GRH in principle envisioned nothing short of a balanced budget over the mid-term. Such a balanced budget did not come about, and the legislation would be supplanted by new deficit control methods in 1990.

The shift from surplus to deficit normality thus occurred not in any predetermined way but rather episodically, over the course of shooting wars, an intensifying arms race that had to be carefully managed, and shifting political tides, which led to sweeping enactments of new tax and social welfare legislation that permanently altered the policymaking landscape. The intellectual approach that policymakers took towards the budget gives some indication of the shift to deficit normality, and here a change is discernable. As administrations struggled to make decisions on the budget, they more and more put their faith in the economy and the boost to revenue from predicted rates of GDP growth and low unemployment. By the early 1990s annual budget requests began to feature whole sections devoted to the economy and "investing in the future," with the implication that a thriving economy could somehow make up the shortfall in receipts. A subtle turn in thinking had occurred across party affiliation that no longer really saw deficits rooted in government's decisions over taxation and spending but rather in the state of the economy and the generation of revenue. A turning point had occurred when even a deficit hawk like Gerald Ford could not plan for an immediate surplus as he introduced the FY 1977 budget, relying instead on anticipated rates of economic growth to hopefully pave the way to a balanced budget by 1980. Ford would no longer be in office by then, and nor would the budget come close to balancing that year. Yet a trend had been set. The government could not totally control its spending habits, and balanced budgets now lay just out of reach.

FACTOR-PERCENTAGE APPROACH

Deficit normality cannot be equated with any one single factor. Defense took the lion's share of the discretionary budget in the late 1940s, 1950s, and early 1960s, with international affairs and presidential leadership uniquely positioned to shape whether the budget would turn in a surplus or deficit in any given year. The Truman and Eisenhower Administrations secured a combined seven balanced budgets over the course of sixteen years when defense dominated discretionary spending. The defense budget continued to grow in real terms, especially in the 1980s, but its relative contribution to deficit normality weakened after the early 1960s. In the years ahead calibrating the tax code into a more potent mechanism of economic policy and creating new entitlements took an increasing share of the contribution to deficit normality.

Computing fluctuations in discrete factors as a percentage of the deficit, specifically defense spending, revenue collected through taxable sources, and entitlements funded from general revenue, offer a means of tracking long-term trends in deficit normality. The concession must be immediately made that this factor-percentage approach is necessarily inexact. It depends on two variables, the shift in spending or revenue on the one hand and the shift in the deficit on the other, the latter of which may be attributable to variable economic circumstances. As a result, this approach can lead to anomalies. A sharp reduction in the deficit tends to cause the percentages for defense or entitlements to jump up if the fall in the deficit is greater than the fall in spending. For instance, even after the Bush Administration put in place the "peace dividend" defense program in the early 1990s, defense as a percentage of the deficit actually increased because the deficit fell faster in these years. On the other hand, a deep recession like in 2007–2009 will cause the deficit to spike upwards, in turn pushing down the spending percentages, even if defense and entitlement spending are not declining in real or nominal dollars. In addition, the rise in revenue as a percentage of the deficit may imply that the tax code is generating more revenue in real terms when that is not necessarily the case. The revenue percentage might simply be rising due to falling deficits. The factor-percentage approach simply has no application in years in which the budget balanced. Even with this inexactness, however, the approach can indicate long-term trends, most importantly the growing share of entitlements funded from general revenue as a percentage of the deficit, which is probably the most significant trend affecting the budget today.

In the 1950s and first half of the 1960s defense and revenue reached startlingly high levels as a percentage of the deficit during expansions but then plunged in the wake of recessions.[1] In 1955, for instance, defense reached 1,044% of the deficit before dropping to 403% in 1959 after economic contraction. Revenue, defined here as being generated from personal and corporate income taxes plus excise taxes, similarly posted a high 1,362% of the deficit in 1955 but then fell by over half to 531% in 1959. The budget could still be described as partially surplus normative in these years, to the extent of budget surpluses resulting from economic expansions. A narrowing deficit during recoveries boosted the defense and revenue percentages while recession helped push them back down. Defense and revenue again notched high percentages at a time of peak economic expansion in 1965, with defense coming to about 3,153% of the deficit and revenue 5,534%. From the early 1970s on, however, defense and revenue assumed on average a downward trajectory. By 1985, a time of robust economic expansion, defense had fallen to 114% of the deficit and revenue to 194%. Entitlements, meanwhile, here taken to include Medicaid and the federal contribution to Medicare Supplemental Insurance (at the time only Part B) continued to rise in nominal dollar amounts through the 1970s. Combined these expenditures frequently reached 30% of the deficit (in 1970 they came to over 40%) but then fell to 18% in 1985. As with defense and revenue, the entitlement percentages depended in part upon the size of deficits, which were enormous by the mid-1980s.

After 1990 entitlements held increasingly higher percentages in relation to deficits. In the long stretch from 1945 to 1991 entitlements either for a while did not contribute to deficits or did so on a more modest scale than defense and revenue. But the critical decisions had been made with the Great Society as more programs received general revenue funding. The creation of Supplemental Security Income in 1972 marked another step in entitlement expansion, while Medicare cost control measures failed to reverse rising spending in the aggregate. Institutional reforms for Medicaid also failed to stem rising costs as states shifted from the fee for service model to health care provided through managed care organizations. Congress officially sanctioned states to adopt managed care for Medicaid with the Balanced Budget Act of 1997, but health care-related entitlements continued to expand with the creation of the Children's Health Insurance Program (CHIP) in 1997, Medicare Part D in 2003, and enlargement of Medicaid under the Affordable Care Act (ACA) in 2010. CHIP provided aid to families with children who earned income beyond the eligibility limits for Medicaid. The Medicare Modernization Act (MMA) of 2003 created a new prescription drug program for seniors, enshrined as Part D, funded in part from premiums and in part from general revenue, while the ACA's expansion of Medicaid conformed to the law's goal of providing universal care through a combination of government assistance and an individual mandate for health insurance.

For a while reduced defense and domestic spending as enforced by the BEA caps, modest tax hikes, and robust economic growth at the end of the decade helped generate four years of budget surpluses from 1997 through FY 2001. The deficit had continued to decline after passage of the BEA. Defense spending, which fell in current dollars, now funded a national security posture oriented around regional stabilization in places such as Somalia, the Balkans, and Haiti rather than the old confrontation at the center of Europe. At home Congress hiked statutory rates in 1993, with the top rate rising back up to 39.6%, while eliminating the Medicare tax wage base. President Clinton signed welfare reform legislation and announced that the age of big government had ended, an initially plausible assertion just preceding the first of the four surpluses. The surpluses of course did not last, ended by tax cuts in 2001 and 2003, which required Congress to waive its own pay-go rules before these rules expired altogether in 2002, increased military expenditures to fund operations in Afghanistan and Iraq, and the continued rise in entitlements funded from general revenue. In many ways the Cold War era, when the federal government failed at times to prioritize between domestic and national security commitments and became sucked into a pattern of fiscal overstretch, continues to this day, especially as great power rivalry heats up with China and Russia. The end of the "peace dividend" and the deployment of military forces to Afghanistan and Iraq drove deficits, but so too did loose tax policy and bigger entitlements.

Defense fell from 120% of the deficit in 1995 to 100% by 2005 while entitlements, now defined as Medicaid plus the federal contribution to Medicare Parts B and D, rose from close to 56% in 1995 to 60% by 2005. The tax cuts of 2001 and 2003 also contributed to revenue losses. The 2001 Economic Growth and Tax Relief Reconciliation Act marginally cut personal income taxes, with the top rate falling back to 35%, while Congress in 2003 cut taxes on dividends and capital gains. The looser tax policy and rising deficits sent revenue from 355% of the deficit in 1995 back to 259% by 2005. The financial crisis of 2008 and subsequent Great Recession, the worst contraction since the Depression, heavily skewed the percentages for defense, revenue, and entitlements, with defense falling to just over 50% of the deficit, revenue to 84%, and entitlements to 35% by 2010. Yet as a modest economic expansion began, the longer-term trend became clear that an aging society translated into ever higher health care costs. By 2017 the federal contribution to Medicare reached $306.54 billion and Medicaid spending came to $374.7 billion for a combined $681.24 billion, larger than defense that year at $598.72 billion. These two entitlements equaled 95% of the deficit compared to defense at under 84%. When including other entitlement programs funded from general revenue like SSI and food stamps, the total for entitlements reached over 110% of the deficit. Moreover, the on-budget deficit in 2017 was not in any way miniscule at $714.78 billion, admittedly smaller than the string of +$1 trillion deficits during or after the Great Recession but still very robust. Revenue by comparison came to 289% for FY 2017.

The Budget Control Act (BCA) of 2011 impacted these trends through another round of deficit control measures in exchange for presidential authority to raise the statutory debt limit. The BCA discretionary spending caps mandated $1 trillion in spending cuts over ten years, in addition to another $1.2 trillion in cuts to be reached through negotiations by a super committee. When the super committee failed to return a workable package, sequestration went into effect in early 2013, triggering $100 billion in annual defense and non-defense spending cuts. The sequester was comprehensive, allocated equally between defense and non-defense spending and affecting some mandatory programs such as Medicare, but it was not totally comprehensive, sparing other entitlements funded from general revenue like Medicaid, CHIP, SSI, and SNAP, the latter a revamped version of food stamps. Government shutdowns, fears of a default on the debt, and the occasional busting of the BCA caps through negotiations across the aisle form a contemporary picture of the deficit to the casual observer, but the larger trend should be noted, an ever increasing financial burden placed on the government due to manifold commitments.

CONTEMPORARY FISCAL CONTEXT, TENTATIVE PROGRAM

Today the budget is frequently thought of in more abstract terms in relation to the economy, with expansionary fiscal policies assumed to carry stimulatory effects and austerity nearly always taken in the context of causing contraction. These assumptions feed the view that the budget and the tax code alike primarily serve as tools to drive economic growth, while they can also be turned against the economy and higher levels of business investment and consumption. This more abstract outlook forces us to view fiscal policy as it should optimally relate to the economy and not what in reality shapes this policy in the first place. Yet the budget sheet and the tax code should be thought of in wholly concrete terms. The budget exists as it does today because of past political decisions intended to serve a multitude of interests. The budget is in that respect organic, ever changing and ever susceptible to external influence. In the American narrative of the past half century, international tensions and domestic politics both forced the budget into a pattern of fiscal overstretch. The tax code should likewise be thought of in concrete terms as a means of collecting revenue, but it very seamlessly morphed into a form, perhaps the single most visible form, of economic policy. The budget and the tax code inevitably impact economic conditions, a point that stands beyond dispute. But that does not mean observers today should fall into the habit of mainly viewing fiscal policy in abstract juxtaposition with the economy.

A traditional view once posited that deficits could not be sustained on a permanent basis for at least two reasons. First, bigger, persistent deficits would trigger higher real interest rates as creditors demanded greater risk premium on the securities they purchased from the government. The larger volume of government securities trading in the secondary market would also tend to put downward pressure on prices, which would in turn push up yields (the yield or profit of a security purchased in the aftermarket is computed from the standpoint of a prospective purchaser). Second, persistent deficits would cause inflation, destabilizing the entire macroeconomic picture and forcing the central bank to hike interest rates. This scenario played out in the late 1960s and 1970s. Inflation had already been building before the oil shocks because of government spending, and only tight monetary policy reversed this trend, albeit at great economic cost. Rising interest rates and inflation would thus impede the government from continuing its profligate spending habits and force a course correction in fiscal policy. One hesitates to infer a self-adjusting pendulum, but rising real interest rates and inflation were at least expected to function as safeguards against out-of-control spending.

These safeguards have not manifested themselves in the twenty-first century. Despite running $1 trillion deficits in the wake of the Great Recession, the federal government encountered little difficulty in finding relatively cheap sources of credit in these years when the recovery still looked tenuous. The ten-year Treasury note yielded less than 3% on average every year from 2009 to 2018, a time of economic expansion when yields should have risen.[2] Even with the huge deficits and the budget brinksmanship on Capitol Hill, creditors apparently had little fear the federal government would ever default on its debt. Lower interest rates and yields signify confidence that the government can handle the rising debt load. Government officials have reinforced these confident assumptions by regularly asserting that the federal government will never default on its debt. The means will always exist to avoid such a calamitous turn of events, including emergency austerity measures like tax hikes and spending cuts if necessary. Nor have the deficits caused inflation. The Federal Reserve has instead toiled to get price growth up to 2% per year during the long expansion. Weak inflation implicates a much more complex phenomenon, perhaps a secular trend that is a byproduct of an ever more globalized economy. In any event, central banks in most of the industrialized world have strenuously worked to stimulate economies and avoid deflation rather than restrain inflation. The European Central Bank has pursued extensive easing through open market operations and setting negative interest rates on the accounts of member banks, causing some government bonds to trade at a negative yield. The Bank of Japan has similarly pursued massive monetary ease in an effort to keep the Japanese economy from contracting. Not only have deficits become normal but so also have negative interest rates and bond yields.

Some economic perspectives assume that in the absence of rising interest rates and inflation the U.S. government can continue to safely incur deficits, which will in turn boost economic growth and generate higher revenue. An expansionary monetary policy further facilitates deficits as the Federal Reserve purchases government securities in the open market, pushing up their market prices and driving down their yields. The Fed's quantitative easing program served as a major driving factor in keeping yields contained after the Great Recession. These stimulus measures are sometimes described as government inflating away its debt, except that in most of today's advanced economies destabilizing inflation does not exist. Given the robust supply of credit through the mechanism of global financial markets, a monetary standard untethered to a commodity such as gold or silver, and a mix of pro-growth fiscal and monetary policies, the goal of trying to actively reduce deficits looks unnecessary or even downright harmful.

These viewpoints appear all too seamless, but more to the point they represent the status quo. The U.S. government today regularly runs deficits precisely because of the lack of an external constraint, whether in the form of higher interest rates or inflation. Perhaps the more interesting inquiry focuses on what differentiates the U.S. from developing nations, where these constraints are more visible, or for how much longer the U.S. government can get away with its current fiscal habits. But undeniably Treasurys remain haven assets for investors around the world while the threat of inflation currently serves as no deterrent to deficits.

Yet simply because the U.S. government right now faces no constraints in running deficits in the hundreds of billions or trillions of dollars does not mean that doing so is advisable. For one, the economic repercussions of deficits should not go ignored. Rising debt burden will threaten to crowd out private investment and reduce output, a long run drag on economic growth and productivity that cannot be easily mitigated. Countries with higher debt may also suffer weaker economic recoveries than those that keep deficits under control. Central banks are often described in terms of their available "ammo," or how much room they have for pumping money into the market and lowering interest rates. The same can be said for the government budget. Available fiscal ammo requires lean budgets during expansions that turn into larger deficits in downturns, further speeding up recovery. If the U.S. government already sustains between $700 billion and $1 trillion in deficits on average every year, even during expansions with +2% GDP growth, then it cannot as easily ramp up spending for countercyclical ends in a recession. That contention does not necessarily imply assumptions of a highly efficient fiscal policy. Rebates for lower income taxpayers could be phased in quickly while attempting to put together a stimulus package for infrastructure projects in Congress would probably lag economic conditions. But in whatever case persistent, bloated deficits render government with less ammo when it is most needed.

The importance of reining in deficits arises not only from economic considerations but also from institutional imperatives. As net interest payments on the debt consume ever larger amounts of budget space, exceeding total discretionary spending within the next thirty years according to CBO projections, policymakers will find it more difficult to respond to various challenges relating to the economy and national security. Deficit normality therefore implicates not merely the economy but effective governance as an organizing principle. Deficits may be thought necessary to grease the wheels of economic and military superpower, but unrestrained deficits will hamper the very necessary or constructive uses of that power, whether for overseas contingency operations, responses to natural disasters, or economic assistance to close trading partners and political allies. The objective should be not so much for the government to literally balance the budget every year but for it to effectively exercise control over its spending and taxation practices. The danger now is that the government has lost control and set off an avalanche of accumulating debt.

Another line of argument opposes budget surpluses from a free market standpoint. It maintains that the government should always transfer its surpluses back to the people through tax cuts. The government would then ideally run very narrow deficits or very narrow surpluses, but it would certainly not plan for large surpluses. The rise in debt would remain stable and negate the need for further tax hikes. Eisenhower expressed these sentiments when calling for tax cuts after coming into office. He wanted the budget to balance in the truest sense possible, meaning government's ability to pay for its expenditures while still giving money back to taxpayers. But deficits, and the resulting growth in debt, cannot be looked at in such stable terms. Deficits fluctuate depending upon various external factors. National emergencies and economic contractions trigger large deficits, and in subsequent years debt needs to be paid down through surpluses. In that sense, the budget should be viewed from a more countercyclical perspective not following a linear path of constant balance.

In the end, the presumptively safe accumulation of debt under conditions of low real interest rates and low inflation should not be carried too far as a policy regime. This scenario can actually be looked at from the opposite perspective, that the federal government now needs low interest rates in order to keep its debt burden from exploding in the event of rising yields, and it further needs low inflation as a check against rising interest rates. With limited means for controlling interest rates, the government depends on the Federal Reserve to ease markets through expansionary operations. As debt keeps growing, and with it the concomitant necessity of holding down borrowing costs, the government may have to start restraining spending just to ensure that the Federal Reserve can safely ease markets on a permanent basis. But if the government continues to increase its spending without letup, the Fed might be less inclined to shift to easy money for fear of igniting inflation. Just because inflation has been subdued in the past decade does not in any way mean that it can go ignored by the central banking authorities. Undeniably, though, the government is today trapped into a dependence on low interest rates, nominal and real, and low inflation. The most sustainable path forward is to cut spending and eliminate any trace of inflationary pressure, in turn giving leeway for the Federal Reserve to press down on borrowing costs. The deficit normative state must evolve to a situation of restrained spending, low inflation, and moderate to low interest rates.

The principle of market confidence continues to apply in an age of deficits, fiat currencies, and negative interest rates. A diminishing level of market confidence can be extrapolated to the extent of debt increasingly engulfing the federal government and bringing it closer to a sovereign debt crisis. The fact that the government may be able to avoid such a crisis is beside the point. The growing fear of such a crisis in markets, especially when exacerbated by financial and economic pressures, may suffice to reduce investor confidence, driving down stock prices but perhaps government bond prices as well, which in theory should be expected to move inversely to stocks. Many observers would argue that such an outlook is unnecessarily dire. The U.S. remains the world's largest economy, the dollar retains its role as a key international reserve asset, and Treasurys are still traded around the world. Conditions would have to be absolutely catastrophic in order for investors to flee the U.S. dollar and Treasurys in a crisis atmosphere. Admittedly, with negative interest rates and slow economic growth prevailing overseas, one cannot help wondering to where investors would flee. But no one can really claim to know what the future will hold in twenty or thirty years. All we can presume today is that confidence in the federal government will erode as the onus of servicing the debt becomes more arduous, in turn impairing confidence in the larger economy.

An improved fiscal situation, on the other hand, would bode well for market confidence. A third path avails itself, beyond the stale dichotomy of pro-growth stimulus and anti-growth austerity, for policies to help bolster market confidence over the long run through debt stabilization. An improved austerity program formulated like the BEA or the BCA might hurt economic growth over the short-term, but any brief contraction would have to result from adjustments in business investment and consumption following the reduction in government spending. The reduction in government spending would also by definition cause a contraction in GDP, but an official contraction in GDP should not always be equated with an actual contraction in the economy. After World War II GDP contracted because of the huge cutback in government spending, but the economy did not truly go into recession. The greater concern instead lies with shifts in business investment and consumption resulting from the reduction in government spending. These short-term trends would still not be detrimental to the overall state of the economy. Austerity has become a pejorative term, but today it should represent a government's attempt to retake control of its budget and the ways in which it spends public money.

The agenda for stable public finance must therefore focus squarely upon deficits. The impending insolvency of the Social Security and Medicare Hospital Insurance trust funds pose closely related challenges that should still not be unnecessarily conflated with current budget deficits. These programs rely on payroll taxes and were never intended to directly affect general revenue. They traditionally invested payroll tax surpluses in Treasury bonds and then used the income from these bonds to help fund payouts to beneficiaries. As both programs start to sustain annual deficits, they must increasingly redeem their trust fund assets to make up the shortfall in funding each year. Recent trust fund reports for Social Security and Medicare predict financing challenges at some point in the 2020s and 2030s when both programs will have exhausted all their remaining assets. Only current revenue from payroll taxes will be able to meet mandatory payments. A common misconception is that, with the depletion of their trust fund assets, Social Security and Medicare will go "bankrupt" and totally implode. That does not appear to be the case, with Social Security and Medicare still expected to pay out anywhere in the range of three quarters to 90% of benefits, though projections can change. These problems will warrant reforms in funding and cost control, but they should not distract public attention from the central challenge today of budget deficits because these deficits are driving up the public debt. A fiscal package today must focus on budget deficits and the factors directly causing them.

The causal roots of today's deficits are comprehensive, a product of vast military commitments not shared by any other country in the world, a tax code viewed more as a tool for economic growth than as a means of collecting revenue, and rising entitlement transfer payments subject to mandatory spending rules. Prescriptions for tackling deficits would have to be commensurately comprehensive, organized in a way similar to the BEA and BCA. The tools exist for a comprehensive approach to deficits. A combination of spending cuts and tax hikes will reduce deficits on an annual basis. What is urgently required now is sheer clarity of purpose. A tentative program replacing the BCA can be sketched out:

- 10% cuts in defense spending and 25% cuts in all non-defense spending funded from general revenue implemented through fixed spending caps.
- The fixed spending caps adjusted once annually for inflation from a current baseline, with narrow exemptions for natural disaster relief and overseas contingency operations.
- 1%–5% progressive income surtax rates across higher-earning tax brackets in order to target optimal tax revenue increases.
- Pay-go rules for all further changes in taxes and entitlements.
- In the event of a breach of the spending caps, automatic 10% cuts in all agency and program budgets funded from general revenue.
- Any resulting surplus revenue automatically transferred to a debt reduction fund.
- Expiration after fifteen years but subject to renewal.

Such a comprehensive approach would no doubt invite criticism from all quarters, including accusations of accelerating a hollowing out of military capabilities and fears of triggering economic contraction. Better long-range budget planning would prevent a "hollowing out" effect for military capabilities, while the legislation would also be phased in incrementally over a five-year period and then remain in effect to the maximum extent for another ten years before automatically expiring. But the legislation would ideally be renewed. The income surtaxes offer a fair and progressive way to increase tax revenue. Depending on the state of the economy, the legislation aims to cut deficits on average by up to $500 billion per year, which would in turn cut deficits somewhere between $5 to $7.5 trillion over fifteen years (depending how quickly the spending cuts and tax hikes would be phased in).

Critics might argue that pay-go rules would hamper countercyclical economic policy in a downturn and in fact leave the budget with no ammo to fight a recession. Congress in these situations could still juice the economy through temporary tax rebates for low income taxpayers, driving up consumption and speeding recovery, provided the rebates are offset by spending cuts or other forms of tax hikes. Admittedly, increased deficit spending would not end recessions, but more limited tax rebates, if offset by other measures, would positively impact the economy with less lag time than spending on longer-term projects. And anyhow the federal government has already run out of ammo. It used it up after the Great Recession, and now the effort should be funneling money directly into consumption and business investment at opportune times without increasing deficits. Nor should the pretense be made that under severe enough conditions Congress would refrain from repealing, temporarily or permanently, its own pay-go rules to fund tax cuts. Congress did so in 2001 and again in 2017 when it waived pay-go rules legislated in 2010 to fund the Tax Cuts and Jobs Act. The proposed legislation could possibly be equipped with a provision granting a temporary exemption from pay-go rules for changes in the tax code if the economy undergoes at least one quarter of negative economic growth. Tax policy might very well lag economic conditions, but such transitory policies, like rebates for lower earning taxpayers, would still help prevent a long recession, especially if coordinated with loose monetary policy.

Unlike the BEA, this proposal would assign a single cap to the extremely broad category of non-defense spending funded from general revenue, not just domestic discretionary spending. Because the proposal assigns a cap to this broad category of spending, benefits funded from general revenue, including Medicare Supplemental Insurance, Medicaid, Supplemental Security Income, and food stamps could very well be implicated. Reformulating eligibility would require changes in mandatory rules outside the appropriations process, but uniformly reducing transfer payments could also be implemented through automatic cuts in reimbursement rates, matching funds, and other transfers. Benefits entirely or partly funded from general revenue should be incorporated into the scheme of spending caps as a matter of principle. These programs do not extend automatic eligibility through payroll taxes. They are partly paid for by taxpayers who may never be enrolled in these programs. Yet incorporating these entitlements into the scheme of spending caps does not imply a specific reduction in benefits. Designating a broad category allows maximum leeway for achieving political compromise, though the difficulty in reaching such a compromise cannot be underestimated.

The other category of spending subject to a cap, defense, is more definite. As a general matter, defense cuts should not somehow signal retreat from the world or the abandonment of treaty commitments in Europe and Asia. The U.S. continues to face asymmetrical threats in the form of terrorism and WMD proliferation as well as great power aggression from China and Russia. Any defense cuts must be carefully applied so as not to degrade core capabilities and research and development in robotics, artificial intelligence, and other cutting-edge technologies. Even with the rise in entitlement spending, defense remains one of the four top recipients of funds along with Social Security, Medicare, and Medicaid. Defense cuts bring to the fore tough dilemmas on which capabilities most effectively protect the domestic population and which are outdated. Additional assessments must focus on ways to marginally cut back non-combat and combat personnel alike without degrading core functions.

Yet the first step in seriously counteracting deficits over the long run is much more straightforward, recognizing the dangers they pose in the public discourse and that they should be addressed at all. Even this preliminary step presents an admittedly difficult challenge when the federal government currently faces no clear impediment to its own profligate tendencies. The proposal mentioned above only sketches out main components and clearly does not form a detailed program. But it still shows that any meaningful approach will have to be comprehensive, impacting all at once defense policy, taxes, and entitlements. The more comprehensive the approach, the more likely it is to be deemed by the public a fair and honest way of reducing the national debt burden. And admittedly such a tentative package as the one mentioned above only constitutes an intermediate agenda. It leads to no permanent reform of the tax code or the entitlement state. But the current historical moment calls for effective governance above all else, a willingness to compromise in the name of the national interest. The ability of the government to exert greater control over spending and revenue would mark a revival in effective liberal democracy.

If deficit control legislation is aggressive enough, then it might produce surplus revenue in years of +2% real GDP growth. The result would not be a return to the surplus normative state as it existed in the late 1800s and early 1900s. Deficits would still be common in years of lower or negative GDP growth, but the at least partial return to surpluses would help slow the accumulating debt burden. Surplus revenue would be diverted into a debt reduction fund for purchasing Treasury debt and cancelling the principal, with interest redeposited into the fund.

Any such program looks a far way off. Under current trends the federal government keeps pushing the limit on how much it can borrow without economic and institutional repercussions, even as it loads more and more debt onto the backs of future generations. The instinctive response in such circumstances should not be to keep pushing the limit but to restrain these excesses through comprehensive measures. Perhaps anti-deficit measures of this magnitude are out of reach in today's divided political environment. Yet one assertion can be safely made, that whatever actions are taken the challenges of fiscal overstretch will continue to be with us down the road.

NOTES

1. All percentages computed from OMB, "Historical Tables."

2. Federal Reserve Bank of St. Louis Economic Data, "10 Year Treasury Constant Maturity Rate," https://fred.stlouisfed.org/series/DGS10, accessed June 2019.

Bibliography

Atrostic, B. K., and James R. Nunns. "Measuring Tax Burden: A Historical Perspective." In *Fifty Years of Economic Measurement: The Jubilee of the Conference on Research in Income and Wealth*, ed. Ernst R. Berndt and Jack E. Triplett. Chicago: University of Chicago Press, 1991.

Auerbach, Alan J., and James M. Poterba. "Why Have Corporate Tax Revenues Declined?" In *Tax Policy and the Economy, Vol. I*, ed. Lawrence H. Summers. Cambridge, MA: MIT Press, 1987.

Bator, Francis M. "No Good Choices: LBJ and the Vietnam/Great Society Connection." *Diplomatic History* 32, no. 3 (June 2008): 309–40.

Condit, Doris M. *History of the Office of the Secretary of Defense, Vol. II, The Test of War: 1950–1953*. Washington, D.C.: Historical Office, Office of the Secretary of Defense, 1988.

Condit, Kenneth W. *History of the Joint Chiefs of Staff, The Joint Chiefs of Staff and National Policy, Vol. II: 1947–1949*. Washington, D.C.: Office of Joint History, Office of the Chairman of the Joint Chiefs of Staff, 1996.

———. *History of the Joint Chiefs of Staff, Vol. VI, The Joint Chiefs of Staff and National Policy: 1955–1956*. Washington, D.C.: Office of Joint History, Office of the Chairman of the Joint Chiefs of Staff, 1998.

Congressional Budget Office. *An Analysis of the Roth-Kemp Tax Proposal*. Washington, D.C.: Congressional Budget Office, 1978.

———. *The 2019 Long-Term Budget Outlook*. Washington, D.C.: Congressional Budget Office, 2019.

Converse, III, Elliot V. *History of Acquisition in the Department of Defense, Vol I., Rearming for the Cold War: 1945–1960*. Washington, D.C.: Historical Office, Office of the Secretary of Defense, 2012.

Drea, Edward J. *Secretaries of Defense Historical Series, Vol. VI., McNamara, Clifford, and the Burdens of Vietnam: 1965–1969*. Washington, D.C.: Historical Office, Office of the Secretary of Defense, 2011.

Forrestal, James. "Functions of the Armed Forces and the Joint Chiefs of Staff." In *The United States Air Force: Basic Documents on Roles and Missions*, ed. Richard I. Wolfe. Washington, D.C.: Office of Air Force History, U.S. Air Force, 1987.

Fullerton, Don, Charls Walker, and Russell Long. "Tax Policy." In *American Economic Policy in the 1980s*, ed. Martin Feldstein. Chicago: University of Chicago Press, 1994.

Futrell, Robert F. "The Influence of the Air Power Concept on Air Force Planning, 1945–1962." In *Military Planning in the Twentieth Century: Proceedings of the Eleventh Military History Symposium*, 10–12 October 1984, ed. Lt. Col. Harry R. Borowski. Washington, D.C.: Office of Air Force History, U.S. Air Force, 1986.

Hunt, Richard A. *Secretaries of Defense Historical Series, Vol. VII, Melvin Laird and the Foundation of the Post-Vietnam Military: 1969–1973*. Washington, D.C.: Historical Office, Office of the Secretary of Defense, 2015.

Irwin, Douglas A. "From Smoot-Hawley to Reciprocal Trade Agreements: Changing the Course of U.S. Trade Policy in the 1930s." In *The Defining Moment: The Great Depression and the American Economy in the Twentieth Century*, ed. Michael D. Bordo, Claudia Goldin, and Eugene N. White. Chicago: University of Chicago Press, 1998.

Kaplan, Lawrence S., Ronald D. Landa, and Edward J. Drea. *History of the Office of the Secretary of Defense, Vol. V, The McNamara Ascendancy: 1961–1965*. Historical Office, Office of the Secretary of Defense, Washington, D.C., 2006.

Keefer, Edward C. *Secretaries of Defense Historical Series, Vol. VIII, Harold Brown, Offsetting the Soviet Military Challenge: 1977–1981*. Washington, D.C.: Historical Office, Office of the Secretary of Defense, 2017.

Keefer, Edward C. and David W. Mabon, eds. *Foreign Relations of the United States, 1958–1960, East Asia-Pacific Region; Cambodia; Laos; Volume XVI*. Washington, D.C.: Government Printing Office, 1992.

Keefer, Edward C. and Charles S. Sampson, eds. *Foreign Relations of the United States, 1964–1968, Volume I, Vietnam, 1964*. Washington, D.C.: Government Printing Office, 1992.

Klingaman, William, David S. Patterson, and Ilana Stern, eds. *Foreign Relations of the United States, Panel, 1955–1957, National Security Policy, Volume XIX*. Washington, D.C.: Government Printing Office, 1990.

Leighton, Richard M. *History of the Office of the Secretary of Defense, Vol. III, Strategy, Money, and the New Look: 1953–1956*. Washington, D.C.: Historical Office, Office of the Secretary of Defense, 2001.

Mabon, David W., ed. *Foreign Relations of the United States, 1961–1963, Volume VIII, National Security Policy*. Washington, D.C.: Government Printing Office, 1996.

Meilinger, Phillip S. *The Admirals' Revolt of 1949: Lessons for Today*. Carlisle, PA: Army War College, 1989.

Moore, John Norton and Robert F. Turner. "The Legal Structure of Defense Organization." Memorandum prepared for the President's Blue Ribbon Commission on Defense Management, January 1986.

Nelson, Ralph L. *Merger Movements in American History, 1995–1956*. Princeton: Princeton University Press, 1959.

Poole, Walter S. *History of the Joint Chiefs of Staff, The Joint Chiefs of Staff and National Policy, Vol. VIII: 1961–1964*. Washington, D.C.: Office of Joint History, Office of the Chairman of the Joint Chiefs of Staff, 2011.

———. *History of Acquisition in the Department of Defense, Vol. II, Adapting to Flexible Response: 1960–1968*. Washington, D.C.: Historical Office, Office of the Secretary of Defense, 2013.

President of the United States. *The Budget of the United States Government for the Fiscal Year Ending June 30, 1947*. Washington, D.C.: Government Printing Office, 1946.

———. *The Budget of the United States Government for the Fiscal Year Ending June 30, 1948*. Washington, D.C.: Government Printing Office, 1947.

———. *The Budget of the United States Government for the Fiscal Year Ending June 30, 1949*. Washington, D.C.: Government Printing Office, 1948.

———. *The Budget of the United States Government for the Fiscal Year Ending June 30, 1950*. Washington, D.C.: Government Printing Office, 1949.

———. *The Budget of the United States Government for the Fiscal Year Ending June 30, 1951*. Washington, D.C.: Government Printing Office, 1950.

———. *The Budget of the United States Government for the Fiscal Year Ending June 30, 1952*. Washington, D.C.: Government Printing Office, 1951.

———. *The Budget of the United States Government for the Fiscal Year Ending June 30, 1954*. Washington, D.C.: Government Printing Office, 1953.

———. *The Budget of the United States Government for the Fiscal Year Ending June 30, 1955*. Washington, D.C.: Government Printing Office, 1954.

———. *The Budget of the United States Government for the Fiscal Year Ending June 30,* 1957. Washington, D.C.: Government Printing Office, 1956.
———. *The Budget of the United States Government for the Fiscal Year Ending June 30, 1959*. Washington, D.C.: Government Printing Office, 1958.
———. *The Budget of the United States Government for the Fiscal Year Ending June 30, 1961*. Washington, D.C.: Government Printing Office, 1960.
———. *The Budget of the United States Government for the Fiscal Year Ending June 30, 1962*. Washington, D.C.: Government Printing Office, 1961.
———. *The Budget of the United States Government for the Fiscal Year Ending June 30, 1963*. Government Printing Office, Washington, D.C., 1962.
———. *The Budget of the United States Government for the Fiscal Year Ending June 30, 1964*. Washington, D.C.: Government Printing Office, 1963.
———. *The Budget of the United States Government for the Fiscal Year Ending June 30, 1965*. Washington, D.C.: Government Printing Office, 1964.
———. *The Budget of the United States Government for the Fiscal Year Ending June 30, 1966*. Washington, D.C.: Government Printing Office, 1965.
———. *The Budget of the United States Government for the Fiscal Year Ending June 30, 1967*. Washington, D.C.: Government Printing Office, 1966.
———. *The Budget of the United States Government for the Fiscal Year Ending June 30, 1970*. Washington, D.C.: Government Printing Office, 1969.
———. *The Budget of the United States Government Fiscal Year 1971*. Washington, D.C.: Government Printing Office, 1970.
———. *The Budget of the United States Government Fiscal Year 1972*. Washington, D.C.: Government Printing Office, 1971.
———. *The Budget of the United States Government Fiscal Year 1973*. Washington, D.C.: Government Printing Office, 1972.
———. *The Budget of the United States Government Fiscal Year 1974*. Washington, D.C.: Government Printing Office, 1973.
———. *The Budget of the United States Government Fiscal Year 1975*. Washington, D.C.: Government Printing Office, 1974.
———. *The Budget of the United States Government Fiscal Year 1976*. Washington, D.C.: Government Printing Office, 1975.
———. *The Budget of the United States Government Fiscal Year 1977*. Washington, D.C.: Government Printing Office, 1976.
———. *The Budget of the United States Government Fiscal Year 1979*. Washington, D.C.: Government Printing Office, 1978.
———. *The Budget of the United States Government Fiscal Year 1981*. Washington, D.C.: Government Printing Office, 1980.
———. *Budget of the United States Government Fiscal Year 1982*. Washington, D.C.: Office of Management and Budget, 1981.
———. *Budget of the United States Government Fiscal Year 1983*. Washington, D.C.: Government Printing Office, 1982.
———. *Budget of the United States Government Fiscal Year 1986*. Washington, D.C.: Government Printing Office, 1985.
———. *Budget of the United States Government Fiscal Year 1987*. Washington, D.C.: Government Printing Office, 1986.
———. *Budget of the United States Government Fiscal Year 1993*. Washington, D.C.: Government Printing Office, 1992.
"Provisions of the Housing Act of 1949." *Monthly Labor Review* 69, no. 2 (August 1949): 155–59.
Rearden, Steven L. *History of the Secretary of Defense, Vol. I, The Formative Years: 1947–1950*. Washington, D.C.: Historical Office, Office of the Secretary of Defense, 1984.
Rose, Lisle A. and Neal H. Petersen, eds. *Foreign Relations of the United States, 1952–1954, National Security Affairs, Volume II, Part I*. Washington, D.C.: Government Printing Office, 1984.

Rothbard, Murray N. "Beginning the Welfare State: Civil War Veterans' Pensions." *The Quarterly Journal of Austrian Economics* 22, no. 1 (Spring 2019): 68–81.

Rowland, Diane, Barbara Lyons, and Jennifer Edwards. "Medicaid: Health Care for the Poor in the Reagan Era." *Annual Review of Public Health* 9 (1988): 427–50.

Sampson, Charles S., ed. *Foreign Relations of the United States, 1961–1963, Volume XIV, Berlin Crisis, 1961–1963*. Washington, D.C.: Government Printing Office, 1993.

Samwick, Andrew A. "Tax Shelters and Passive Losses after the Tax Reform Act of 1986." In *Empirical Foundations of Household Taxation*, ed. Martin Feldstein and James Poterba. Chicago: University of Chicago Press, 1986.

Schaffel, Kenneth. *The Emerging Shield: The Air Force and the Evolution of Continental Air Defense: 1945–1960*. Washington, D.C.: Office of Air Force History, U.S. Air Force, 1991.

Schnabel, James F. and Robert J. Watson. *History of the Joint Chiefs of Staff, The Joint Chiefs of Staff and National Policy, Vol. III: 1950–1951*. Washington, D.C.: Office of Joint History, Office of the Chairman of the Joint Chiefs of Staff, 1998.

Secretary of Defense. *Fiscal Year 1971 Defense Program and Budget*. Washington, D.C.: Government Printing Office, 1970.

———. *Annual Defense Department Report FY 1973*. Washington, D.C.: Government Printing Office, 1972.

———. *Annual Defense Department Report FY 1977*. Washington, D.C.: Government Printing Office, 1976.

———. *Annual Defense Department Report FY 1978*. Washington, D.C.: Government Printing Office, 1977.

———. *Department of Defense Annual Report Fiscal Year 1979*. Washington, D.C.: Government Printing Office, 1978.

———. *Department of Defense Annual Report Fiscal Year 1981*. Washington, D.C.: Government Printing Office, 1980.

Secretary of the Navy. *Report of the Secretary of the Navy. 1889. In Two Parts. Part I*. Washington, D.C.: Government Printing Office, 1890.

Secretary of the Treasury. *Annual Report of the Secretary of the Treasury on the State of the Finances for the Year 1890*. Washington, D.C.: Government Printing Office, 1891.

———. *Annual Report of the Secretary of the Treasury on the State of the Finances for the Year 1892*. Washington, D.C.: Government Printing Office, 1892.

———. *Annual Report of the Secretary of the Treasury on the State of the Finances for the Fiscal Year Ended June 30, 1905*. Washington, D.C.: Government Printing Office, 1906.

———. *Annual Report of the Secretary of the Treasury on the State of the Finances for the Fiscal Year Ended June 30, 1924*. Washington, D.C.: Government Printing Office, 1925.

———. *Annual Report of the Secretary of the Treasury on the State of the Finances for the Fiscal Year Ended June 30, 1926*. Washington, D.C.: Government Printing Office, 1927.

———. *Annual Report of the Secretary of the Treasury on the State of the Finances for the Fiscal Year Ended June 30, 1946*. Washington, D.C.: Government Printing Office, 1947.

———. *Annual Report of the Secretary of the Treasury on the State of the Finances for the Fiscal Year Ended June 30, 1947*. Washington, D.C.: Government Printing Office, 1948.

———. *Annual Report of the Secretary of the Treasury on the State of the Finances for the Fiscal Year Ended June 30, 1948*. Washington, D.C.: Government Printing Office, 1949.

———. *Annual Report of the Secretary of the Treasury on the State of the Finances for the Fiscal Year Ended June 30, 1950*. Washington, D.C.: Government Printing Office, 1951.

———. *Annual Report of the Secretary of the Treasury on the State of the Finances for the Fiscal Year Ended June 30, 1951*. Washington, D.C.: Government Printing Office, 1952.

———. *Annual Report of the Secretary of the Treasury on the State of the Finances for the Fiscal Year Ended June 30, 1954*. Washington, D.C.: Government Printing Office, 1955.

———. *Annual Report of the Secretary of the Treasury on the State of the Finances for the Fiscal Year Ended June 30, 1961*. Washington, D.C.: Government Printing Office, 1962.

———. *Annual Report of the Secretary of the Treasury on the State of the Finances for the Fiscal Year Ended June 30, 1962*. Washington, D.C.: Government Printing Office, 1963.

———. *Annual Report of the Secretary of the Treasury on the State of the Finances for the Fiscal Year Ended June 30, 1963*. Washington, D.C.: Government Printing Office, 1964.

———. *Annual Report of the Secretary of the Treasury on the State of the Finances for the Fiscal Year Ended June 30, 1964*. Washington, D.C.: Government Printing Office, 1965.
———. *Annual Report of the Secretary of the Treasury on the State of the Finances for the Fiscal Year Ended June 30, 1967*. Washington, D.C.: Government Printing Office, 1968.
———. *Annual Report of the Secretary of the Treasury on the State of the Finances for the Fiscal Year Ended June 30, 1968*. Washington, D.C.: Government Printing Office, 1969.
———. *Annual Report of the Secretary of the Treasury on the State of the Finances for the Fiscal Year Ended June 30, 1969*. Washington, D.C.: Government Printing Office, 1970.
———. *Annual Report of the Secretary of the Treasury on the State of the Finances for the Fiscal Year Ended June 30, 1970*. Washington, D.C.: Government Printing Office, 1970.
———. *Annual Report of the Secretary of the Treasury on the State of the Finances for the Fiscal Year Ended June 30, 1972*. Washington, D.C.: Government Printing Office, 1972.
———. *Annual Report of the Secretary of the Treasury on the State of the Finances for the Fiscal Year Ended June 30, 1975*. Washington, D.C.: Government Printing Office, 1975.
———. *Annual Report of the Secretary of the Treasury on the State of the Finances for the Fiscal Year Ended June 30, 1976 and Transition Quarter*. Washington, D.C.: Government Printing Office, 1977.
———. *Annual Report of the Secretary of the Treasury on the State of the Finances Fiscal Year 1977*. Washington, D.C.: Government Printing Office, 1978.
———. *Annual Report of the Secretary of the Treasury on the State of the Finances Fiscal Year 1978*. Washington, D.C.: Government Printing Office, 1979.
———. *Annual Report of the Secretary of the Treasury on the State of the Finances Fiscal Year 1979*. Washington, D.C.: Government Printing Office, 1980.
Survival in the Air Age: A Report by the President's Air Policy Commission. Washington, D.C.: Government Printing Office, 1948.
Tempalski, Jerry. "Revenue Effects of Major Tax Bills." Office of Tax Analysis, U.S. Treasury Department, Working Paper No. 81 (September 2006).
Walker, James, Lewis Bernstein, and Sharon Lang. *Seize the High Ground: The Army in Space and Missile Defense*. Washington, D.C.: Historical Office, U.S. Army Space and Defense Command, 2003.
Watson, Robert J. *History of the Office of the Secretary of Defense, Vol. IV, Into the Missile Age: 1956–1960*. Washington, D.C.: Historical Office, Office of the Secretary of Defense, 1997.
———. *History of the Joint Chiefs of Staff, Vol. V, The Joint Chiefs of Staff and National Policy, 1953–1954*. Washington, D.C.: Office of Joint History, Office of the Chairman of the Joint Chiefs of Staff, 1998.

COLLECTIONS

Collection: The Korean War and Its Origins. Series: President's Secretary's Files. Harry S. Truman Presidential Library & Museum.
Folder: "A Report to the National Security Council—NSC 68, April 12, 1950." Collection: Ideological Foundations of the Cold War. Series: President's Secretary's Files. Harry S. Truman Presidential Library & Museum.
Folder: "Report to the National Security Council: U.S. Military Courses of Action with Respect to the Situation in Berlin, July 28 1948." Collection: The Berlin Airlift. Series: President's Secretary's Files. Harry S. Truman Presidential Library & Museum.
John F. Kennedy Library Oral History Program.
"Memo re CIA estimate of probable consequences of the death of Stalin, April 10, 1953." NSC Staff Papers. Special Staff File. Box 7, Special Staff Memos (2). Dwight Eisenhower Presidential Library and Museum.
"Memorandum for the Military Representatives: Force Goals for 1952, 1953, and 1954." SGM-0648–52, Standing Group Memoranda. NATO Archives, Brussels, Belgium.
Military Committee Series. NATO Archives, Brussels, Belgium.
NSC Meeting File. Gerald R. Ford Presidential Library.

Papers of John F. Kennedy. Presidential Papers. National Security Files. John F. Kennedy Presidential Library and Museum.

Papers of John F. Kennedy. Presidential Papers. President's Office Files. John F. Kennedy Presidential Library and Museum.

"Report from the Military Committee to the North Atlantic Defense Committee on North Atlantic Treaty Organization Medium Term Plan." DC 013, DC, Subject Files Defence Committee. NATO Archives, Brussels, Belgium.

"Report on Army's R&D programs including nuclear and non-nuclear firepower, mines, chemical warfare, SSMs, air defense, space and satellites, air and surface mobility, combat surveillance and nuclear research, undated." Office of the Staff Secretary Records. Subject Series. Alphabetical Subseries. Box 2, Army [Vol. I] (10). Dwight Eisenhower Presidential Library and Museum.

Standing Group Series. NATO Archives, Brussels, Belgium.

White House Office of the Special Assistant for Science and Technology. Dwight Eisenhower Presidential Library and Museum.

Index

About the Author

William Mannen is also the author of *Efficient Macro Concept: U.S. Monetary, Industrial, and Foreign Exchange Policies*.

www.ingramcontent.com/pod-product-compliance
Ingram Content Group UK Ltd.
Pitfield, Milton Keynes, MK11 3LW, UK
UKHW041843031026
15587UKWH00002B/969

9 781793 607096